Henry James

Henry James OM (15 April 1843 – 28 February 1916) was an American-British author regarded as a key transitional figure between literary realism and literary modernism, and is considered by many to be among the greatest novelists in the English language. He was the son of Henry James Sr. and the brother of renowned philosopher and psychologist William James and diarist Alice James.

He is best known for a number of novels dealing with the social and marital interplay between émigré Americans, English people, and continental Europeans. Examples of such novels include The Portrait of a Lady, The Ambassadors, and The Wings of the Dove. His later works were increasingly experimental. In describing the internal states of mind and social dynamics of his characters, James often made use of a style in which ambiguous or contradictory motives and impressions were overlaid or juxtaposed in the discussion of a character's psyche. (Source: Wikipedia)

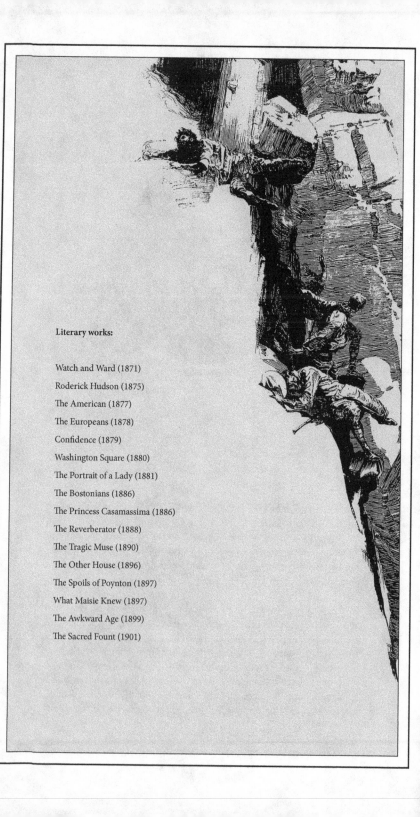

Literary works:

Watch and Ward (1871)

Roderick Hudson (1875)

The American (1877)

The Europeans (1878)

Confidence (1879)

Washington Square (1880)

The Portrait of a Lady (1881)

The Bostonians (1886)

The Princess Casamassima (1886)

The Reverberator (1888)

The Tragic Muse (1890)

The Other House (1896)

The Spoils of Poynton (1897)

What Maisie Knew (1897)

The Awkward Age (1899)

The Sacred Fount (1901)

THE
WORKS
OF
HENRY JAMES

VOL. 35 (OF 36)

VIEWS AND REVIEWS
WASHINGTON SQUARE

An Imprint of Moon Classics LLC

A Wholly Owned Subsidiary of Queenior LLC

A Melodragon Company

First Printing: 2020

ISBN 978-1-6627-1616-4 (Paperback)

ISBN 978-1-6627-1617-1 (Hardcover)

Published by Moon Classics

www.moonclassics.com

Contents

THE
WORKS
OF
HENRY JAMES
VOL. 35 (OF 36)

VIEWS AND REVIEWS

INTRODUCTION

Those whose palates are accustomed to the subtle flavours of the wines of the Rhine and Moselle can smack their lips and name the vintage at the first taste. Likewise any one fairly familiar with the work of Mr. James during his forty years of literary activity can, after the reading of a single page taken at random, judge with a remarkable accuracy the date of its composition. Yet the transition has not been abrupt and the styles of writing which the author has adopted, early, middle and late, have blended in such a way that he has been bringing many of his earlier readers, though some have fallen by the wayside, along with him to a genuine appreciation of his present work.

It is not unnatural but disappointing that those of the present generation who chance to meet Mr. James in one of the later novels are not as likely to seek a second volume as those who read Daisy Miller *some thirty years ago when that study first appeared, so fresh in its note of charm and pathos, in the now almost unfindable brown wrappers of Harper's Half Hour Series, for they may forever miss a rare enjoyment.*

In the critical papers which make up the contents of this book, the characteristics of the author's later style are wholly absent. Without the date of the original appearance of these essays in periodical form being indicated, the chronological setting of this work is apparent. No sentences with marvelously intricate complications of construction and with expressions involved are in the author's method at this time, while for clearness and charm these views and reviews are admirable specimens, showing qualities which brought Mr. James his early readers and first made his name an essential feature of the announcements of publishers of the more discriminating periodicals forty years ago.

The earliest authenticated magazine article by Mr. James—printed when he was twenty-one—is a critical notice of Nassau W. Senior's Essays on Fiction *in* The North American Review *for October, 1864. From this time until the appearance of his first volume—*A Passionate Pilgrim and Other Tales, *Boston: 1875—as many as one hundred and twenty-five serious literary notices contributed to periodicals can be traced to him.*

During this period it must also be remembered that Mr. James was equally employed in writing short stories, art criticism and notes of travel, both at home and abroad, and that these were also distinctive features of the widely scattered journals in which they appeared.

In The North American Review, The Atlantic Monthly, The Galaxy, Lippincott's Magazine, The New York Tribune, The Independent *and some other periodicals, the authorship of such work was attributed to Mr. James on the publication of the articles or in regularly issued indexes.*

The articles in The Nation *are seldom signed, and there is no published index showing the contributors to its files. In preparing a recent*[*] *Bibliography of the writings of Henry James I had access to a record which the late Wendell Phillips Garrison, who was Mr. Godkin's associate from the founding of the paper and after 1881 editor in charge until June 28, 1906, had carefully kept of every author's work which his paper had published since its first issue. The amount of matter which Mr. James had provided, and the variety of interests concerning which he wrote, made an amazing array of notes. It is from the early issues of* The Nation *that much of the contents of this volume is reprinted. Of Mr. James's contributions to periodicals those to this paper were perhaps the most notable as well as the most frequent. He was represented in its first number—July 6, 1865—by some critical notes on Henry W. Kingsley's novel, "*The Hillyars and the Bartons: A Story of Two Families," *under the title,* "The Noble School of Fiction," *and the name "Henry James" appears in the publisher's announced list of contributors to the early volumes. Many of these papers which first appeared in* The Nation *have been reprinted, but few readers at this distance can realize how much the esteem in which that journal was immediately held under the editorial supervision of Mr. Godkin was due to perhaps its youngest regular contributor.*

[*] *A Bibliography of the Writings of Henry James. Boston and New York: Houghton, Mifflin and Company, 1906.*

*Volumes of the collected critical papers have already appeared,—*French Poets and Novelists, London: *1878, and* Partial Portraits, *London: 1888, are the more notable,—but by far the greater part of these contemporary Essays on the* *literature of the late sixties and the seventies are now almost lost in the files of old or extinct periodicals.*

We are accustomed these later years to think of Mr. James as novelist rather than literary essayist and he has been cited by a recent writer as an author of fiction who becomes a critic on occasion and, he also adds, that his analytical system of novel writing excellently fits him for the office of critic; but, on the contrary, the papers in this volume seem to show that his early self-training as a critic has been the preparation for the creation of his characters in fiction.

The true lover of Mr. James's work feels the same delightful sense of intimate discovery in touching these early papers that an artist does in finding a portfolio of early sketches by a beloved master whose developed power and strength is known to him. There is the recognition of the characteristic touch even here—the insight, the thought within a thought, (more lately the despair of privileged psychologic athletes), the mystery of seeing—not what is apparent to the outward eye but what we fancied we concealed successfully within our inmost selves. There is the extraordinary sense of his having put on paper what we really thought—what we now think—that gives us more faith than ever in our artist who is expression for us who feel, but who are yet dumb.

LE ROY PHILLIPS.

Boston, April 10, 1908.

THE NOVELS OF GEORGE ELIOT

THE critic's first duty in the presence of an author's collective works is to seek out some key to his method, some utterance of his literary convictions, some indication of his ruling theory. The amount of labour involved in an inquiry of this kind will depend very much upon the author. In some cases the critic will find express declarations; in other cases he will have to content himself with conscientious inductions. In a writer so fond of digressions as George Eliot, he has reason to expect that broad evidences of artistic faith will not be wanting. He finds in *Adam Bede* the following passage:—

"Paint us an angel if you can, with a floating violet robe and a face paled by the celestial light; paint us yet oftener a Madonna, turning her mild face upward, and opening her arms to welcome the divine glory; but do not impose on us any æsthetic rules which shall banish from the region of art those old women scraping carrots with their work-worn hands,—those heavy clowns taking holiday in a dingy pot-house,—those rounded backs and stupid weather-beaten faces that have bent over the spade and done the rough work of the world,—those homes with their tin cans, their brown pitchers, their rough curs, and their clusters of onions. In this world there are so many of these common, coarse people, who have no picturesque, sentimental wretchedness. It is so needful we should remember their existence, else we may happen to leave them quite out of our religion and philosophy, and frame lofty theories which only fit a world of extremes....

"There are few prophets in the world,—few sublimely beautiful women,—few heroes. I can't afford to give all my love and reverence to such rarities; I want a great deal of those feelings for my every-day fellowmen, especially for the few in the foreground of the great multitude, whose faces I know, whose hands I touch, for whom I have to make way with kindly courtesy....

"I herewith discharge my conscience," our author continues, "and declare that I have had quite enthusiastic movements of admiration toward old gentlemen who spoke the worst English, who were occasionally fretful in their temper, and who had never moved in a higher sphere of influence than that of parish overseer; and that the way in which I have come to the conclusion that human nature is loveable—the way I have learnt something of its deep pathos, its sublime mysteries—has been by living a great deal among people more or less commonplace and vulgar, of whom you would perhaps hear nothing very surprising if you were to inquire about them in the neighbourhoods where they dwelt."

But even in the absence of any such avowed predilections as these, a brief glance over the principal figures of her different works would assure us that our author's sympathies are with common people. Silas Marner is a linen-weaver, Adam Bede is a carpenter, Maggie Tulliver is a miller's daughter, Felix Holt is a watchmaker, Dinah Morris works in a factory, and Hetty Sorrel is a dairy-maid. Esther Lyon, indeed, is a daily governess; but Tito Melema alone is a scholar. In the *Scenes of Clerical Life*, the author is constantly slipping down from the clergymen, her heroes, to the most ignorant and obscure of their parishioners. Even in *Romola* she consecrates page after page to the conversation of the Florentine populace. She is as unmistakably a painter of *bourgeois* life as Thackeray was a painter of the life of drawing-rooms.

Her opportunities for the study of the manners of the solid lower classes have evidently been very great. We have her word for it that she has lived much among the farmers, mechanics, and small traders of that central region of England which she has made known to us under the name of Loamshire. The conditions of the popular life in this district in that already distant period to which she refers the action of most of her stories—the end of the last century and the beginning of the present—were so different from any that have been seen in America, that an American, in treating of her books, must be satisfied not to touch upon the question of their accuracy and fidelity as pictures of manners and customs. He can only say that they bear strong internal evidence of truthfulness.

If he is a great admirer of George Eliot, he will indeed be tempted to affirm that they must be true. They offer a completeness, a rich density of detail, which could be the fruit only of a long term of conscious contact,—

such as would make it much more difficult for the author to fall into the perversion and suppression of facts, than to set them down literally. It is very probable that her colours are a little too bright, and her shadows of too mild a gray, that the sky of her landscapes is too sunny, and their atmosphere too redolent of peace and abundance. Local affection may be accountable for half of this excess of brilliancy; the author's native optimism is accountable for the other half.

I do not remember, in all her novels, an instance of gross misery of any kind not directly caused by the folly of the sufferer. There are no pictures of vice or poverty or squalor. There are no rags, no gin, no brutal passions. That average humanity which she favours is very *borné* in intellect, but very genial in heart, as a glance at its representatives in her pages will convince us. In *Adam Bede*, there is Mr. Irwine, the vicar, with avowedly no qualification for his profession, placidly playing chess with his mother, stroking his dogs, and dipping into Greek tragedies; there is the excellent Martin Poyser at the Farm, good-natured and rubicund; there is his wife, somewhat too sharply voluble, but only in behalf of cleanliness and honesty and order; there is Captain Donnithorne at the Hall, who does a poor girl a mortal wrong, but who is, after all, such a nice, good-looking fellow; there are Adam and Seth Bede, the carpenter's sons, the strongest, purest, most discreet of young rustics. The same broad felicity prevails in *The Mill on the Floss*. Mr. Tulliver, indeed, fails in business; but his failure only serves as an offset to the general integrity and prosperity. His son is obstinate and wilful; but it is all on the side of virtue. His daughter is somewhat sentimental and erratic; but she is more conscientious yet.

Conscience, in the classes from which George Eliot recruits her figures, is a universal gift. Decency and plenty and good-humour follow contentedly in its train. The word which sums up the common traits of our author's various groups is the word *respectable*. Adam Bede is pre-eminently a respectable young man; so is Arthur Donnithorne; so, although he will persist in going without a cravat, is Felix Holt. So, with perhaps the exception of Maggie Tulliver and Stephen Guest, is every important character to be found in our author's writings. They all share this fundamental trait,—that in each of them passion proves itself feebler than conscience.

The first work which made the name of George Eliot generally known, contains, to my perception, only a small number of the germs of her future power. From the *Scenes of Clerical Life* to *Adam Bede* she made not so much a step as a leap. Of the three tales contained in the former work, I think the first is much the best. It is short, broadly descriptive, humourous, and exceedingly pathetic. "The Sad Fortunes of the Reverend Amos Barton" are fortunes which clever story-tellers with a turn for pathos, from Oliver Goldsmith downward, have found of very good account,—the fortunes of a hapless clergyman of the Church of England in daily contention with the problem how upon eighty pounds a year to support a wife and six children in all due ecclesiastical gentility.

"Mr. Gilfil's Love-Story," the second of the tales in question, I cannot hesitate to pronounce a failure. George Eliot's pictures of drawing-room life are only interesting when they are linked or related to scenes in the tavern parlour, the dairy, and the cottage. Mr. Gilfil's love-story is enacted entirely in the drawing-room, and in consequence it is singularly deficient in force and reality. Not that it is vulgar,—for our author's good taste never forsakes her,—but it is thin, flat, and trivial. But for a certain family likeness in the use of language and the rhythm of the style, it would be hard to believe that these pages are by the same hand as *Silas Marner*.

In "Janet's Repentance," the last and longest of the three clerical stories, we return to middle life,—the life represented by the Dodsons in *The Mill on the Floss*. The subject of this tale might almost be qualified by the French epithet *scabreux*. It would be difficult for what is called *realism* to go further than in the adoption of a heroine stained with the vice of intemperance. The theme is unpleasant; the author chose it at her peril. It must be added, however, that Janet Dempster has many provocations. Married to a brutal drunkard, she takes refuge in drink against his ill-usage; and the story deals less with her lapse into disgrace than with her redemption, through the kind offices of the Reverend Edgar Tryan,—by virtue of which, indeed, it takes its place in the clerical series. I cannot help thinking that the stern and tragical character of the subject has been enfeebled by the over-diffuseness of the narrative and the excess of local touches. The abundance of the author's recollections and observations of village life clogs the dramatic movement, over which she has as yet a comparatively slight control. In her subsequent works the stouter fabric of the story is better able to support this heavy drapery of humour and digression.

To a certain extent, I think *Silas Marner* holds a higher place than any of the author's works. It is more nearly a masterpiece; it has more of that simple, rounded, consummate aspect, that absence of loose ends and gaping issues, which marks a classical work. What was attempted in it, indeed, was within more immediate reach than the heart-trials of Adam Bede and Maggie Tulliver. A poor, dull-witted, disappointed Methodist cloth-weaver; a little golden-haired foundling child; a well-meaning, irresolute country squire, and his patient, childless wife;—these, with a chorus of simple, beer-loving villagers, make up the *dramatis personae*. More than any of its brother-works, *Silas Marner*, I think, leaves upon the mind a deep impression of the grossly material life of agricultural England in the last days of the old *régime*,—the days of full-orbed Toryism, of Trafalgar and of Waterloo, when the invasive spirit of French domination threw England back upon a sense of her own insular solidity, and made her for the time doubly, brutally, morbidly English. Perhaps the best pages in the work are the first thirty, telling the story of poor Marner's disappointments in friendship and in love, his unmerited disgrace, and his long, lonely twilight-life at Raveloe, with the sole companionship of his loom, in which his muscles moved "with such even repetition, that their pause seemed almost as much a constraint as the holding of his breath."

Here, as in all George Eliot's books, there is a middle life and a low life; and here, as usual, I prefer the low life. In *Silas Marner*, in my opinion, she has come nearest the mildly rich tints of brown and gray, the mellow lights and the undreadful corner-shadows of the Dutch masters whom she emulates. One of the chapters contains a scene in a pot-house, which frequent reference has made famous. Never was a group of honest, garrulous village simpletons more kindly and humanely handled. After a long and somewhat chilling silence, amid the pipes and beer, the landlord opens the conversation "by saying in a doubtful tone to his cousin the butcher:—

"'Some folks 'ud say that was a fine beast you druv in yesterday, Bob?'

"The butcher, a jolly, smiling, red-haired man, was not disposed to answer rashly. He gave a few puffs before he spat, and replied, 'And they wouldn't be fur wrong, John.'

"After this feeble, delusive thaw, silence set in as severely as before.

"'Was it a red Durham?' said the farrier, taking up the thread of discourse after the lapse of a few minutes.

"The farrier looked at the landlord, and the landlord looked at the butcher, as the person who must take the responsibility of answering.

"'Red it was,' said the butcher, in his good-humoured husky treble,— 'and a Durham it was.'

"'Then you needn't tell me who you bought it of,' said the farrier, looking round with some triumph; 'I know who it is has got the red Durhams o' this country-side. And she'd a white star on her brow, I'll bet a penny?'

"'Well; yes—she might,' said the butcher, slowly, considering that he was giving a decided affirmation. 'I don't say contrairy.'

"'I knew that very well,' said the farrier, throwing himself back defiantly; 'if I don't know Mr. Lammeter's cows, I should like to know who does,— that's all. And as for the cow you bought, bargain or no bargain, I've been at the drenching of her,—contradick me who will.'

"The farrier looked fierce, and the mild butcher's conversational spirit was roused a little.

"'I'm not for contradicking no man,' he said; 'I'm for peace and quietness. Some are for cutting long ribs. I'm for cutting 'em short myself; but I don't quarrel with 'em. All I say is, it's a lovely carkiss,—and anybody as was reasonable, it'ud bring tears into their eyes to look at it.'

"'Well, it's the cow as I drenched, whatever it is,' pursued the farrier, angrily; 'and it was Mr. Lammeter's cow, else you told a lie when you said it was a red Durham.'

"'I tell no lies,' said the butcher, with the same mild huskiness as before; 'and I contradick none,—not if a man was to swear himself black; he's no meat of mine, nor none of my bargains. All I say is, it's a lovely carkiss. And what I say I'll stick to; but I'll quarrel wi' no man.'

"'No,' said the farrier, with bitter sarcasm, looking at the company generally; 'and p'rhaps you didn't say the cow was a red Durham; and p'rhaps you didn't say she'd got a star on her brow,—stick to that, now you are at it.'"

Matters having come to this point, the landlord interferes *ex officio* to preserve order. The Lammeter family having come up, he discreetly invites Mr. Macey, the parish clerk and tailor, to favour the company with his recollections on the subject. Mr. Macey, however, "smiled pityingly in answer to the landlord's appeal, and said: 'Ay, ay; I know, I know: but I let other folks talk. I've laid by now, and gev up to the young uns. Ask them as have been to school at Tarley: they've learn't pernouncing; that's came up since my day.'"

Mr. Macey is nevertheless persuaded to dribble out his narrative; proceeding by instalments, and questioned from point to point, in a kind of Socratic manner, by the landlord. He at last arrives at Mr. Lammeter's marriage, and how the clergyman, when he came to put the questions, inadvertently transposed the position of the two essential names, and asked, "Wilt thou have this man to be thy wedded wife?" etc.

"'But the partic'larest thing of all,' pursues Mr. Macey, 'is, as nobody took any notice on it but me, and they answered straight off "Yes," like as if it had been me saying "Amen" i' the right place, without listening to what went before.'

"'But *you* knew what was going on well enough, didn't you, Mr. Macey? You were live enough, eh?' said the butcher.

"'Yes, bless you!' said Mr. Macey, pausing, and smiling in pity at the impatience of his hearer's imagination,—'why, I was all of a tremble; it was as if I'd been a coat pulled by two tails, like; for I couldn't stop the parson, I couldn't take upon me to do that; and yet I said to myself, I says, "Suppose they shouldn't be fast married," 'cause the words are contrairy, and my head went working like a mill, for I was always uncommon for turning things over and seeing all round 'em; and I says to myself, "Is't the meaning or the words as makes folks fast i' wedlock?" For the parson meant right, and the bride and bride-groom meant right. But then, when I came to think on it, meaning goes but a little way i' most things, for you may mean to stick things together and your glue may be bad, and then where are you?'"

Mr. Macey's doubts, however, are set at rest by the parson after the service, who assures him that what does the business is neither the meaning nor the words, but the register. Mr. Macey then arrives at the chapter—or rather is gently inducted thereunto by his hearers—of the ghosts who frequent certain of the Lammeter stables. But ghosts threatening to prove as pregnant a theme of contention as Durham cows, the landlord again meditates: "'There's folks i' my opinion, they can't see ghos'es, not if they stood as plain as a pikestaff before 'em. And there's reason i' that. For there's my wife, now, can't smell, not if she'd the strongest o' cheese under her nose. I never seed a ghost myself, but then I says to myself, "Very like I haven't the smell for 'em." I mean, putting a ghost for a smell or else contrairiways. And so I'm for holding with both sides.... For the smell's what I go by.'"

The best drawn of the village worthies in *Silas Marner* are Mr. Macey, of the scene just quoted, and good Dolly Winthrop, Marner's kindly patroness. I have room for only one more specimen of Mr. Macey. He is looking on at a New Year's dance at Squire Cass's, beside Ben Winthrop, Dolly's husband.

"'The Squire's pretty springy, considering his weight,' said Mr. Macey, 'and he stamps uncommon well. But Mr. Lammeter beats 'em all for shapes; you see he holds his head like a sodger, and he isn't so cushiony as most o' the oldish gentlefolks,—they run fat in gineral;—and he's got a fine leg. The parson's nimble enough, but he hasn't got much of a leg: it is a bit too thick downward, and his knees might be a bit nearer without damage; but he might do worse, he might do worse. Though he hasn't that grand way o' waving his hand as the Squire has.'

"'Talk o' nimbleness, look at Mrs. Osgood,' said Ben Winthrop.... 'She's the finest made woman as is, let the next be where she will.'

24

"'I don't heed how the women are made,' said Mr. Macey, with some contempt. 'They wear nayther coat nor breeches; you can't make much out o' their shapes!'"

Mrs. Winthrop, the wheelwright's wife who, out of the fullness of her charity, comes to comfort Silas in the season of his distress, is in her way one of the most truthfully sketched of the author's figures. "She was in all respects a woman of scrupulous conscience, so eager for duties that life seemed to offer them too scantily unless she rose at half past four, though this threw a scarcity of work over the more advanced hours of the morning, which it was a constant problem for her to remove.... She was a very mild, patient woman, whose nature it was to seek out all the sadder and more serious elements of life and pasture her mind upon them." She stamps I. H. S. on her cakes and loaves without knowing what the letters mean, or indeed without knowing that they are letters, being very much surprised that Marner can "read 'em off,"—chiefly because they are on the pulpit cloth at church. She touches upon religions themes in a manner to make the superficial reader apprehend that she cultivates some polytheistic form of faith,—extremes meet. She urges Marner to go to church, and describes the satisfaction which she herself derives from the performance of her religious duties.

"If you've niver had no church, there 's no telling what good it'll do you. For I feel as set up and comfortable as niver was, when I've been and heard the prayers and the singing to the praise and glory o' God, as Mr. Macey gives out,—and Mr. Crackenthorp saying good words and more partic'lar on Sacramen' day; and if a bit o' trouble comes, I feel as I can put up wi' it, for I've looked for help i' the right quarter, and giv myself up to Them as we must all give ourselves up to at the last: and if we've done our part, it isn't to be believed as Them as are above us 'ud be worse nor we are, and come short o' Theirn."

"The plural pronoun," says the author, "was no heresy of Dolly's, but only her way of avoiding a presumptuous familiarity." I imagine that there is in no other English novel a figure so simple in its elements as this of Dolly Winthrop, which is so real without being contemptible, and so quaint without being ridiculous.

In all those of our author's books which have borne the name of the hero or heroine,—*Adam Bede, Silas Marner, Romola,* and *Felix Holt,*—the person so put forward has really played a subordinate part. The author may have set out with the intention of maintaining him supreme; but her material has become rebellious in her hands, and the technical hero has been eclipsed by the real one. Tito is the leading figure in *Romola.* The story deals predominantly, not with Romola as affected by Tito's faults, but with Tito's faults as affecting first himself, and incidentally his wife. Godfrey Cass, with his lifelong secret, is by right the hero of *Silas Marner.* Felix Holt, in the work which bears his name, is little more than an occasional apparition; and indeed the novel has no hero, but only a heroine.

The same remark applies to *Adam Bede,* as the work stands. The central figure of the book, by virtue of her great misfortune, is Hetty Sorrel. In the presence of that misfortune no one else, assuredly, has a right to claim dramatic pre-eminence. The one person for whom an approach to equality may be claimed is, not Adam Bede, but Arthur Donnithorne. If the story had ended, as I should have infinitely preferred to see it end, with Hetty's execution, or even with her reprieve, and if Adam had been left to his grief, and Dinah Morris to the enjoyment of that distinguished celibacy for which she was so well suited, then I think Adam might have shared the honours of pre-eminence with his hapless sweetheart. But as it is, the continuance of the book in his interest is fatal to him. His sorrow at Hetty's misfortune is not a *sufficient* sorrow for the situation. That his marriage at some future time was quite possible, and even natural, I readily admit; but that was matter for a new story.

This point illustrates, I think, the great advantage of the much-censured method, introduced by Balzac, of continuing his heroes' adventures from tale to tale. Or, admitting that the author was indisposed to undertake, or even to conceive, in its completeness, a new tale, in which Adam, healed of his wound by time, should address himself to another woman, I yet hold that it would be possible tacitly to foreshadow some such event at the close of the tale which we are supposing to end with Hetty's death,—to make it the logical consequence of Adam's final state of mind. Of course circumstances would have much to do with bringing it to pass, and these circumstances could not be foreshadowed; but apart from the action of circumstances would stand the fact that, to begin with, the event was *possible*.

The assurance of this possibility is what I should have desired the author to place the sympathetic reader at a stand-point to deduce for himself. In every novel the work is divided between the writer and the reader; but the writer makes the reader very much as he makes his characters. When he makes him ill, that is, makes him different, he does no work; the writer does all. When he makes him well, that is, makes him interested, then the reader does quite half the labour. In making such a deduction as I have just indicated, the reader would be doing but his share of the task; the grand point is to get him to make it. I hold that there is a way. It is perhaps a secret; but until it is found out, I think that the art of story-telling cannot be said to have approached perfection.

When you re-read coldly and critically a book which in former years you have read warmly and carelessly, you are surprised to see how it changes its proportions. It falls away in those parts which have been pre-eminent in your memory, and it increases in the small portions. Until I lately read *Adam Bede* for a second time, Mrs. Poyser was in my mind its representative figure; for I remembered a number of her epigrammatic sallies. But now, after a second reading, Mrs. Poyser is the last figure I think of, and a fresh perusal of her witticisms has considerably diminished their classical flavour. And if I must tell the truth, Adam himself is next to the last, and sweet Dinah Morris third from the last. The person immediately evoked by the title of the work is poor Hetty Sorrel.

Mrs. Poyser is *too* epigrammatic; her wisdom smells of the lamp. I do not mean to say that she is not natural, and that women of her class are not often gifted with her homely fluency, her penetration, and her turn for forcible analogies. But she is too sustained; her morality is too shrill,—too much in *staccato*; she too seldom subsides into the commonplace. Yet it cannot be denied that she puts things very happily. Remonstrating with Dinah Morris on the undue disinterestedness of her religious notions, "But for the matter o' that," she cries, "if everybody was to do like you, the world must come to a stand-still; for if everybody tried to do without house and home and eating and drinking, and was always talking as we must despise the things o' the world, as you say, I should like to know where the pick of the stock, and the corn, and the best new milk-cheeses 'ud have to go? *Everybody 'ud be wanting to make bread o' tail ends*, and everybody 'ud be running after everybody else to preach to 'em, i'stead o' bringing up their families and laying by against a bad harvest." And when Hetty comes home late from the Chase, and alleges in excuse that the clock at home is so much earlier than the clock at the great house: "What, you'd be wanting the clock set by gentlefolks' time, would you? an' sit up burning candle, and lie a-bed wi' the sun a-bakin' you, like a cowcumber i' the frame?" Mrs. Poyser has something almost of Yankee shrewdness and angularity; but the figure of a New England rural housewife would lack a whole range of Mrs. Poyser's feelings, which, whatever may be its effect in real life, gives its subject in a novel at least a very picturesque richness of colour; the constant sense, namely, of a superincumbent layer of "gentlefolks," whom she and her companions can never raise their heads unduly without hitting.

My chief complaint with Adam Bede himself is that he is too good. He is meant, I conceive, to be every inch a man; but, to my mind, there are several inches wanting. He lacks spontaneity and sensibility, he is too stiff-backed. He lacks that supreme quality without which a man can never be interesting to men,—the capacity to be tempted. His nature is without richness or responsiveness. I doubt not that such men as he exist, especially in the author's thrice-English Loamshire; she has partially described them as a class, with a felicity which carries conviction. She claims for her hero that, although a plain man, he was as little an ordinary man as he was a genius.

"He was not an average man. Yet such men as he are reared here and there in every generation of our peasant artisans, with an inheritance of affections nurtured by a simple family life of common need and common industry, and an inheritance of faculties trained in skillful, courageous labour; they make their way upward, rarely as geniuses, most commonly as painstaking, honest men, with the skill and conscience to do well the tasks that lie before them. Their lives have no discernible echo beyond the neighbourhood where they dwelt; but you are almost sure to find there some good piece of road, some building, some application of mineral produce, some improvement in farming practice, some reform of parish abuses, with which their names are associated by one or two generations after them. Their employers were the richer for them; the work of their hands has worn well, and the work of their brains has guided well the hands of other men."

One cannot help feeling thankful to the kindly writer who attempts to perpetuate their memories beyond the generations which profit immediately by their toil. If she is not a great dramatist, she is at least an exquisite describer. But one can as little help feeling that it is no more than a strictly logical retribution, that in her hour of need (dramatically speaking) she should find them indifferent to their duties as heroes. I profoundly doubt whether the central object of a novel may successfully be a passionless creature. The ultimate eclipse, both of Adam Bede and of Felix Holt would seem to justify my question. Tom Tulliver is passionless, and Tom Tulliver lives gratefully in the memory; but this, I take it, is because he is strictly a subordinate figure, and awakens no reaction of feeling on the reader's part by usurping a position which he is not the man to fill.

Dinah Morris is apparently a study from life; and it is warm praise to say, that, in spite of the high key in which she is conceived, morally, she retains many of the warm colours of life. But I confess that it is hard to conceive of a woman so exalted by religious fervour remaining so cool-headed and so temperate. There is in Dinah Morris too close an agreement between her distinguished natural disposition and the action of her religious faith. If by nature she had been passionate, rebellious, selfish, I could better understand her actual self-abnegation. I would look upon it as the logical fruit of a profound religious experience. But as she stands, heart and soul go easily hand in hand. I believe it to be very uncommon for what is called a religious conversion merely to intensify and consecrate pre-existing inclinations. It is usually a change, a wrench; and the new life is apt to be the more sincere as the old one had less in common with it. But, as I have said, Dinah Morris bears so many indications of being a reflection of facts well known to the author,—and the phenomena of Methodism, from the frequency with which their existence is referred to in her pages, appear to be so familiar to her,—that I hesitate to do anything but thankfully accept her portrait.

About Hetty Sorrel I shall have no hesitation whatever: I accept her with all my heart. Of all George Eliot's female figures she is the least ambitious, and on the whole, I think, the most successful. The part of the story which concerns her is much the most forcible; and there is something infinitely tragic in the reader's sense of the contrast between the sternly prosaic life of the good people about her, their wholesome decency and their noon-day probity, and the dusky sylvan path along which poor Hetty is tripping, light-footed, to her ruin. Hetty's conduct throughout seems to me to be thoroughly consistent. The author has escaped the easy error of representing her as in any degree made serious by suffering. She is vain and superficial by nature; and she remains so to the end.

As for Arthur Donnithorne, I would rather have had him either better or worse. I would rather have had a little more premeditation before his fault, or a little more repentance after it; that is, while repentance could still be of use. Not that, all things considered, he is not a very fair image of a frank-hearted, well-meaning, careless, self-indulgent young gentleman; but the author has in his case committed the error which in Hetty's she avoided,—the error of showing him as redeemed by suffering. I cannot but think that he was as weak as she. A weak woman, indeed, is weaker than a weak man; but Arthur Donnithorne was a superficial fellow, a person emphatically not to be moved by a shock of conscience into a really interesting and dignified attitude, such as he is made to assume at the close of the book. Why not see things in their nakedness? the impatient reader is tempted to ask. Why not let passions and foibles play themselves out?

It is as a picture, or rather as a series of pictures, that I find *Adam Bede* most valuable. The author succeeds better in drawing attitudes of feeling than in drawing movements of feeling. Indeed, the only attempt at development of character or of purpose in the book occurs in the case of Arthur Donnithorne, where the materials are of the simplest kind. Hetty's lapse into disgrace is not gradual, it is immediate: it is without struggle and without passion. Adam himself has arrived at perfect righteousness when the book opens; and it is impossible to go beyond that. In his case too, therefore, there is no dramatic progression. The same remark applies to Dinah Morris.

It is not in her conceptions nor her composition that George Eliot is strongest: it is in her *touches*. In these she is quite original. She is a good deal of a humourist, and something of a satirist; but she is neither Dickens nor Thackeray. She has over them the great advantage that she is also a good deal of a philosopher; and it is to this union of the keenest observation with the ripest reflection, that her style owes its essential force. She is a thinker,— not, perhaps, a passionate thinker, but at least a serious one; and the term can be applied with either adjective neither to Dickens nor Thackeray. The constant play of lively and vigourous thought about the objects furnished by her observation animates these latter with a surprising richness of colour and a truly human interest. It gives to the author's style, moreover, that lingering, affectionate, comprehensive quality which is its chief distinction; and perhaps occasionally it makes her tedious. George Eliot is so little tedious, however, because, if, on the one hand, her reflection never flags, so, on the other, her observation never ceases to supply it with material. Her observation, I think, is decidedly of the feminine kind: it deals, in preference, with small things. This fact may be held to explain the excellence of what I have called her pictures, and the comparative feebleness of her dramatic movement.

The contrast here indicated, strong in *Adam Bede*, is most striking in *Felix Holt, the Radical*. The latter work is an admirable tissue of details; but it seems to me quite without character as a composition. It leaves upon the mind no single impression. Felix Holt's radicalism, the pretended motive of the story, is utterly choked amidst a mass of subordinate interests. No representation is attempted of the growth of his opinions, or of their action upon his character; he is marked by the same singular rigidity of outline and fixedness of posture which characterized Adam Bede,—except, perhaps, that there is a certain inclination towards poetry in Holt's attitude. But if the general outline is timid and undecided in *Felix Holt*, the different parts are even richer than in former works. There is no person in the book who attains to triumphant vitality; but there is not a single figure, of however little importance, that has not caught from without a certain reflection of life. There is a little old waiting-woman to a great lady,—Mrs. Denner by name,—who does not occupy five pages in the story, but who leaves upon the mind a most vivid impression of decent, contented, intelligent, half-stoical servility.

"There were different orders of beings,—so ran Denner's creed,—and she belonged to another order than that to which her mistress belonged. She had a mind as sharp as a needle, and would have seen through and through the ridiculous pretensions of a born servant who did not submissively accept the rigid fate which had given her born superiors. She would have called such pretensions the wrigglings of a worm that tried to walk on its tail.... She was a hard-headed, godless little woman, but with a character to be reckoned on as you reckon on the qualities of iron."

"I'm afraid of ever expecting anything good again," her mistress says to her in a moment of depression.

"'That's weakness, madam. Things don't happen because they are bad or good, else all eggs would be addled or none at all, and at the most it is but six to the dozen. There's good chances and bad chances, and nobody's luck is pulled only by one string.... There's a good deal of pleasure in life for you yet.'

"'Nonsense! There's no pleasure for old women.... What are your pleasures, Denner, besides being a slave to me?'

"O, there's pleasure in knowing one is not a fool, like half the people one sees about. And managing one's husband is some pleasure, and doing one's business well. Why, if I've only got some orange-flowers to candy, I shouldn't like to die till I see them all right. Then there's the sunshine now and then; I like that, as the cats do. I look upon it life is like our game at whist, when Banks and his wife come to the still-room of an evening. I don't enjoy the game much, but I like to play my cards well, and see what will be the end of it; and I want to see you make the best of your hand, madam, for your luck has been mine these forty years now."

And, on another occasion, when her mistress exclaims, in a fit of distress, that "God was cruel when he made women," the author says:—

"The waiting-woman had none of that awe which could be turned into defiance; the sacred grove was a common thicket to her.

"'It mayn't be good luck to be a woman,' she said. 'But one begins with it from a baby; one gets used to it. And I shouldn't like to be a man,—to cough so loud, and stand straddling about on a wet day, and be so wasteful with meat and drink. *They're a coarse lot, I think.*'"

I should think they were, beside Mrs. Denner.

This glimpse of her is made up of what I have called the author's *touches*. She excels in the portrayal of homely stationary figures for which her well-stored memory furnishes her with types. Here is another touch, in which satire predominates. Harold Transome makes a speech to the electors at Treby.

"Harold's only interruption came from his own party. The oratorical clerk at the Factory, acting as the tribune of the dissenting interest, and feeling bound to put questions, might have been troublesome; *but his voice being unpleasantly sharp, while Harold's was full and penetrating, the questioning was cried down.*"

Of the four English stories, *The Mill on the Floss* seems to me to have most dramatic continuity, in distinction from that descriptive, discursive method of narration which I have attempted to indicate. After Hetty Sorrel, I think Maggie Tulliver the most successful of the author's young women, and after Tito Melema, Tom Tulliver the best of her young men. English novels abound in pictures of childhood; but I know of none more truthful and touching than the early pages of this work. Poor erratic Maggie is worth a hundred of her positive brother, and yet on the very threshold of life she is compelled to accept him as her master. He falls naturally into the man's privilege of always being in the right. The following scene is more than a reminiscence; it is a real retrospect. Tom and Maggie are sitting upon the bough of an elder-tree, eating jam-puffs. At last only one remains, and Tom undertakes to divide it.

"The knife descended on the puff, and it was in two; but the result was not satisfactory to Tom, for he still eyed the halves doubtfully. At last he said, 'Shut your eyes, Maggie.'

"'What for?'

"'You never mind what for,—shut 'em when I tell you.'

"Maggie obeyed.

"'Now, which'll you have, Maggie, right hand or left?'

"'I'll have that one with the jam run out,' said Maggie, keeping her eyes shut to please Tom.

"'Why, you don't like that, you silly. You may have it if it comes to you fair, but I sha'n't give it to you without. Right or left,—you choose now. Ha-a-a!' said Tom, in a tone of exasperation, as Maggie peeped. 'You keep your eyes shut now, else you sha'n't have any.'

"Maggie's power of sacrifice did not extend so far; indeed, I fear she cared less that Tom should enjoy the utmost possible amount of puff, than that he should be pleased with her for giving him the best bit. So she shut her eyes quite close until Tom told her to 'say which,' and then she said, 'Left hand.'

"'You've got it,' said Tom, in rather a bitter tone.

"'What! the bit with the jam run out?'

"'No; here, take it,' said Tom, firmly, handing decidedly the best piece to Maggie.

"'O, please, Tom, have it; I don't mind,—I like the other; please take this.'

"'No, I sha'n't,' said Tom, almost crossly, beginning on his own inferior piece.

"Maggie, thinking it was of no use to contend further, began too, and ate up her half puff with considerable relish as well as rapidity. But Tom had finished first, and had to look on while Maggie ate her last morsel or two, feeling in himself a capacity for more. *Maggie didn't know Tom was looking at her: she was see-sawing on the elder-bough, lost to everything but a vague sense of jam and idleness.*

"'O, you greedy thing!' said Tom, when she had swallowed the last morsel."

The portions of the story which bear upon the Dodson family are in their way not unworthy of Balzac; only that, while our author has treated its peculiarities humourously, Balzac would have treated them seriously, almost solemnly. We are reminded of him by the attempt to classify the Dodsons socially in a scientific manner, and to accumulate small examples of their idiosyncrasies, I do not mean to say that the resemblance is very deep.

The chief defect—indeed, the only serious one—in *The Mill on the Floss* is its conclusion. Such a conclusion is in itself assuredly not illegitimate, and there is nothing in the fact of the flood, to my knowledge, essentially unnatural: what I object to is its relation to the preceding part of the story. The story is told as if it were destined to have, if not a strictly happy termination, at least one within ordinary probabilities. As it stands, the *dénouement* shocks the reader most painfully. Nothing has prepared him for it; the story does not move towards it; it casts no shadow before it. Did such a *dénouement* lie within the author's intentions from the first, or was it a tardy expedient for the solution of Maggie's difficulties? This question the reader asks himself, but of course he asks it in vain.

For my part, although, as long as humanity is subject to floods and earthquakes, I have no objection to see them made use of in novels, I would in this particular case have infinitely preferred that Maggie should have been left to her own devices. I understand the author's scruples, and to a certain degree I respect them. A lonely spinsterhood seemed but a dismal consummation of her generous life; and yet, as the author conceives, it was unlikely that she would return to Stephen Guest. I respect Maggie profoundly; but nevertheless I ask, Was this after all so unlikely? I will not try to answer the question. I have shown enough courage in asking it. But one thing is certain: a *dénouement* by which Maggie should have called Stephen back would have been extremely interesting, and would have had far more in its favour than can be put to confusion by a mere exclamation of horror.

I have come to the end of my space without speaking of *Romola*, which, as the most important of George Eliot's works, I had kept in reserve. I have only room to say that on the whole I think it *is* decidedly the most important,—not the most entertaining nor the most readable, but the one in which the largest things are attempted and grasped. The figure of Savonarola, subordinate though it is, is a figure on a larger scale than any which George Eliot has elsewhere undertaken; and in the career of Tito Melema there is a fuller representation of the development of a character.

Considerable as are our author's qualities as an artist, and largely as they are displayed in "Romola," the book strikes me less as a work of art than as a work of morals. Like all of George Eliot's works, its dramatic construction is feeble; the story drags and halts,—the setting is too large for the picture; but I remember that, the first time I read it, I declared to myself that much should be forgiven it for the sake of its generous feeling and its elevated morality. I still recognize this latter fact, but I think I find it more on a level than I at first found it with the artistic conditions of the book.

"Our deeds determine us," George Eliot says somewhere in *Adam Bede*, "as much as we determine our deeds." This is the moral lesson of *Romola*. A man has no associate so intimate as his own character, his own career,—his present and his past; and if he builds up his career of timid and base actions, they cling to him like evil companions, to sophisticate, to corrupt, and to damn him. As in Maggie Tulliver we had a picture of the elevation of the moral tone by honesty and generosity, so that when the mind found itself face to face with the need for a strong muscular effort, it was competent to perform it; so in Tito we have a picture of that depression of the moral tone by falsity and self-indulgence, which gradually evokes on every side of the subject some implacable claim, to be avoided or propitiated. At last all his unpaid debts join issue before him, and he finds the path of life a hideous blind alley.

Can any argument be more plain? Can any lesson be more salutary? "Under every guilty secret," writes the author, with her usual felicity, "there is a hidden brood of guilty wishes, whose unwholesome, infecting life is cherished by the darkness. The contaminating effect of deeds often lies less in the commission than in the consequent adjustment of our desires,—the enlistment of self-interest on the side of falsity; as, on the other hand, the purifying influence of public confession springs from the fact, that by it the hope in lies is forever swept away, *and the soul recovers the noble attitude of simplicity.*" And again: "Tito was experiencing that inexorable law of human souls, that we prepare ourselves for sudden deeds by the reiterated choice of good or evil that gradually determines character." Somewhere else I think she says, in purport, that our deeds are like our children; we beget them, and rear them and cherish them, and they grow up and turn against us and misuse us.

The fact that has led me to a belief in the fundamental equality between the worth of *Romola* as a moral argument and its value as a work of art, is the fact that in each character it seems to me essentially prosaic. The excellence both of the spirit and of the execution of the book is emphatically an obvious excellence. They make no demand upon the imagination of the reader. It is true of both of them that he who runs may read them. It may excite surprise that I should intimate that George Eliot is deficient in imagination; but I believe that I am right in so doing. Very readable novels have been written without imagination; and as compared with writers who, like Mr. Trollope, are totally destitute of the faculty, George Eliot may be said to be richly endowed with it. But as compared with writers whom we are tempted to call decidedly imaginative, she must, in my opinion, content herself with the very solid distinction of being exclusively an observer. In confirmation of this I would suggest a comparison of those chapters in *Adam Bede* which treat of Hetty's flight and wanderings, and those of Miss Brontë's *Jane Eyre* which describe the heroine's escape from Rochester's house and subsequent perambulations. The former are throughout admirable prose; the latter are in portions very good poetry.

One word more. Of all the impressions—and they are numerous—which a reperusal of George Eliot's writings has given me, I find the strongest to be this: that (with all deference to *Felix Holt, the Radical*) the author is in morals and æsthetics essentially a conservative. In morals her problems are still the old, passive problems. I use the word "old" with all respect. What moves her most is the idea of a conscience harassed by the memory of slighted obligations. Unless in the case of Savonarola, she has made no attempt to depict a conscience taking upon itself great and novel responsibilities. In her last work, assuredly such an attempt was—considering the title—conspicuous by its absence.

Of a corresponding tendency in the second department of her literary character,—or perhaps I should say in a certain middle field where morals and æsthetics move in concert,—it is very difficult to give an example. A tolerably good one is furnished by her inclination to compromise with the old tradition—and here I use the word "old" *without* respect—which exacts that a serious story of manners shall close with the factitious happiness of a fairy-tale. I know few things more irritating in a literary way than each of her final chapters,—for even in *The Mill on the Floss* there is a fatal "Conclusion." Both as an artist and a thinker, in other words, our author is an optimist; and although a conservative is not necessarily an optimist, I think an optimist is pretty likely to be a conservative.

ON A DRAMA OF MR. BROWNING

THIS is a decidedly irritating and displeasing performance. It is growing more difficult every year for Mr. Browning's old friends to fight his battles for him, and many of them will feel that on this occasion the cause is really too hopeless, and the great poet must himself be answerable for his indiscretions.

Nothing that Mr. Browning writes, of course, can be vapid; if this were possible, it would be a much simpler affair. If it were a case of a writer "running thin," as the phrase is, there would be no need for criticism; there would be nothing in the way of matter to criticise, and old readers would have no heart to reproach. But it may be said of Mr. Browning that he runs thick rather than thin, and he need claim none of the tenderness granted to those who have used themselves up in the service of their admirers. He is robust and vigorous; more so now, even, than heretofore, and he is more prolific than in the earlier part of his career. But his wantonness, his wilfulness, his crudity, his inexplicable want of secondary thought, as we may call it, of the stage of reflection that follows upon the first outburst of the idea, and smooths, shapes, and adjusts it—all this alloy of his great genius is more sensible now than ever.

The Inn Album reads like a series of rough notes for a poem—of hasty hieroglyphics and symbols, decipherable only to the author himself. A great poem might perhaps have been made of it, but assuredly it is not a great poem, nor any poem whatsoever. It is hard to say very coherently what it is. Up to a certain point, like everything of Mr. Browning's, it is highly dramatic and vivid and beyond that point, like all its companions, it is as little dramatic as possible. It is not narrative, for there is not a line of comprehensible, consecutive statement in the two hundred and eleven pages of the volume. It is not lyrical, for there is not a phrase which in any degree does the office of the poetry that comes lawfully into the world—chants itself, images itself, or lingers in the memory.

"That bard's a Browning; he neglects the form!" one of the characters exclaims with irresponsible frankness. That Mr. Browning knows he "neglects the form," and does not particularly care, does not very much help matters; it only deepens the reader's sense of the graceless and thankless and altogether unavailable character of the poem. And when we say unavailable, we make the only reproach which is worth addressing to a writer of Mr. Browning's intellectual power. A poem with so many presumptions in its favour as such an authorship carries with it is a thing to make some intellectual use of, to care for, to remember, to return to, to linger over, to become intimate with. But we can as little imagine a reader (who has not the misfortune to be a reviewer) addressing himself more than once to the perusal of *The Inn Album*, as we fancy cultivating for conversational purposes the society of a person afflicted with a grievous impediment of speech.

Two gentlemen have been playing cards all night in an inn-parlour, and the peep of day finds one of them ten thousand pounds in debt to the other. The tables have been turned, and the victim is the actual victor. The elder man is a dissolute and penniless nobleman, who has undertaken the social education of the aspiring young heir of a great commercial fortune, and has taught him so well that the once ingenuous lad knows more than his clever master. The young man has come down into the country to see his cousin, who lives, hard by at the Hall, with her aunt, and with whom his aristocratic preceptor recommends him, for good worldly reasons, to make a match.

Infinite discourse, of that formidable full-charged sort that issues from the lips of all Mr. Browning's characters, follows the play, and as the morning advances the two gentlemen leave the inn and go for a walk. Lord K. has meanwhile related to his young companion the history of one of his own earlier loves—how he had seduced a magnificent young woman, and she had fairly frightened him into offering her marriage. On learning that he had meant to go free if he could, her scorn for him becomes such that she rejects his offer of reparation (a very fine stroke) and enters into wedlock with a "smug, crop-haired, smooth-chinned sort of curate-creature." The young man replies that he himself was once in love with a person that quite answers to this description, and then the companions separate—the pupil to call at the Hall, and the preceptor to catch the train for London.

The reader is then carried back to the inn-parlour, into which, on the departure of the gentlemen, two ladies have been ushered. One of them is the young man's cousin, who is playing at cross-purposes with her suitor; the other is her intimate friend, arrived on a flying visit. The intimate friend is of course the ex-victim of Lord K. The ladies have much conversation—all of it rather more ingeniously inscrutable than that of their predecessors; it terminates in the exit of the cousin and the entrance of the young man. He recognizes the curate's wife as the object of his own stifled affection, and the two have, as the French say, an *intime* conversation.

At last Lord K. comes back, having missed his train, and finds himself confronted with his stormy mistress. Very stormy she proves to be, and her outburst of renewed indignation and irony contains perhaps the most successful writing in the poem. Touched by the lady's eloquence, the younger man, who has hitherto professed an almost passionate admiration for his companion, begins to see him in a less interesting light, and in fact promptly turns and reviles him. The situation is here extremely dramatic. Lord K. is a cynic of a sneaking pattern, but he is at any rate a man of ideas. He holds the destiny of his adversaries in his hands, and, snatching up the inn album (which has been knocking about the table during the foregoing portions of the narrative), he scrawls upon it his ultimatum. Let the lady now bestow her affection on his companion, and let the latter accept this boon as a vicarious payment of the gambling debt, otherwise Lord K. will enlighten the lady's husband as to the extent of her acquaintance with himself.

He presents the open page to the heroine, who reads it aloud, and for an answer her younger and more disinterested lover, "with a tiger-flash yell, spring, and scream," throws himself on the insulter, half an hour since, his guide, philosopher, and friend, and, by some means undescribed by Mr. Browning puts an end to his life. This incident is related in two pregnant lines, which, judged by the general standard of style of the *Inn Album*, must be considered fine:

"A tiger-flash, yell, spring and scream: halloo!

Death's out and on him, has and holds him—ugh!"

The effect is of course augmented if the reader is careful to make the "ugh!" rhyme correctly with the "halloo!" The lady takes poison, which she carries on her person and which operates instantaneously, and the young man's cousin, re-entering the room, has a sufficiently tremendous surprise.

The whole picture indefinably appeals to the imagination. There is something very curious about it and even rather arbitrary, and the reader wonders how it came, in the poet's mind, to take exactly that shape. It is very much as if he had worked backwards, had seen his dénouement first, as a mere picture—the two corpses in the inn-parlour, and the young man and his cousin confronted above them—and then had traced back the possible motives and sources. In looking for these Mr. Browning has of course encountered a vast number of deep discriminations and powerful touches of portraitures. He deals with human character as a chemist with his acids and alkalies, and while he mixes his coloured fluids in a way that surprises the profane, knows perfectly well what he is about. But there is too apt to be in his style that hiss and sputter and evil aroma which characterise the proceedings of the laboratory. The idea, with Mr. Browning, always tumbles out into the world in some grotesque hind-foremost manner; it is like an unruly horse backing out of his stall, and stamping and plunging as he comes. His thought knows no simple stage—at the very moment of its birth it is a terribly complicated affair.

We frankly confess, at the risk of being accused of deplorable levity of mind, that we have found this want of clearness of explanation, of continuity, of at least superficial verisimilitude, of the smooth, the easy, the agreeable, quite fatal to our enjoyment of *The Inn Album*. It is all too argumentative, too curious and recondite. The people talk too much in long set speeches, at a moment's notice, and the anomaly so common in Browning, that the talk of the women is even more rugged and insoluble than that of the men, is here greatly exaggerated. We are reading neither prose nor poetry; it is too real for the ideal, and too ideal for the real. The author of *The Inn Album* is not a writer to whom we care to pay trivial compliments, and, it is not a trivial complaint to say that his book is only barely comprehensible. Of a successful dramatic poem one ought to be able to say more.

SWINBURNE'S ESSAYS

MR. SWINBURNE has by this time impressed upon the general public a tolerably vivid image of his literary personality. His line is a definite one; his note is familiar, and we know what to expect from him. He was at pains, indeed, a year ago to quicken the apprehension of American readers by an effusion directed more or less explicitly to themselves. This piece of literature was brief, but it was very remarkable. Mr. Emerson had had occasion to speak of Mr. Swinburne with qualified admiration and this circumstance, coming to Mr. Swinburne's ears, had prompted him to uncork on the spot the vials of his wrath. He addressed to a newspaper a letter of which it is but a colourless account to say that it embodied the very hysterics of gross vituperation.

Mr. Swinburne has some extremely just remarks about Byron's unamenableness to quotation, his having to be taken in the gross. This is almost equally true of our author himself; he must be judged by all he has done, and we must allow, in our judgment, the weight he would obviously claim for it to his elaborate tribute to the genius of Mr. Emerson. His tone has two distinct notes—the note of measureless praise and the note of furious denunciation. Each is in need of a correction, but we confess that, with all its faults, we prefer the former. That Mr. Swinburne has a kindness for his more restrictive strain is, however, very obvious. He is over-ready to sound it, and he is not particular about his pretext.

Some people, he says, for instance, affirm that a writer may have a very effective style, yet have nothing of value to express with it. Mr. Swinburne demands that they prove their assertion. "This flattering unction the very foolishest of malignants will hardly, in this case (that of Mr. D. G. Rossetti), be able to lay upon the corrosive sore which he calls his soul; the ulcer of ill-will must rot unrelieved by the rancid ointment of such fiction." In Mr. W. M. Rossetti's edition of Shelley there is in a certain line, an interpolation of the word "autumn." "For the conception of this atrocity the editor is not responsible; for its adoption he is. A thousand years of purgatorial fire would be insufficient expiation for the criminal on whose deaf and desperate head must rest the original guilt of defacing the text of Shelley with this most damnable corruption."

The essays before us are upon Victor Hugo, D. G. Rossetti, William Morris, Matthew Arnold as a poet, Shelley, Byron, Coleridge, and John Ford. To these are added two papers upon pictures—the drawings of the old masters at Florence and the Royal Academy Exhibition of 1868. Mr. Swinburne, in writing of poets, cannot fail to say a great many felicitous things. His own insight into the poetic mystery is so deep, his perception in matters of language so refined, his power of appreciation so large and active, his imagination, especially, so sympathetic and flexible, that we constantly feel him to be one who has a valid right to judge and pass sentence. The variety of his sympathies in poetry is especially remarkable, and is in itself a pledge of criticism of a liberal kind. Victor Hugo is his divinity—a divinity whom indeed, to our sense, he effectually conceals and obliterates in the suffocating fumes of his rhetoric. On the other hand, one of the best papers in the volume is a disquisition on the poetry of Mr. Matthew Arnold, of which his relish seems hardly less intense and for whom he states the case with no less prodigious a redundancy of phrase.

Matthew Arnold's canons of style, we should have said, are a positive negation of those of Mr. Swinburne's, and it is to the credit of the latter's breadth of taste that he should have entered into an intellectual temperament which is so little his own. The other articles contain similar examples of his vivacity and energy of perception, and offer a number of happy judgments and suggestive observations. His estimate of Byron as a poet (not in the least as a man—on this point his utterances are consummately futile) is singularly discriminating; his measurement of Shelley's lyric force is eloquently adequate; his closing words upon John Ford are worth quoting as a specimen of strong apprehension and solid statement. Mr. Swinburne is by no means always solid, and this passage represents him at his best:—

"No poet is less forgettable than Ford; none fastens (as it were) the fangs of his genius and his will more deeply in your memory. You cannot shake hands with him and pass him by; you cannot fall in with him and out again at pleasure; if he touch you once he takes you, and what he takes he keeps his hold of; his work becomes a part of your thought and parcel of your spiritual furniture for ever; he signs himself upon you as with a seal of deliberate and decisive power. His force is never the force of accident; the casual divinity of beauty which falls, as though direct from heaven, upon stray lines and phrases of some poets, fails never by any such heavenly chance on his; his strength of impulse is matched by his strength of will; he never works more by instinct than by resolution; he knows what he would have and what he will do, and gains his end and does his work with full conscience of purpose and insistence of design. By the might of a great will seconded by the force of a great hand he won the place he holds against all odds of rivalry in a race of rival giants."

On the other hand, Mr. Swinburne is constantly liable on this same line to lapse into flagrant levity and perversity of taste; as in saying that he cannot consider Wordsworth "as mere poet" equal to Coleridge as mere poet; in speaking of Alfred de Musset as "the female page or attendant dwarf" of Byron, and his poems as "decoctions of watered Byronism"; or in alluding jauntily and *en passant* to Gautier's *Mademoiselle de Maupin* as "the most perfect and exquisite book of modern times."

To note, however, the points at which Mr. Swinburne's judgment hits the mark, or the points at which it misses it, is comparatively superfluous, inasmuch as both of these cases seem to us essentially accidental. His book is not at all a book of judgment; it is a book of pure imagination. His genius is for style simply, and not in the least for thought nor for real analysis; he goes through the motions of criticism, and makes a considerable show of logic and philosophy, but with deep appreciation his writing seems to us to have very little to do.

He is an imaginative commentator, often of a very splendid kind, but he is never a real interpreter and rarely a trustworthy guide. He is a writer, and a writer in constant quest of a theme. He has an inordinate sense of the picturesque, and he finds his theme in those subjects and those writers which gratify it. When they gratify it highly, he conceives a boundless relish for them; they give him his chance, and he turns-on the deluge of his exorbitant homage. His imagination kindles, he abounds in their own sense, when they give him an inch he takes an ell, and quite loses sight of the subject in the entertainment he finds in his own word-spinning. In this respect he is extraordinarily accomplished: he very narrowly misses having a magnificent style. On the imaginative side, his style is almost complete, and seems capable of doing everything that picturesqueness demands. There are few writers of our day who could have produced this description of a thunderstorm at sea. Mr. Swinburne gives it to us as the likeness of Victor Hugo's genius:—

"About midnight, the thundercloud was full overhead, full of incessant sound and fire, lightening and darkening so rapidly that it seemed to have life, and a delight in its life. At the same hour, the sky was clear to the west, and all along the sea-line there sprang and sank as to music a restless dance or chase of summer lightnings across the lower sky: a race and riot of lights, beautiful and rapid as a course of shining Oceanides along the tremulous floor of the sea. Eastward, at the same moment, the space of clear sky was higher and wider, a splendid semicircle of too intense purity to be called blue; it was of no colour nameable by man; and midway in it, between the stars and the sea, hung the motionless full moon; Artemis watching with serene splendour of scorn the battle of Titans and the revel of nymphs from her stainless and Olympian summit of divine indifferent light. Underneath and about us, the sea was paved with flame; the whole water trembled and hissed with phosphoric fire; even through the wind and thunder I could hear the crackling and sputtering of the water-sparks. In the same heaven and in the same hour there shone at once the three contrasted glories, golden and fiery and white, of moonlight, and of the double lightning, forked and sheet; and under all this miraculous heaven lay a flaming floor of water."

But with this extravagant development of the imagination there is no commensurate development either of the reason or of the moral sense. One of these defects is, to our mind, fatal to Mr. Swinburne's style; the other is fatal to his tone, to his temper, to his critical pretensions. His style is without measure, without discretion, without sense of what to take and what to leave; after a few pages, it becomes intolerably fatiguing. It is always listening to itself—always turning its head over its shoulders to see its train flowing behind it. The train shimmers and tumbles in a very gorgeous fashion, but the rustle of its embroidery is fatally importunate.

Mr. Swinburne is a dozen times too verbose; at least one-half of his phrases are what the French call phrases in the air. One-half of his sentence is always a repetition, for mere fancy's sake and nothing more, of the meaning of the other half—a play upon its words, an echo, a reflection, a duplication. This trick, of course, makes a writer formidably prolix. What we have called the absence of the moral sense of the writer of these essays is, however, their most disagreeable feature. By this we do not mean that Mr. Swinburne is not didactic, nor edifying, nor devoted to pleading the cause of virtue. We mean simply that his moral plummet does not sink at all, and that when he pretends to drop it he is simply dabbling in the relatively very shallow pool of the picturesque.

A sense of the picturesque so refined as Mr. Swinburne's will take one a great way, but it will by no means, in dealing with things whose great value is in what they tell us of human character, take one all the way. One breaks down with it (if one treats it as one's sole support) sooner or later in æsthetics; one breaks down with it very soon indeed in psychology.

We do not remember in this whole volume a single instance of delicate moral discrimination—a single case in which the moral note has been struck, in which the idea betrays the smallest acquaintance with the conscience. The moral realm for Mr. Swinburne is simply a brilliant chiaroscuro of costume and posture. This makes all Mr. Swinburne's magnificent talk about Victor Hugo's great criminals and monstrosities, about Shelley's Count Cenci, and Browning's Guido Franchesini, and about dramatic figures generally, quite worthless as anything but amusing fantasy. As psychology it is, to our sense, extremely puerile; for we do not mean simply to say that the author does not understand morality—a charge to which he would be probably quite indifferent; but that he does not at all understand immorality. Such a passage as his rhapsody upon Victor Hugo's Josiane ("such a pantheress may be such a poetess," etc.) means absolutely nothing. It is entertaining as pictorial writing—though even in this respect as we have said, thanks to excess and redundancy, it is the picturesque spoiled rather than achieved; but as an attempt at serious analysis it seems to us, like many of its companions, simply ghastly—ghastly in its poverty of insight and its pretension to make mere lurid imagery do duty as thought.

THE POETRY OF WILLIAM MORRIS

I. THE LIFE AND DEATH OF JASON

IN this poetical history of the fortunate—the unfortunate—Jason, Mr. Morris has written a book of real value. It is some time since we have met with a work of imagination of so thoroughly satisfactory a character,—a work read with an enjoyment so unalloyed and so untempered by the desire to protest and to criticise. The poetical firmament within these recent years has been all alive with unprophesied comets and meteors, many of them of extraordinary brilliancy, but most of them very rapid in their passage. Mr. Morris gives us the comfort of feeling that he is a fixed star, and that his radiance is not likely to be extinguished in a draught of wind,—after the fashion of Mr. Alexander Smith, Mr. Swinburne and Miss Ingelow.

Mr. Morris's poem is ushered into the world with a very florid birthday speech from the pen of the author of the too famous *Poems and Ballads*,—a circumstance, we apprehend, in no small degree prejudicial to its success. But we hasten to assure all persons whom the knowledge of Mr. Swinburne's enthusiasm may have led to mistrust the character of the work, that it has to our perception nothing in common with this gentleman's own productions, and that his article proves very little more than that his sympathies are wiser than his performance. If Mr. Morris's poem may be said to remind us of the manner of any other writer, it is simply of that of Chaucer; and to resemble Chaucer is a great safeguard against resembling Swinburne.

The Life and Death of Jason, then, is a narrative poem on a Greek subject, written in a genuine English style. With the subject all reading people are familiar, and we have no need to retrace its details. But it is perhaps not amiss to transcribe the few pregnant lines of prose into which, at the outset, Mr. Morris has condensed the argument of his poem:—

"Jason the son of Æson, king of Iolchos, having come to man's estate, demanded of Pelias his father's kingdom, which he held wrongfully. But Pelias answered, that if he would bring from Colchis the golden fleece of the ram that had carried Phryxus thither, he would yield him his right. Whereon Jason sailed to Colchis in the ship Argo, with other heroes, and by means of Medea, the king's daughter, won the fleece; and carried off also Medea; and so, after many troubles, came back to Iolchos again. There, by Medea's wiles, was Pelias slain; but Jason went to Corinth, and lived with Medea happily, till he was taken with the love of Glauce, the king's daughter of Corinth, and must needs wed her; whom also Medea destroyed, and fled to Ægeus at Athens; and not long after Jason died strangely."

The style of this little fragment of prose is not an unapt measure of the author's poetical style,—quaint, but not too quaint, more Anglo-Saxon than Latin, and decidedly laconic. For in spite of the great length of his work, his manner is by no means diffuse. His story is a long one, and he wishes to do it justice; but the movement is rapid and business-like, and the poet is quite guiltless of any wanton lingering along the margin of the subject matter,—after the manner, for instance, of Keats,—to whom, individually, however, we make this tendency no reproach. Mr. Morris's subject is immensely rich,—heavy with its richness,—and in the highest degree romantic and poetical. For the most part, of course, he found not only the great *contours*, but the various incidents and episodes, ready drawn to his hand; but still there was enough wanting to make a most exhaustive drain upon his ingenuity and his imagination. And not only these faculties have been brought into severe exercise, but the strictest good taste and good sense were called into play, together with a certain final gift which we hardly know how to name, and which is by no means common, even among very clever poets,—a comprehensive sense of form, of proportion, and of real completeness, without which the most brilliant efforts of the imagination are a mere agglomeration of ill-reconciled beauties. The legend of Jason is full of strangely constructed marvels and elaborate prodigies and horrors, calculated to task heavily an author's adroitness.

We have so pampered and petted our sense of the ludicrous of late years, that it is quite the spoiled child of the house, and without its leave no guest can be honourably entertained. It is very true that the atmosphere of Grecian mythology is so entirely an artificial one, that we are seldom tempted to refer its weird anomalous denizens to our standard of truth and beauty. Truth, indeed, is at once put out of the question; but one would say beforehand, that many of the creations of Greek fancy were wanting even in beauty, or at least in that ease and simplicity which has been acquired in modern times by force of culture. But habit and tradition have reconciled us to these things in their native forms, and Mr. Morris's skill reconciles us to them in his modern and composite English.

The idea, for instance, of a *flying ram*, seems, to an undisciplined fancy, a not especially happy creation, nor a very promising theme for poetry; but Mr. Morris, without diminishing its native oddity, has given it an ample romantic dignity. So, again, the sowing of the dragon's teeth at Colchis, and the springing up of mutually opposed armed men, seems too complex and recondite a scene to be vividly and gracefully realized; but as it stands, it is one of the finest passages in Mr. Morris's poem. His great stumbling-block, however, we take it, was the necessity of maintaining throughout the dignity and prominence of his hero. From the moment that Medea comes into the poem, Jason falls into the second place, and keeps it to the end. She is the all-wise and all-brave helper and counsellor at Colchis, and the guardian angel of the returning journey. She saves her companions from the Circean enchantments, and she withholds them from the embraces of the Sirens. She effects the death of Pelias, and assures the successful return of the Argonauts. And finally—as a last claim upon her interest—she is slighted and abandoned by the man of her love. Without question, then, she is the central figure of the poem,—a powerful and enchanting figure,—a creature of barbarous arts, and of exquisite human passions. Jason accordingly possesses only that indirect hold upon our attention which belongs to the Virgilian Æneas; although Mr. Morris has avoided Virgil's error of now and then allowing his hero to be contemptible.

A large number, however, of far greater drawbacks than any we are able to mention could not materially diminish the powerful beauty of this fantastic legend. It is as rich in adventure as the Odyssey, and very much simpler. Its prime elements are of the most poetical and delightful kind. What can be more thrilling than the idea of a great boatful of warriors embarking upon dreadful seas, not for pleasure, nor for conquest, nor for any material advantage, but for the simple discovery of a jealously watched, magically guarded relic? There is in the character of the object of their quest something heroically unmarketable, or at least unavailable.

But of course the story owes a vast deal to its episodes, and these have lost nothing in Mr. Morris's hands. One of the most beautiful—the well known adventure of Hylas—occurs at the very outset. The beautiful young man, during a halt of the ship, wanders inland through the forest, and, passing beside a sylvan stream, is espied and incontinently loved by the water nymphs, who forthwith "detach" one of their number to work his seduction. This young lady assumes the disguise and speech of a Northern princess, clad in furs, and in this character sings to her victim "a sweet song, sung not yet to any man." Very sweet and truly lyrical it is like all the songs scattered through Mr. Morris's narrative. We are, indeed, almost in doubt whether the most beautiful passages in the poem do not occur in the series of songs in the fourteenth book.

The ship has already touched at the island of Circe, and the sailors, thanks to the earnest warnings of Medea, have abstained from setting foot on the fatal shore; while Medea has, in turn, been warned by the enchantress against the allurements of the Sirens. As soon as the ship draws nigh, these fair beings begin to utter their irresistible notes. All eyes are turned lovingly on the shore, the rowers' charmed muscles relax, and the ship drifts landward. But Medea exhorts and entreats her companions to preserve their course. Jason himself is not untouched, as Mr. Morris delicately tells us,—"a moment Jason gazed." But Orpheus smites his lyre before it is too late, and stirs the languid blood of his comrades. The Sirens strike their harps amain, and a conflict of song arises. The Sirens sing of the cold, the glittering, the idle delights of their submarine homes; while Orpheus tells of the warm and pastoral landscapes of Greece. We have no space for quotation; of course Orpheus carries the day. But the finest and most delicate practical sense is shown in the alternation of the two lyrical arguments,—the soulless sweetness of the one, and the deep human richness of the other.

There is throughout Mr. Morris's poem a great unity and evenness of excellence, which make selection and quotation difficult; but of impressive touches in our reading we noticed a very great number. We content ourselves with mentioning a single one. When Jason has sown his bag of dragon's teeth at Colchis, and the armed fighters have sprung up along the furrows, and under the spell contrived by Medea have torn each other to death:—

> "One man was left alive, but wounded sore,
>
> Who, staring round about and seeing no more
>
> His brothers' spears against him, fixed his eyes
>
> Upon the queller of those mysteries.
>
> Then dreadfully they gleamed, and with no word,
>
> He tottered towards him with uplifted sword.
>
> But scarce he made three paces down the field,
>
> Ere chill death seized his heart, and on his shield
>
> Clattering he fell."

We have not spoken of Mr. Morris's versification nor of his vocabulary. We have only room to say that, to our perception, the first in its facility and harmony, and the second in its abundance and studied simplicity, leave nothing to be desired. There are of course faults and errors in his poem, but there are none that are not trivial and easily pardoned in the light of the fact that he has given us a work of consummate art and of genuine beauty. He has foraged in a treasure-house; he has visited the ancient world, and come back with a massive cup of living Greek wine. His project was no light task, but he has honourably fulfilled it. He has enriched the language with a narrative poem which we are sure that the public will not suffer to fall into the ranks of honoured but uncherished works,—objects of vague and sapient reference,—but will continue to read and to enjoy. In spite of its length, the interest of the story never flags, and as a work of art it never ceases to be pure. To the jaded intellects of the present moment, distracted with the strife of creeds and the conflict of theories, it opens a glimpse into a world where they will be called upon neither to choose, to criticise, nor to believe, but simply to feel, to look, and to listen.

II. THE EARTHLY PARADISE

This new volume of Mr. Morris is, we think, a book for all time; but it is especially a book for these ripening summer days. To sit in the open shade, inhaling the heated air, and, while you read these perfect fairy tales, these rich and pathetic human traditions to glance up from your page at the clouds and the trees, is to do as pleasant a thing as the heart of man can desire. Mr. Morris's book abounds in all the sounds and sights and sensations of nature, in the warmth of the sunshine, the murmur of forests, and the breath of ocean-scented breezes. The fullness of physical existence which belongs to climates where life is spent in the open air, is largely diffused through its pages:

... "Hot July was drawing to an end,

And August came the fainting year to mend

With fruit and grain; so 'neath the trellises,

Nigh blossomless, did they lie well at ease,

And watched the poppies burn across the grass,

And o'er the bindweed's bells the brown bee pass,

Still murmuring of his gains: windless and bright

The morn had been, to help their dear delight.

... Then a light wind arose

That shook the light stems of that flowery close,

And made men sigh for pleasure."

This is a random specimen. As you read, the fictitious universe of the poem seems to expand and advance out of its remoteness, to surge musically about your senses, and merge itself utterly in the universe which surrounds you. The summer brightness of the real world goes halfway to meet it; and the beautiful figures which throb with life in Mr. Morris's stories pass lightly to and fro between the realm of poetry and the mild atmosphere of fact. This quality was half the charm of the author's former poem, *The Life and Death of Jason*, published last summer. We seemed really to follow, beneath the changing sky, the fantastic boatload of wanderers in their circuit of the ancient world. For people compelled to stay at home, the perusal of the book in a couple of mornings was very nearly as good as a fortnight's holiday. The poem appeared to reflect so clearly and forcibly the poet's natural sympathies with the external world, and his joy in personal contact with it, that the reader obtained something very like a sense of physical transposition, without either physical or intellectual weariness.

This ample and direct presentment of the joys of action and locomotion seems to us to impart to these two works a truly national and English tone. They taste not perhaps of the English soil, but of those strong English sensibilities which the great insular race carry with them through their wanderings, which they preserve and apply with such energy in every terrestrial clime, and which make them such incomparable travellers. We heartily recommend such persons as have a desire to accommodate their reading to the season—as are vexed with a delicate longing to place themselves intellectually in relation with the genius of the summer—to take this *Earthly Paradise* with them to the country.

The book is a collection of tales in verse—found, without exception, we take it, rather than imagined, and linked together, somewhat loosely, by a narrative prologue. The following is the "argument" of the prologue—already often enough quoted, but pretty enough, in its ingenious prose, to quote again:—

"Certain gentlemen and mariners of Norway, having considered all that they had heard of the Earthly Paradise, set sail to find it, and, after many troubles and the lapse of many years, came old men to some western land, of which they had never before heard: there they died, when they had dwelt there certain years, much honoured of the strange people."

The adventures of these wanderers, told by one of their number, Rolf the Norseman, born at Byzantium—a happy origin for the teller of a heroic tale, as the author doubtless felt—make, to begin with, a poem of considerable length, and of a beauty superior perhaps to that of the succeeding tales. An admirable romance of adventure has Mr. Morris unfolded in the melodious energy of this half-hurrying, half-lingering narrative—a romance to make old hearts beat again with the boyish longing for transmarine mysteries, and to plunge boys themselves into a delicious agony of unrest.

The story is a tragedy, or very near it—as what story of the search for an Earthly Paradise could fail to be? Fate reserves for the poor storm-tossed adventurers a sort of fantastic compromise between their actual misery and their ideal bliss, whereby a kindly warmth is infused into the autumn of their days, and to the reader, at least, a very tolerable Earthly Paradise is laid open. The elders and civic worthies of the western land which finally sheltered them summon them every month to a feast, where, when all grosser desires have been duly pacified, the company sit at their ease and listen to the recital of stories. Mr. Morris gives in this volume the stories of the six midmonths of the year, two tales being allotted to each month—one from the Greek Mythology, and one, to express it broadly, of a Gothic quality. He announces a second series in which, we infer, he will in the same manner give us the stories rehearsed at the winter fireside.

The Greek stories are the various histories of Atalanta, of Perseus, of Cupid and Psyche, of Alcestis, of Atys, the hapless son of Crœsus, and of Pygmalion. The companion pieces, which always serve excellently well to place in relief the perfect pagan character of their elder mates, deal of course with elements less generally known.

"Atalanta's Race," the first of Mr. Morris's Greek legends, is to our mind almost the best. There is something wonderfully simple and childlike in the story, and the author has given it ample dignity, at the same time that he has preserved this quality.

Most vividly does he present the mild invincibility of his fleet-footed heroine and the half-boyish simplicity of her demeanour—a perfect model of a *belle inhumaine*. But the most beautiful passage in the poem is the description of the vigil of the love-sick Milanion in the lonely sea-side temple of Venus. The author has conveyed with exquisite art the sense of devout stillness and of pagan sanctity which invests this remote and prayerful spot. The yellow torch-light,

"Wherein with fluttering gown and half-bared limb

The temple damsels sung their evening hymn;"

the sound of the shallow flowing sea without, the young man's restless sleep on the pavement, besprinkled with the ocean spray, the apparition of the goddess with the early dawn, bearing the golden apple—all these delicate points are presented in the light of true poetry.

The narrative of the adventures of Danaë and of Perseus and Andromeda is, with the exception of the tale of Cupid and Psyche which follows it, the longest piece in the volume. Of the two, we think we prefer the latter. Unutterably touching is the career of the tender and helpless Psyche, and most impressive the terrible hostility of Venus. The author, we think, throughout manages this lady extremely well. She appears to us in a sort of rosy dimness, through which she looms as formidable as she is beautiful, and gazing with "gentle eyes and unmoved smiles,"

> "Such as in Cyprus, the fair blossomed isle,
>
> When on the altar in the summer night
>
> They pile the roses up for her delight,
>
> Men see within their hearts."

"The Love of Alcestis" is the beautiful story of the excellent wife who, when her husband was ill, gave up her life, so that he might recover and live for ever. Half the interest here, however, lies in the servitude of Apollo in disguise, and in the touching picture of the radiant god doing in perfection the homely work of his office, and yet from time to time emitting flashes, as it were, of genius and deity, while the good Admetus observes him half in kindness and half in awe.

The story of the "Son of Crœsus," the poor young man who is slain by his best friend because the gods had foredoomed it, is simple, pathetic, and brief. The finest and sweetest poem in the volume, to our taste, is the tale of "Pygmalion and the Image." The merit of execution is perhaps not appreciably greater here than in the other pieces, but the legend is so unutterably charming that it claims precedence of its companions. As beautiful as anything in all our later poetry, we think, is the description of the growth and dominance in the poor sculptor's heart of his marvellous passion for the stony daughter of his hands. Borne along on the steady, changing flow of his large and limpid verse, the author glides into the situation with an ease and grace and fullness of sympathy worthy of a great master. Here, as elsewhere, there is no sign of effort or of strain. In spite of the studied and *recherché* character of his diction, there is not a symptom of affectation in thought or speech. We seem in this tale of "Pygmalion" truly to inhabit the bright and silent workroom of a great Greek artist, and, standing among shapes and forms of perfect beauty, to breathe the incense-tainted air in which lovely statues were conceived and shining stones chiselled into immortality.

Mr. Morris is indubitably a sensuous poet, to his credit be it said; his senses are constantly proffering their testimony and crying out their delight. But while they take their freedom, they employ it in no degree to their own debasement. Just as there is modesty of temperament we conceive there is modesty of imagination, and Mr. Morris possesses the latter distinction. The total absence of it is, doubtless, the long and short of Mr. Swinburne's various troubles. We may imagine Mr. Swinburne making a very clever poem of this story of "Pygmalion," but we cannot fancy him making it anything less than utterly disagreeable. The thoroughly agreeable way in which Mr. Morris tells it is what especially strikes us. We feel that his imagination is equally fearless and irreproachable, and that while he tells us what we may call a sensuous story in all its breadth, he likewise tells it in all its purity. It has, doubtless, an impure side; but of the two he prefers the other. While Pygmalion is all aglow with his unanswered passion, he one day sits down before his image:

> "And at the last drew forth a book of rhymes,
>
> Wherein were writ the tales of many climes,
>
> And read aloud the sweetness hid therein
>
> Of lovers' sorrows and their tangled sin."

He reads aloud to his marble torment: would Mr. Swinburne have touched that note?

We have left ourselves no space to describe in detail the other series of tales—"The Man born to be King," "The Proud King," "The Writing on the Image," "The Lady of the Land," "The Watching of the Falcon," and "Ogier the Dane."

The author in his *Jason* identified himself with the successful treatment of Greek subjects to such a degree as to make it easy to suppose that these matters were the specialty of his genius. But in these romantic modern stories the same easy power is revealed, the same admirable union of natural gifts and cultivated perceptions. Mr. Morris is evidently a poet in the broad sense of the word—a singer of human joys and sorrows, whenever and wherever found. His somewhat artificial diction, which would seem to militate against our claim that his genius is of the general and comprehensive order, is, we imagine, simply an achievement of his own. It is not imposed from without, but developed from within. Whatever may be said of it, it certainly will not be accused of being unpoetical; and except this charge, what serious one can be made?

The author's style—according to our impression—is neither Chaucerian, Spenserian, nor imitative; it is literary, indeed, but it has a freedom and irregularity, an adaptability to the movements of the author's mind, which make it an ample vehicle of poetical utterance. He says in this language of his own the most various and the most truthful things; he moves, melts, and delights. Such at least, is our own experience. Other persons, we know, find it difficult to take him entirely *au sérieux*. But we, taking him—and our critical duties too—in the most serious manner our mind permits of, feel strongly impelled, both by gratitude and by reflection, to pronounce him a noble and delightful poet. To call a man healthy nowadays is almost an insult—invalids learn so many secrets. But the health of the intellect is often promoted by physical disability. We say therefore, finally, that however the faculty may have been promoted—with the minimum of suffering, we certainly hope— Mr. Morris is a supremely healthy writer. This poem is marked by all that is broad and deep in nature, and all that is elevating, profitable, and curious in art.

MATTHEW ARNOLD'S ESSAYS

MR. ARNOLD'S *Essays in Criticism* come to American readers with a reputation already made,—the reputation of a charming style, a great deal of excellent feeling, and an almost equal amount of questionable reasoning. It is for us either to confirm the verdict passed in the author's own country, or to judge his work afresh. It is often the fortune of English writers to find mitigation of sentence in the United States.

The Essays contained in this volume are on purely literary subjects; which is for us, by itself, a strong recommendation. English literature, especially contemporary literature, is, compared with that of France and Germany, very poor in collections of this sort. A great deal of criticism is written, but little of it is kept; little of it is deemed to contain any permanent application. Mr. Arnold will doubtless find in this fact—if indeed he has not already signalized it—but another proof of the inferiority of the English to the Continental school of criticism, and point to it as a baleful effect of the narrow practical spirit which animates, or, as he would probably say, paralyzes, the former. But not only is his book attractive as a whole, from its exclusively literary character; the subject of each essay is moreover particularly interesting. The first paper is on the function of Criticism at the present time; a question, if not more important, perhaps more directly pertinent here than in England. The second, discussing the literary influence of Academies, contains a great deal of valuable observation and reflection in a small compass and under an inadequate title. The other essays are upon the two De Guérins, Heinrich Heine, Pagan and Mediæval Religious Sentiment, Joubert, Spinoza, and Marcus Aurelius. The first two articles are, to our mind, much the best; the next in order of excellence is the paper on Joubert; while the others, with the exception, perhaps, of that on Spinoza, are of about equal merit.

Mr. Arnold's style has been praised at once too much and too little. Its resources are decidedly limited; but if the word had not become so cheap, we should nevertheless call it fascinating. This quality implies no especial force; it rests in this case on the fact that, whether or not you agree with the matter beneath it, the manner inspires you with a personal affection for the author. It expresses great sensibility, and at the same time great good-nature; it indicates a mind both susceptible and healthy. With the former element alone it would savour of affectation; with the latter, it would be coarse. As it stands, it represents a spirit both sensitive and generous. We can best describe it, perhaps, by the word sympathetic. It exhibits frankly, and without detriment to its national character, a decided French influence. Mr. Arnold is too wise to attempt to write French English; he probably knows that a language can only be indirectly enriched; but as nationality is eminently a matter of form, he knows too that he can really violate nothing so long as he adheres to the English letter.

His Preface is a striking example of the intelligent amiability which animates his style. His two leading Essays were, on their first appearance, made the subject of much violent contention, their moral being deemed little else than a wholesale schooling of the English press by the French programme. Nothing could have better proved the justice of Mr. Arnold's remarks upon the "provincial" character of the English critical method than the reception which they provoked. He now acknowledges this reception in a short introduction, which admirably reconciles smoothness of temper with sharpness of wit. The taste of this performance has been questioned; but wherever it may err, it is assuredly not in being provincial; it is essentially civil. Mr. Arnold's amiability is, in our eye, a strong proof of his wisdom. If he were a few degrees more short-sighted, he might have less equanimity at his command. Those who sympathise with him warmly will probably like him best as he is; but with such as are only half his friends, this freedom from party passion, from what is after all but a lawful professional emotion, will argue against his sincerity.

For ourselves, we doubt not that Mr. Arnold possesses thoroughly what the French call the courage of his opinions. When you lay down a proposition which is forthwith controverted, it is of course optional with you to take up the cudgels in its defence. If you are deeply convinced of its truth, you will perhaps be content to leave it to take care of itself; or, at all events, you will not go out of your way to push its fortunes; for you will reflect that in the long run an opinion often borrows credit from the forbearance of its patrons. In the long run, we say; it will meanwhile cost you an occasional pang to see your cherished theory turned into a football by the critics. A football is not, as such, a very respectable object, and the more numerous the players, the more ridiculous it becomes. Unless, therefore, you are very confident of your ability to rescue it from the chaos of kicks, you will best consult its interests by not mingling in the game. Such has been Mr. Arnold's choice. His opponents say that he is too much of a poet to be a critic; he is certainly too much of a poet to be a disputant. In the Preface in question he has abstained from reiterating any of the views put forth in the two offensive Essays; he has simply taken a delicate literary vengeance upon his adversaries.

For Mr. Arnold's critical feeling and observation, used independently of his judgment, we profess a keen relish. He has these qualities, at any rate, of a good critic, whether or not he have the others,—the science and the logic. It is hard to say whether the literary critic is more called upon to understand or to feel. It is certain that he will accomplish little unless he can feel acutely; although it is perhaps equally certain that he will become weak the moment that he begins to "work," as we may say, his natural sensibilities. The best critic is probably he who leaves his feelings out of account, and relies upon reason for success. If he actually possesses delicacy of feeling, his work will be delicate without detriment to its solidity. The complaint of Mr. Arnold's critics is that his arguments are too sentimental. Whether this complaint is well founded, we shall hereafter inquire; let us determine first what sentiment has done for him. It has given him, in our opinion, his greatest charm and his greatest worth. Hundreds of other critics have stronger heads; few, in England at least, have more delicate perceptions. We regret that we have not the space to confirm this assertion by extracts. We must refer the reader to the book itself, where he will find on every page an illustration of our meaning. He will find one, first of all, in the apostrophe to the University of Oxford, at the close of the Preface,—"home of lost causes and forsaken beliefs and unpopular names and impossible loyalties." This is doubtless nothing but sentiment, but it seizes a shade of truth, and conveys it with a directness which is not at the command of logical demonstration. Such a process might readily prove, with the aid of a host of facts, that the University is actually the abode of much retarding conservatism; a fine critical instinct alone, and the measure of audacity which accompanies such an instinct, could succeed in placing her on the side of progress by boldly saluting her as the Queen of Romance: romance being the deadly enemy of the commonplace; the commonplace being the fast ally of Philistinism, and Philistinism the heaviest drag upon the march of civilisation.

Mr. Arnold is very fond of quoting Goethe's eulogy upon Schiller, to the effect that his friend's greatest glory was to have left so far behind him *was uns alle bändigt, das Gemeine*, that bane of mankind, the common. Exactly how much the inscrutable Goethe made of this fact, it is hard at this day to determine; but it will seem to many readers that Mr. Arnold makes too much of it. Perhaps he does, for himself; but for the public in general he decidedly does not. One of the chief duties of criticism is to exalt the importance of the ideal; and Goethe's speech has a long career in prospect before we can say with the vulgar that it is "played out." Its repeated occurrence in Mr. Arnold's pages is but another instance of poetic feeling subserving the ends of criticism.

The famous comment upon the girl Wragg, over which the author's opponents made so merry, we likewise owe—we do not hesitate to declare it—to this same poetic feeling. Why cast discredit upon so valuable an instrument of truth? Why not wait at least until it is used in the service of error? The worst that can be said of the paragraph in question is, that it is a great ado about nothing. All thanks, say we, to the critic who will pick up such nothings as these; for if he neglects them, they are blindly trodden under foot. They may not be especially valuable, but they are for that very reason the critic's particular care. Great truths take care of themselves; great truths are carried aloft by philosophers and poets; the critic deals in contributions to truth.

Another illustration of the nicety of Mr. Arnold's feeling is furnished by his remarks upon the quality of *distinction* as exhibited in Maurice and Eugénie de Guérin, "that quality which at last inexorably corrects the world's blunders and fixes the world's ideals, [which] procures that the popular poet shall not pass for a Pindar, the popular historian for a Tacitus, nor the popular preacher for a Bossuet." Another is offered by his incidental remarks upon

Coleridge, in the article on Joubert; another, by the remarkable felicity with which he has translated Maurice de Guérin's *Centaur*; and another, by the whole body of citations with which, in his second Essay, he fortifies his proposition that the establishment in England of an authority answering to the French Academy would have arrested certain evil tendencies of English literature,—for to nothing more offensive than this, as far as we can see, does this argument amount.

In the first and most important of his Essays Mr. Arnold puts forth his views upon the actual duty of criticism. They may be summed up as follows. Criticism has no concern with the practical; its function is simply to get at the best thought which is current,—to see things in themselves as they are,—to be disinterested. Criticism can be disinterested, says Mr. Arnold,

"by keeping from practice; by resolutely following the law of its own nature, which is to be a free play of the mind on all subjects which it touches, by steadily refusing to lend itself to any of those ulterior political, practical considerations about ideas which plenty of people will be sure to attach to them, which perhaps ought often to be attached to them, which in this country, at any rate, are certain to be attached to them, but which criticism has really nothing to do with. Its business is simply to know the best that is known and thought in the world, and, by in its turn making this known, to create a current of true and fresh ideas. Its business is to do this with inflexible honesty, with due ability; but its business is to do no more, and to leave alone all questions of practical consequences and applications,—questions which will never fail to have due prominence given to them."

We used just now a word of which Mr. Arnold is very fond,—a word of which the general reader may require an explanation, but which, when explained, he will be likely to find indispensable; we mean the word *Philistine*. The term is of German origin, and has no English synonym. "At Soli," remarks

Mr. Arnold, "I imagined they did not talk of solecisms; and here, at the very head-quarters of Goliath, nobody talks of Philistinism." The word *épicier*, used by Mr. Arnold as a French synonyme, is not so good as *bourgeois*, and to those who know that *bourgeois* means a citizen, and who reflect that a citizen is a person seriously interested in the maintenance of order, the German term may now assume a more special significance. An English review briefly defines it by saying that "it applies to the fat-headed respectable public in general." This definition must satisfy us here. The Philistine portion of the English press, by which we mean the considerably larger portion, received Mr. Arnold's novel programme of criticism with the uncompromising disapprobation which was to be expected from a literary body, the principle of whose influence, or indeed of whose being is its subservience, through its various members, to certain political and religious interests.

Mr. Arnold's general theory was offensive enough; but the conclusions drawn by him from the fact that English practice has been so long and so directly at variance with it, were such as to excite the strongest animosity. Chief among these was the conclusion that this fact has retarded the development and vulgarised the character of the English mind, as compared with the French and the German mind. This rational inference may be nothing but a poet's flight; but for ourselves, we assent to it. It reaches us too. The facts collected by Mr. Arnold on this point have long wanted a voice. It has long seemed to us that, as a nation, the English are singularly incapable of large, of high, of general views. They are indifferent to pure truth, to *la verité vraie*. Their views are almost exclusively practical, and it is in the nature of practical views to be narrow. They seldom indeed admit a fact but on compulsion; they demand of an idea some better recommendation, some longer pedigree, than that it is true. That this lack of spontaneity in the English intellect is caused by the tendency of English criticism, or that it is to be corrected by a diversion, or even by a complete reversion, of this tendency, neither Mr. Arnold nor ourselves suppose, nor do we look upon such a result as desirable. The part which Mr. Arnold assigns to his reformed method of criticism is a purely tributary part. Its indirect result will be to quicken the naturally irrational action of the English mind; its direct result will be to furnish that mind with a larger stock of ideas than it has enjoyed under the time-honoured *régime* of Whig and Tory, High-Church and Low-Church organs.

We may here remark, that Mr. Arnold's statement of his principles is open to some misinterpretation,—an accident against which he has, perhaps, not sufficiently guarded it. For many persons the word *practical* is almost identical with the word *useful,* against which, on the other hand, they erect the word *ornamental.* Persons who are fond of regarding these two terms as irreconcilable, will have little patience with Mr. Arnold's scheme of criticism. They will look upon it as an organised preference of unprofitable speculation to common sense. But the great beauty of the critical movement advocated by Mr. Arnold is that in either direction its range of action is unlimited. It deals with plain facts as well as with the most exalted fancies; but it deals with them only for the sake of the truth which is in them, and not for *your* sake, reader, and that of your party. It takes *high ground,* which is the ground of theory. It does not busy itself with consequences, which are all in all to you. Do not suppose that it for this reason pretends to ignore or to undervalue consequences; on the contrary, it is because it knows that consequences are inevitable that it leaves them alone. It cannot do two things at once; it cannot serve two masters. Its business is to make truth generally accessible, and not to apply it. It is only on condition of having its hands free, that it can make truth generally accessible. We said just now that its duty was, among other things, to exalt, if possible, the importance of the ideal. We should perhaps have said the intellectual; that is, of the principle of understanding things. Its business is to urge the claims of all things to be understood. If this is its function in England, as Mr. Arnold represents, it seems to us that it is doubly its function in this country. Here is no lack of votaries of the practical, of experimentalists, of empirics. The tendencies of our civilisation are certainly not such as foster a preponderance of morbid speculation. Our national genius inclines yearly more and more to resolve itself into a vast machine for sifting, in all things, the wheat from the chaff. American society is so shrewd, that we may safely allow it to make application of the truths of the study. Only let us keep it supplied with the truths of the study, and not with the half-truths of the forum. Let criticism take the stream of truth at its source, and then practice can take it half-way down. When criticism takes it half-way down, practice will come poorly off.

If we have not touched upon the faults of Mr. Arnold's volume, it is because they are faults of detail, and because, when, as a whole, a book commands our assent, we do not incline to quarrel with its parts. Some of the parts in these Essays are weak, others are strong; but the impression which they all combine to leave is one of such beauty as to make us forget, not only their particular faults, but their particular merits. If we were asked what is the particular merit of a given essay, we should reply that it is a merit much less common at the present day than is generally supposed,—the merit which pre-eminently characterises Mr. Arnold's poems, the merit, namely, of having a *subject*. Each essay is *about* something. If a literary work now-a-days start with a certain topic, that is all that is required of it; and yet it is a work of art only on condition of ending with that topic, on condition of being written, not from it, but to it. If the average modern essay or poem were to wear its title at the close, and not at the beginning, we wonder in how many cases the reader would fail to be surprised by it. A book or an article is looked upon as a kind of Staubbach waterfall, discharging itself into infinite space.

If we were questioned as to the merit of Mr. Arnold's book as a whole, we should say that it lay in the fact that the author takes high ground. The manner of his Essays is a model of what criticisms should be. The foremost English critical journal, the Saturday Review, recently disposed of a famous writer by saying, in a parenthesis, that he had done nothing but write nonsense all his life. Mr. Arnold does not pass judgment in parenthesis. He is too much of an artist to use leading propositions for merely literary purposes. The consequence is, that he says a few things in such a way as that almost in spite of ourselves we remember them, instead of a number of things which we cannot for the life of us remember. There are many things which we wish he had said better. It is to be regretted, for instance, that, when Heine is for once in a way seriously spoken of, he should not be spoken of more as the great poet which he is, and which even in New England he will one day be admitted to be, than with reference to the great moralist which he is not, and which he never claimed to be. But here, as in other places, Mr. Arnold's excellent spirit reconciles us with his shortcomings. If he has not spoken of Heine exhaustively, he has at all events spoken of him seriously, which for an Englishman is a good deal.

Mr. Arnold's supreme virtue is that he speaks of all things seriously, or, in other words, that he is not offensively clever. The writers who are willing to resign themselves to this obscure distinction are in our opinion the only writers who understand their time. That Mr. Arnold thoroughly understands his time we do not mean to say, for this is the privilege of a very select few; but he is, at any rate, profoundly conscious of his time. This fact was clearly apparent in his poems, and it is even more apparent in these Essays. It gives them a peculiar character of melancholy,—that melancholy which arises from the spectacle of the old-fashioned instinct of enthusiasm in conflict (or at all events in contact) with the modern desire to be fair,—the melancholy of an age which not only has lost its *naïveté*, but which knows it has lost it.

MR. WALT WHITMAN

IT has been a melancholy task to read this book; and it is a still more melancholy one to write about it. Perhaps since the day of Mr. Tupper's *Philosophy* there has been no more difficult reading of the poetic sort. It exhibits the effort of an essentially prosaic mind to lift itself, by a prolonged muscular strain, into poetry. Like hundreds of other good patriots, during the last four years, Mr. Walt Whitman has imagined that a certain amount of violent sympathy with the great deeds and sufferings of our soldiers, and of admiration for our national energy, together with a ready command of picturesque language, are sufficient inspiration for a poet. If this were the case, we had been a nation of poets. The constant developments of the war moved us continually to strong feeling and to strong expression of it. But in those cases in which these expressions were written out and printed with all due regard to prosody, they failed to make poetry, as any one may see by consulting now in cold blood the back volumes of the *Rebellion Record*.

Of course the city of Manhattan, as Mr. Whitman delights to call it, when regiments poured through it in the first months of the war, and its own sole god, to borrow the words of a real poet, ceased for a while to be the millionaire, was a noble spectacle, and a poetical statement to this effect is possible. *Of course* the tumult of a battle is grand, the results of a battle tragic, and the untimely deaths of young men a theme for elegies. But he is not a poet who merely reiterates these plain facts *ore rotundo*. He only sings them worthily who views them from a height. Every tragic event collects about it a number of persons who delight to dwell upon its superficial points—of minds which are bullied by the *accidents* of the affair. The temper of such minds seems to us to be the reverse of the poetic temper; for the poet, although he incidentally masters, grasps, and uses the superficial traits of his theme, is really a poet only in so far as he extracts its latent meaning and holds it up to common eyes. And yet from such minds most of our war-verses have come, and Mr. Whitman's utterances, much as the assertion may surprise his friends, are in this respect no exception to general fashion. They are an exception, however, in that they openly pretend to be something better; and this it is that makes them melancholy reading.

Mr. Whitman is very fond of blowing his own trumpet, and he has made very explicit claims for his books. "Shut not your doors," he exclaims at the outset—

"Shut not your doors to me, proud libraries,

For that which was lacking among you all, yet needed most, I bring;

A book I have made for your dear sake, O soldiers,

And for you, O soul of man, and you, love of comrades;

The words of my book nothing, the life of it everything;

A book separate, not link'd with the rest, nor felt by the intellect;

But you will feel every word, O Libertad! arm'd Libertad!

It shall pass by the intellect to swim the sea, the air,

With joy with you, O soul of man."

These are great pretensions, but it seems to us that the following are even greater:

"From Paumanok starting, I fly like a bird,

Around and around to soar, to sing the idea of all;

To the north betaking myself, to sing there arctic songs,

To Kanada, 'till I absorb Kanada in myself—to Michigan then,

To Wisconsin, Iowa, Minnesota, to sing their songs (they are inimitable);

Then to Ohio and Indiana, to sing theirs—to Missouri and Kansas and Arkansas to sing theirs,

To Tennessee and Kentucky—to the Carolinas and Georgia, to sing theirs,

To Texas, and so along up toward California, to roam accepted everywhere;

To sing first (to the tap of the war-drum, if need be)

The idea of all—of the western world, one and inseparable,

And then the song of each member of these States."

Mr. Whitman's primary purpose is to celebrate the greatness of our armies; his secondary purpose is to celebrate the greatness of the city of New York. He pursues these objects through a hundred pages of matter which remind us irresistibly of the story of the college professor who, on a venturesome youth bringing him a theme done in blank verse, reminded him that it was not customary in writing prose to begin each line with a capital. The frequent capitals are the only marks of verse in Mr. Whitman's writings. There is, fortunately, but one attempt at rhyme. We say fortunately, for if the inequality of Mr. Whitman's lines were self-registering, as it would be in the case of an anticipated syllable at their close, the effect would be painful in the extreme. As the case stands, each line stands off by itself, in resolute independence of its companions, without a visible goal.

But if Mr. Whitman does not write verse, he does not write ordinary prose. The reader has seen that liberty is "libertad." In like manner, comrade is "camerado"; Americans are "Americanos"; a pavement is a "trottoir," and Mr. Whitman himself is a "chansonnier." If there is one thing that Mr. Whitman is not, it is this, for Béranger was a *chansonnier*. To appreciate the force of our conjunction, the reader should compare his military lyrics with Mr. Whitman's declamations. Our author's novelty, however, is not in his words, but in the form of his writing. As we have said, it begins for all the world like verse and turns out to be arrant prose. It is more like Mr. Tupper's proverbs than anything we have met.

But what if, in form, it *is* prose? it may be asked. Very good poetry has come out of prose before this. To this we would reply that it must first have gone into it. Prose, in order to be good poetry, must first be good prose. As a general principle, we know of no circumstance more likely to impugn a writer's earnestness than the adoption of an anomalous style. He must have something very original to say if none of the old vehicles will carry his thoughts. Of course he *may* be surprisingly original. Still, presumption is against him. If on examination the matter of his discourse proves very valuable, it justifies, or at any rate excuses, his literary innovation.

But if, on the other hand, it is of a common quality, with nothing new about it but its manners, the public will judge the writer harshly. The most that can be said of Mr. Whitman's vaticinations is, that, cast in a fluent and familiar manner, the average substance of them might escape unchallenged. But we have seen that Mr. Whitman prides himself especially on the substance—the life—of his poetry. It may be rough, it may be grim, it may be clumsy—such we take to be the author's argument—but it is sincere, it is sublime, it appeals to the soul of man, it is the voice of a people. He tells us, in the lines quoted, that the words of his book are nothing. To our perception they are everything, and very little at that.

A great deal of verse that is nothing but words has, during the war, been sympathetically sighed over and cut out of newspaper corners, because it has possessed a certain simple melody. But Mr. Whitman's verse, we are confident, would have failed even of this triumph, for the simple reason that no triumph, however small, is won but through the exercise of art, and that this volume is an offence against art. It is not enough to be grim and rough and careless; common sense is also necessary, for it is by common sense that we are judged. There exists in even the commonest minds, in literary matters, a certain precise instinct of conservatism, which is very shrewd in detecting wanton eccentricities.

To this instinct Mr. Whitman's attitude seems monstrous. It is monstrous because it pretends to persuade the soul while it slights the intellect; because it pretends to gratify the feelings while it outrages the taste. The point is that it does this *on theory*, wilfully, consciously, arrogantly. It is the little nursery game of "open your mouth and shut your eyes." Our hearts are often touched through a compromise with the artistic sense, but never in direct violation of it. Mr. Whitman sits down at the outset and counts out the intelligence. This were indeed a wise precaution on his part if the intelligence were only submissive! But when she is deliberately insulted, she takes her revenge by simply standing erect and open-eyed. This is assuredly the best she can do. And if she could find a voice she would probably address Mr. Whitman as follows:—

"You came to woo my sister, the human soul. Instead of giving me a kick as you approach, you should either greet me courteously, or, at least, steal in unobserved. But now you have me on your hands. Your chances are poor. What the human heart desires above all is sincerity, and you do not appear to me sincere. For a lover you talk entirely too much about yourself. In one place you threaten to absorb Kanada. In another you call upon the city of New York to incarnate you, as you have incarnated it. In another you inform us that neither youth pertains to you nor 'delicatesse,' that you are awkward in the parlour, that you do not dance, and that you have neither bearing, beauty, knowledge, nor fortune. In another place, by an allusion to your 'little songs,' you seem to identify yourself with the third person of the Trinity.

"For a poet who claims to sing 'the idea of all,' this is tolerably egotistical. We look in vain, however, through your book for a single idea. We find nothing but flashy imitations of ideas. We find a medley of extravagances and commonplaces. We find art, measure, grace, sense sneered at on every page, and nothing positive given us in their stead. To be positive one must have something to say; to be positive requires reason, labour, and art; and art requires, above all things, a suppression of one's self, a subordination of one's self to an idea. This will never do for you, whose plan is to adapt the scheme of the universe to your own limitations. You cannot entertain and exhibit ideas; but, as we have seen, you are prepared to incarnate them. It is for this reason, doubtless, that when once you have planted yourself squarely before the public, and in view of the great service you have done to the ideal, have become, as you say, 'accepted everywhere,' you can afford to deal exclusively in words. What would be bald nonsense and dreary platitudes in any one else becomes sublimity in you.

"But all this is a mistake. To become adopted as a national poet, it is not enough to discard everything in particular and to accept everything in general, to amass crudity upon crudity, to discharge the undigested contents of your blotting-book into the lap of the public. You must respect the public which you address; for it has taste, if you have not. It delights in the grand, the heroic, and the masculine; but it delights to see these conceptions cast into worthy form. It is indifferent to brute sublimity. It will never do for you to thrust your hands into your pockets and cry out that, as the research of form is an intolerable bore, the shortest and most economical way for the public to embrace its idols—for the nation to realise its genius—is in your own person.

"This democratic, liberty-loving, American populace, this stern and war-tried people, is a great civiliser. It is devoted to refinement. If it has sustained a monstrous war, and practised human nature's best in so many ways for the last five years, it is not to put up with spurious poetry afterwards. To sing aright our battles and our glories it is not enough to have served in a hospital (however praiseworthy the task in itself), to be aggressively careless, inelegant, and ignorant, and to be constantly preoccupied with yourself. It is not enough to be rude, lugubrious, and grim. You must also be serious. You must forget yourself in your ideas. Your personal qualities—the vigour of your temperament, the manly independence of your nature, the tenderness of your heart—these facts are impertinent. You must be *possessed*, and you must thrive to possess your possession. If in your striving you break into divine eloquence, then you are a poet. If the idea which possesses you is the idea of your country's greatness, then you are a national poet; and not otherwise."

THE POETRY OF GEORGE ELIOT

I. THE SPANISH GYPSY

IKNOW not whether George Eliot has any enemies, nor why she should have any; but if perchance she has, I can imagine them to have hailed the announcement of a poem from her pen as a piece of particularly good news. "Now, finally," I fancy them saying, "this sadly over-rated author will exhibit all the weakness that is in her; now she will prove herself what we have all along affirmed her to be—not a serene, self-directing genius of the first order, knowing her powers and respecting them, and content to leave well enough alone, but a mere showy rhetorician, possessed and prompted, not by the humble spirit of truth, but by an insatiable longing for applause." Suppose Mr. Tennyson were to come out with a novel, or Madame George Sand were to produce a tragedy in French alexandrines. The reader will agree with me, that these are hard suppositions; yet the world has seen stranger things, and been reconciled to them. Nevertheless, with the best possible will toward our illustrious novelist, it is easy to put ourselves in the shoes of these hypothetical detractors. No one, assuredly, but George Eliot could mar George Eliot's reputation; but there was room for the fear that she might do it. This reputation was essentially prose-built, and in the attempt to insert a figment of verse of the magnitude of *The Spanish Gypsy*, it was quite possible that she might injure its fair proportions.

In consulting her past works, for approval of their hopes and their fears, I think both her friends and her foes would have found sufficient ground for their arguments. Of all our English prose-writers of the present day, I think I may say, that, as a writer simply, a mistress of style, I have been very near preferring the author of *Silas Marner* and of *Romola*,—the author, too, of *Felix Holt*. The motive of my great regard for her style I take to have been that I fancied it such perfect solid prose. Brilliant and lax as it was in tissue, it seemed to contain very few of the silken threads of poetry; it lay on the ground like a carpet, instead of floating in the air like a banner. If my impression was correct, *The Spanish Gypsy* is not a genuine poem. And yet, looking over the author's novels in memory, looking them over in the light of her unexpected assumption of the poetical function, I find it hard at times not to mistrust my impression. I like George Eliot well enough, in fact, to admit, for the time, that I might have been in the wrong. If I had liked her less, if I had rated lower the quality of her prose, I should have estimated coldly the possibilities of her verse. Of course, therefore, if, as I am told many persons do in England, who consider carpenters and weavers and millers' daughters no legitimate subject for reputable fiction, I had denied her novels any qualities at all, I should have made haste, on reading the announcement of her poem, to speak of her as the world speaks of a lady, who, having reached a comfortable middle age, with her shoulders decently covered, "for reasons deep below the reach of thought," (to quote our author), begins to go out to dinner in a low-necked dress "of the period," and say in fine, in three words, that she was going to make a fool of herself.

But here, meanwhile, is the book before me, to arrest all this *a priori* argumentation. Time enough has elapsed since its appearance for most readers to have uttered their opinions, and for the general verdict of criticism to have been formed. In looking over several of the published reviews, I am struck with the fact that those immediately issued are full of the warmest delight and approval, and that, as the work ceases to be a novelty, objections, exceptions, and protests multiply. This is quite logical. Not only does it take a much longer time than the reviewer on a weekly journal has at his command to properly appreciate a work of the importance of *The Spanish Gypsy*, but the poem was actually much more of a poem than was to be expected. The foremost feeling of many readers must have been—it was certainly my own— that we had hitherto only half known George Eliot. Adding this dazzling new half to the old one, readers constructed for the moment a really splendid literary figure. But gradually the old half began to absorb the new, and to assimilate its virtues and failings, and critics finally remembered that the cleverest writer in the world is after all nothing and no one but himself.

The most striking quality in *The Spanish Gypsy*, on a first reading, I think, is its extraordinary rhetorical energy and elegance. The richness of the author's style in her novels gives but an inadequate idea of the splendid generosity of diction displayed in the poem. She is so much of a thinker and an observer that she draws very heavily on her powers of expression, and one may certainly say that they not only never fail her, but that verbal utterance almost always bestows upon her ideas a peculiar beauty and fullness, apart from their significance. The result produced in this manner, the reader will see, may come very near being poetry; it is assuredly eloquence. The faults in the present work are very seldom faults of weakness, except in so far as it is weak to lack an absolute mastery of one's powers; they arise rather from an excess of rhetorical energy, from a desire to attain to perfect fullness and roundness of utterance; they are faults of overstatement. It is by no means uncommon to find a really fine passage injured by the addition of a clause which dilutes the idea under pretence of completing it. The poem opens, for instance, with a description of

"Broad-breasted Spain, leaning with equal love

(A calm earth-goddess crowned with corn and vines)

On the Mid Sea that moans with memories,

And on the untravelled Ocean, whose vast tides

Pant dumbly passionate with dreams of youth."

The second half of the fourth line and the fifth, here, seem to me as poor as the others are good. So in the midst of the admirable description of Don Silva, which precedes the first scene in the castle:—

"A spirit framed

Too proudly special for obedience,

Too subtly pondering for mastery:

Born of a goddess with a mortal sire,

Heir of flesh-fettered, weak divinity,

Doom-gifted with long resonant consciousness

And perilous heightening of the sentient soul."

The transition to the lines in Italic is like the passage from a well-ventilated room into a vacuum. On reflection, we see "long resonant consciousness" to be a very good term; but, as it stands, it certainly lacks breathing-space. On the other hand, there are more than enough passages of the character of the following to support what I have said of the genuine splendour of the style:—

"I was right!

These gems have life in them: their colours speak,

Say what words fail of. So do many things,—

The scent of jasmine and the fountain's plash,

The moving shadows on the far-off hills,

The slanting moonlight and our clasping hands.

O Silva, there's an ocean round our words,

That overflows and drowns them. Do you know.

Sometimes when we sit silent, and the air

Breathes gently on us from the orange-trees,

It seems that with the whisper of a word

Our souls must shrink, get poorer, more apart?

Is it not true?

DON SILVA.

Yes, dearest, it is true.

Speech is but broken light upon the depth

Of the unspoken: even your loved words

Float in the larger meaning of your voice

As something dimmer."

I may say in general, that the author's admirers must have found in *The Spanish Gypsy* a presentment of her various special gifts stronger and fuller, on the whole, than any to be found in her novels. Those who valued her chiefly for her humour—the gentle humour which provokes a smile, but deprecates a laugh—will recognise that delightful gift in Blasco, and Lorenzo, and Roldan, and Juan,—slighter in quantity than in her prose-writings, but quite equal, I think, in quality. Those who prize most her descriptive powers will see them wondrously well embodied in these pages. As for those who have felt compelled to declare that she possesses the Shakespearian touch, they must consent, with what grace they may, to be disappointed. I have never thought our author a great dramatist, nor even a particularly dramatic writer. A real dramatist, I imagine, could never have reconciled himself to the odd mixture of the narrative and dramatic forms by which the present work is distinguished; and that George Eliot's genius should have needed to work under these conditions seems to me strong evidence of the partial and incomplete character of her dramatic instincts. An English critic lately described her, with much correctness, as a critic rather than a creator of characters. She puts her figures into action very successfully, but on the whole she thinks for them more than they think for themselves. She thinks, however, to wonderfully good purpose. In none of her works are there two more distinctly human representations than the characters of Silva and Juan.

The latter, indeed, if I am not mistaken, ranks with Tito Melema and Hetty Sorrel, as one of her very best conceptions.

What is commonly called George Eliot's humour consists largely, I think, in a certain tendency to epigram and compactness of utterance,—not the short-clipped, biting, ironical epigram, but a form of statement in which a liberal dose of truth is embraced in terms none the less comprehensive for being very firm and vivid. Juan says of Zarca that

> He is one of those
>
> Who steal the keys from snoring Destiny,
>
> And make the prophets lie."

Zarca himself, speaking of "the steadfast mind, the undivided will to seek the good," says most admirably,—

> "'Tis that compels the elements, *and wrings*
>
> *A human music from the indifferent air.*"

When the Prior pronounces Fedalma's blood "unchristian as the leopard's," Don Silva retorts with,—

> "Unchristian as the Blessed Virgin's blood.
>
> Before the angel spoke the word, 'All hail!'"

Zarca qualifies his daughter's wish to maintain her faith to her lover, at the same time that she embraces her father's fortunes, as

80

"A woman's dream,—who thinks by smiling well

To ripen figs in frost."

This happy brevity of expression is frequently revealed in those rich descriptive passages and touches in which the work abounds. Some of the lines taken singly are excellent:—

"And bells make Catholic the trembling air";

and,

"Sad as the twilight, all his clothes ill-girt";

and again

"Mournful professor of high drollery."

Here is a very good line and a half:—

"The old rain-fretted mountains in their robes

Of shadow-broken gray."

Here, finally, are three admirable pictures:—

"The stars thin-scattered made the heavens large,

Bending in slow procession; in the east,

Emergent from the dark waves of the hills,

Seeming a little sister of the moon,

Glowed Venus all unquenched."

"Spring afternoons, when delicate shadows fall

Pencilled upon the grass; high summer morns,

When white light rains upon the quiet sea,

And cornfields flush for ripeness."

"Scent the fresh breath of the height-loving herbs,

That, trodden by the pretty parted hoofs

Of nimble goats, sigh at the innocent bruise,

And with a mingled difference exquisite

Pour a sweet burden on the buoyant air."

But now to reach the real substance of the poem, and to allow the reader to appreciate the author's treatment of human character and passion, I must speak briefly of the story. I shall hardly misrepresent it, when I say that it is a very old one, and that it illustrates that very common occurrence in human affairs,—the conflict of love and duty. Such, at least, is the general impression made by the poem as it stands. It is very possible that the author's primary intention may have had a breadth which has been curtailed in the execution of the work,—that it was her wish to present a struggle between nature and culture, between education and the instinct of race. You can detect in such a theme the stuff of a very good drama,—a somewhat stouter stuff, however, than *The Spanish Gypsy* is made of. George Eliot, true to that didactic tendency for which she has hitherto been remarkable, has preferred to make her heroine's predicament a problem in morals, and has thereby, I think, given herself hard work to reach a satisfactory solution. She has, indeed, committed herself to a signal error, in a psychological sense,—that of making a Gypsy girl with a conscience. Either Fedalma was a perfect Zincala in temper and instinct,—in which case her adhesion to her father and her race was a blind, passionate, sensuous movement, which is almost expressly contradicted,—or else she was a pure and intelligent Catholic, in which case nothing in the nature of a struggle can be predicated. The character of Fedalma, I may say, comes very near being a failure,—a very beautiful one; but in point of fact it misses it.

It misses it, I think, thanks to that circumstance which in reading and criticising *The Spanish Gypsy* we must not cease to bear in mind, the fact that the work is emphatically a *romance*. We may contest its being a poem, but we must admit that it is a romance in the fullest sense of the word. Whether the term may be absolutely defined I know not; but we may say of it, comparing it with the novel, that it carries much farther that compromise with reality which is the basis of all imaginative writing. In the romance this principle of compromise pervades the superstructure as well as the basis. The most that we exact is that the fable be consistent with itself. Fedalma is not a real Gypsy maiden. The conviction is strong in the reader's mind that a genuine Spanish Zincala would have somehow contrived both to follow her tribe and to keep her lover. If Fedalma is not real, Zarca is even less so. He is interesting, imposing, picturesque; but he is very far, I take it, from being a genuine *Gypsy* chieftain. They are both ideal figures,—the offspring of a strong mental desire for creatures well rounded in their elevation and heroism,— creatures who should illustrate the nobleness of human nature divorced from its smallness. Don Silva has decidedly more of the common stuff of human feeling, more charming natural passion and weakness. But he, too, is largely a vision of the intellect; his constitution is adapted to the atmosphere and the climate of romance. Juan, indeed, has one foot well planted on the lower earth; but Juan is only an accessory figure. I have said enough to lead the reader to perceive that the poem should not be regarded as a rigid transcript of actual or possible fact,—that the action goes on in an artificial world, and that properly to comprehend it he must regard it with a generous mind.

Viewed in this manner, as efficient figures in an essentially ideal and romantic drama, Fedalma and Zarca seem to gain vastly, and to shine with a brilliant radiance. If we reduce Fedalma to the level of the heroines of our modern novels, in which the interest aroused by a young girl is in proportion to the similarity of her circumstances to those of the reader, and in which none but the commonest feelings are required, provided they be expressed with energy, we shall be tempted to call her a solemn and cold-blooded jilt. In a novel it would have been next to impossible for the author to make the heroine renounce her lover. In novels we not only forgive that weakness which is common and familiar and human, but we actually demand it. But in poetry, although we are compelled to adhere to the few elementary passions of our nature, we do our best to dress them in a new and exquisite garb. Men and women in a poetical drama are nothing, if not distinguished.

"Our dear young love,—its breath was happiness!

But it had grown upon a larger life,

Which tore its roots asunder."

These words are uttered by Fedalma at the close of the poem, and in them she emphatically claims the distinction of having her own private interests invaded by those of a people. The manner of her kinship with the Zincali is in fact a very much "larger life" than her marriage with Don Silva. We may, indeed, challenge the probability of her relationship to her tribe impressing her mind with a force equal to that of her love,—her "dear young love." We may declare that this is an unnatural and violent result. For my part, I think it is very far from violent; I think the author has employed her art in reducing the apparently arbitrary quality of her preference for her tribe. I say reducing; I do not say effacing; because it seems to me, as I have intimated, that just at this point her art has been wanting, and we are not sufficiently prepared for Fedalma's movement by a sense of her Gypsy temper and instincts. Still, we are in some degree prepared for it by various passages in the opening scenes of the book,—by all the magnificent description of her dance in the Plaza:—

"All gathering influences culminate

And urge Fedalma. Earth and heaven seem one,

Life a glad trembling on the outer edge

Of unknown rapture. Swifter now she moves,

Filling the measure with a double beat

And widening circle; now she seems to glow

With more declaréd presence, glorified.

Circling, she lightly bends, and lifts on high

The multitudinous-sounding tambourine,

And makes it ring and boom, then lifts it higher,

Stretching her left arm beauteous."

We are better prepared for it, however, than by anything else, by the whole impression we receive of the exquisite refinement and elevation of the young girl's mind,—by all that makes her so bad a Gypsy. She possesses evidently a very high-strung intellect, and her whole conduct is in a higher key, as I may say, than that of ordinary women, or even ordinary heroines. She is natural, I think, in a poetical sense. She is consistent with her own prodigiously superfine character. From a lower point of view than that of the author, she lacks several of the desirable feminine qualities,—a certain womanly warmth and petulance, a graceful irrationality. Her mind is very much too lucid, and her aspirations too lofty. Her conscience, especially, is decidedly over-active. But this is a distinction which she shares with all the author's heroines,—Dinah Morris, Maggie Tulliver, Romola, and Esther Lyon,—a distinction, moreover, for which I should be very sorry to hold George Eliot to account. There are most assuredly women and women. While Messrs. Charles Reade and Wilkie Collins, and Miss Braddon and her school, tell one half the story, it is no more than fair that the author of *The Spanish Gypsy* should, all unassisted, attempt to relate the other.

Whenever a story really interests one, he is very fond of paying it the compliment of imagining it otherwise constructed, and of capping it with a different termination. In the present case, one is irresistibly tempted to fancy *The Spanish Gypsy* in prose,—a compact, regular drama: not in George Eliot's prose, however: in a diction much more nervous and heated and rapid, written with short speeches as well as long. (The reader will have observed the want of brevity, retort, interruption, rapid alternation, in the dialogue of the poem. The characters all talk, as it were, standing still.) In such a play as the one indicated one imagines a truly dramatic Fedalma,—a passionate, sensuous, irrational Bohemian, as elegant as good breeding and native good taste could make her, and as pure as her actual sister in the poem,—but rushing into her father's arms with a cry of joy, and losing the sense of her lover's sorrow in what the author has elsewhere described as "the hurrying ardour of action." Or in the way of a different termination, suppose that Fedalma should for the time value at once her own love and her lover's enough to make her prefer the latter's destiny to that represented by her father. Imagine, then, that, after marriage, the Gypsy blood and nature should begin to flow and throb in quicker pulsations,—and that the poor girl should sadly contrast the sunny freedom and lawless joy of her people's lot with the splendid rigidity and formalism of her own. You may conceive at this point that she should pass from sadness to despair, and from despair to revolt. Here the catastrophe may occur in a dozen different ways. Fedalma may die before her husband's eyes, of unsatisfied longing for the fate she has rejected; or she may make an attempt actually to recover her fate, by wandering off and seeking out her people. The cultivated mind, however, it seems to me, imperiously demands, that, on finally overtaking them, she shall die of mingled weariness and shame, as neither a good Gypsy nor a good Christian, but simply a good figure for a tragedy. But there is a degree of levity which almost amounts to irreverence in fancying this admirable performance as anything other than it is.

After Fedalma comes Zarca, and here our imagination flags. Not so George Eliot's: for as simple imagination, I think that in the conception of this impressive and unreal figure it appears decidedly at its strongest. With Zarca, we stand at the very heart of the realm of romance. There is a truly grand simplicity, to my mind, in the outline of his character, and a remarkable air of majesty in his poise and attitude. He is a *père noble* in perfection. His speeches have an exquisite eloquence. In strictness, he is to the last degree unreal, illogical, and rhetorical; but a certain dramatic unity is diffused through his character by the depth and energy of the colours in which he is painted. With a little less simplicity, his figure would be decidedly modern. As it stands, it is neither modern nor mediæval; it belongs to the world of intellectual dreams and visions. The reader will admit that it is a vision of no small beauty, the conception of a stalwart chieftain who distils the cold exaltation of his purpose from the utter loneliness and obloquy of his race:—

"Wanderers whom no God took knowledge of,

To give them laws, to fight for them, or blight

Another race to make them ampler room;

A people with no home even in memory,

No dimmest lore of giant ancestors

To make a common hearth for piety";

a people all ignorant of

"The rich heritage, the milder life,

Of nations fathered by a mighty Past."

Like Don Silva, like Juan, like Sephardo, Zarca is decidedly a man of intellect.

Better than Fedalma or than Zarca is the remarkably beautiful and elaborate portrait of Don Silva, in whom the author has wished to present a young nobleman as splendid in person and in soul as the dawning splendour of his native country. In the composition of his figure, the real and the romantic, brilliancy and pathos, are equally commingled. He cannot be said to stand out in vivid relief. As a piece of painting, there is nothing commanding, aggressive, brutal, as I may say, in his lineaments. But they will bear close scrutiny. Place yourself within the circumscription of the work, breathe its atmosphere, and you will see that Don Silva is portrayed with a delicacy to which English story-tellers, whether in prose or verse, have not accustomed us. There are better portraits in Browning, but there are also worse; in Tennyson there are none as good; and in the other great poets of the present century there are no attempts, that I can remember, to which we may compare it. In spite of the poem being called in honour of his mistress, Don Silva is in fact the central figure in the work. Much more than Fedalma, he is the passive object of the converging blows of Fate. The young girl, after all, did what was easiest; but he is entangled in a network of agony, without choice or compliance of his own. It is an admirable subject admirably treated. I may describe it by saying that it exhibits a perfect aristocratic nature (born and bred at a time when democratic aspirations were quite irrelevant to happiness), dragged down by no fault of its own into the vulgar mire of error and expiation. The interest which attaches to Don Silva's character revolves about its exquisite human weakness, its manly scepticism, its antipathy to the trenchant, the absolute, and arbitrary. At the opening of the book, the author rehearses his various titles:—

"Such titles with their blazonry are his

Who keeps this fortress, sworn Alcaÿde,

Lord of the valley, master of the town,

Commanding whom he will, himself commanded

By Christ his Lord, who sees him from the cross,

And from bright heaven where the Mother pleads;

By good Saint James, upon the milk-white steed,

Who leaves his bliss to fight for chosen Spain;

By the dead gaze of all his ancestors;

And by the mystery of his Spanish blood,

Charged with the awe and glories of the past."

Throughout the poem, we are conscious, during the evolution of his character, of the presence of these high mystical influences, which, combined with his personal pride, his knightly temper, his delicate culture, form a splendid background for passionate dramatic action. The finest pages in the book, to my taste, are those which describe his lonely vigil in the Gypsy camp, after he has failed in winning back Fedalma, and has pledged his faith to Zarca. Placed under guard, and left to his own stern thoughts, his soul begins to react against the hideous disorder to which he has committed it, to proclaim its kinship with "customs and bonds and laws," and its sacred need of the light of human esteem:—

"Now awful Night,

Ancestral mystery of mysteries, came down

Past all the generations of the stars,

And visited his soul with touch more close

Than when he kept that closer, briefer watch,

Under the church's roof, beside his arms,

And won his knighthood."

To be appreciated at their worth, these pages should be attentively read. Nowhere has the author's marvellous power of expression, the mingled dignity and pliancy of her style, obtained a greater triumph. She has reproduced the expression of a mind with the same vigorous distinctness as that with which a great painter represents the expression of a countenance.

The character which accords best with my own taste is that of the minstrel Juan, an extremely generous conception. He fills no great part in the drama; he is by nature the reverse of a man of action; and, strictly, the story could very well dispense with him. Yet, for all that, I should be sorry to lose him, and lose thereby the various excellent things which are said of him and by him. I do not include his songs among the latter. Only two of the lyrics in the work strike me as good: the song of Pablo, "The world is great: the birds all fly from me"; and, in a lower degree, the chant of the Zincali, in the fourth book. But I do include the words by which he is introduced to the reader:—

"Juan was a troubadour revived,

Freshening life's dusty road with babbling rills

Of wit and song, living 'mid harnessed men

With limbs ungalled by armour, ready so

To soothe them weary and to cheer them sad.

Guest at the board, companion in the camp,

A crystal mirror to the life around:

Flashing the comment keen of simple fact

Defined in words; lending brief lyric voice

To grief and sadness; hardly taking note

Of difference betwixt his own and others';

But, rather singing as a listener

To the deep moans, the cries, the wildstrong joys

Of universal Nature, old, yet young."

When Juan talks at his ease, he strikes the note of poetry much more surely than when he lifts his voice in song:—

"Yet if your graciousness will not disdain

A poor plucked songster, shall he sing to you?

Some lay of afternoons,—some ballad strain

Of those who ached once, but are sleeping now

Under the sun-warmed flowers?"

Juan's link of connection with the story is, in the first place, that he is in love with Fedalma, and, in the second, as a piece of local colour. His attitude with regard to Fedalma is indicated with beautiful delicacy:—

"O lady, constancy has kind and rank.

One man's is lordly, plump, and bravely clad,

Holds its head high, and tells the world its name:

Another man's is beggared, must go bare,

And shiver through the world, the jest of all,

But that it puts the motley on, and plays

Itself the jester."

Nor are his merits lost upon her, as she declares, with no small force,—

"No! on the close-thronged spaces of the earth

A battle rages; Fate has carried me

'Mid the thick arrows: I will keep my stand,—

91

Nor shrink, and let the shaft pass by my breast

To pierce another. O, 'tis written large,

The thing I have to do. But you, dear Juan,

Renounce, endure, are brave, unurged by aught

Save the sweet overflow of your good-will."

In every human imbroglio, be it of a comic or a tragic nature, it is good to think of an observer standing aloof, the critic, the idle commentator of it all, taking notes, as we may say, in the interest of truth. The exercise of this function is the chief ground of our interest in Juan. Yet as a man of action, too, he once appeals most irresistibly to our sympathies: I mean in the admirable scene with Hinda, in which he wins back his stolen finery by his lute-playing. This scene, which is written in prose, has a simple realistic power which renders it a truly remarkable composition.

Of the different parts of *The Spanish Gypsy* I have spoken with such fullness as my space allows: it remains to add a few remarks upon the work as a whole. Its great fault is simply that it is not a genuine poem. It lacks the hurrying quickness, the palpitating warmth, the bursting melody of such a creation. A genuine poem is a tree that breaks into blossom and shakes in the wind. George Eliot's elaborate composition is like a vast mural design in mosaic-work, where great slabs and delicate morsels of stone are laid together with wonderful art, where there are plenty of noble lines and generous hues, but where everything is rigid, measured, and cold,—nothing dazzling, magical, and vocal. The poem contains a number of faulty lines,—lines of twelve, of eleven, and of eight syllables,—of which it is easy to suppose that a more sacredly commissioned versifier would not have been guilty. Occasionally, in the search for poetic effect, the author decidedly misses her way:—

"All her being paused

In resolution, *as some leonine wave,*" etc.

A "leonine" wave is rather too much of a lion and too little of a wave. The work possesses imagination, I think, in no small measure. The description of Silva's feelings during his sojourn in the Gypsy camp is strongly pervaded by it; or if perchance the author achieved these passages without rising on the wings of fancy, her glory is all the greater. But the poem is wanting in passion. The reader is annoyed by a perpetual sense of effort and of intellectual tension. It is a characteristic of George Eliot, I imagine, to allow her impressions to linger a long time in her mind, so that by the time they are ready for use they have lost much of their original freshness and vigour. They have acquired, of course, a number of artificial charms, but they have parted with their primal natural simplicity. In this poem we see the landscape, the people, the manners of Spain as through a glass smoked by the flame of meditative vigils, just as we saw the outward aspect of Florence in *Romola*. The brightness of colouring is there, the artful chiaroscuro, and all the consecrated properties of the scene; but they gleam in an artificial light. The background of the action is admirable in spots, but is cold and mechanical as a whole. The immense rhetorical ingenuity and elegance of the work, which constitute its main distinction, interfere with the faithful, uncompromising reflection of the primary elements of the subject.

The great merit of the characters is that they are marvellously well *understood*,—far better understood than in the ordinary picturesque romance of action, adventure, and mystery. And yet they are not understood to the bottom; they retain an indefinably factitious air, which is not sufficiently justified by their position as ideal figures. The reader who has attentively read the closing scene of the poem will know what I mean. The scene shows remarkable talent; it is eloquent, it is beautiful; but it is arbitrary and fanciful, more than unreal,—untrue. The reader silently chafes and protests, and finally breaks forth and cries, "O for a blast from the outer world!" Silva and Fedalma have developed themselves so daintily and elaborately within the close-sealed precincts of the author's mind, that they strike us at last as acting not as simple human creatures, but as downright *amateurs* of the morally graceful and picturesque. To say that this is the ultimate impression of the poem is to say that it is not a great work. It is in fact not a great drama. It is, in the first place, an admirable study of character,—an essay, as they say, toward the solution of a given problem in conduct. In the second, it is a noble literary performance. It can be read neither without interest in the former respect, nor without profit for its signal merits of style,—and this in spite of the fact that the versification is, as the French say, as little *réussi* as was to be expected in a writer beginning at a bound with a kind of verse which is very much more difficult than even the best prose,—the author's own prose. I shall indicate most of its merits and defects, great and small, if I say it is a romance,—a romance written by one who is emphatically a thinker.

II. THE LEGEND OF JUBAL AND OTHER POEMS

When the author of *Middlemarch* published, some years since, her first volume of verse, the reader, in trying to judge it fairly, asked himself what he should think of it if she had never published a line of prose. The question, perhaps, was not altogether a help to strict fairness of judgment, but the author was protected from illiberal conclusions by the fact that, practically, it was impossible to answer it. George Eliot belongs to that class of pre-eminent writers in relation to whom the imagination comes to self-consciousness only to find itself in subjection. It was impossible to disengage one's judgment from the permanent influence of *Adam Bede* and its companions, and it was necessary, from the moment that the author undertook to play the poet's part, to feel that her genius was all of one piece.

People have often asked themselves how they would estimate Shakespeare if they knew him only by his comedies, Homer if his name stood only for the *Odyssey*, and Milton if he had written nothing but "Lycidas" and the shorter pieces. The question of necessity, inevitable though it is, leads to nothing. George Eliot is neither Homer nor Shakespeare nor Milton; but her work, like theirs, is a massive achievement, divided into a supremely good and a less good, and it provokes us, like theirs, to the fruitless attempt to estimate the latter portion on its own merits alone.

The little volume before us gives us another opportunity; but here, as before, we find ourselves uncomfortably divided between the fear, on the one hand, of being bribed into favour, and, on the other, of giving short measure of it. The author's verses are a narrow manifestation of her genius, but they are an unmistakeable manifestation. *Middlemarch* has made us demand even finer things of her than we did before, and whether, as patented readers of *Middlemarch*, we like "Jubal" and its companions the less or the more, we must admit that they are characteristic products of the same intellect.

We imagine George Eliot is quite philosopher enough, having produced her poems mainly as a kind of experimental entertainment for her own mind, to let them commend themselves to the public on any grounds whatever which will help to illustrate the workings of versatile intelligence,—as interesting failures, if nothing better. She must feel they are interesting; an exaggerated modesty cannot deny that.

We have found them extremely so. They consist of a rhymed narrative, of some length, of the career of Jubal, the legendary inventor of the lyre; of a short rustic idyl in blank verse on a theme gathered in the Black Forest of Baden; of a tale, versified in rhyme, from Boccaccio; and of a series of dramatic scenes called "Armgart,"—the best thing, to our sense, of the four. To these are added a few shorter pieces, chiefly in blank verse, each of which seems to us proportionately more successful than the more ambitious ones. Our author's verse is a mixture of spontaneity of thought and excessive reflectiveness of expression and its value is generally more in the idea than in the form. In whatever George Eliot writes you have the comfortable certainty, infrequent in other quarters, of finding an idea, and you get the substance of her thought in the short poems, without the somewhat rigid envelope of her poetic diction.

If we may say, broadly, that the supreme merit of a poem is in having warmth, and that it is less and less valuable in proportion as it cools by too long waiting upon either fastidious skill or inefficient skill, the little group of verses entitled "Brother and Sister" deserve our preference. They have extreme loveliness, and the feeling they so abundantly express is of a much less intellectualised sort than that which prevails in the other poems. It is seldom that one of our author's compositions concludes upon so simply sentimental a note as the last lines of "Brother and Sister":—

> "But were another childhood-world my share,
>
> I would be born a little sister there!"

This will be interesting to many readers as proceeding more directly from the writer's personal experience than anything else they remember. George Eliot's is a personality so enveloped in the mists of reflection that it is an uncommon sensation to find one's self in immediate contact with it. This charming poem, too, throws a grateful light on some of the best pages the author has written,—those in which she describes her heroine's childish years in *The Mill on the Floss*. The finest thing in that admirable novel has always been, to our taste, not its portrayal of the young girl's love-struggles as regards her lover, but those as regards her brother. The former are fiction,—skilful fiction; but the latter are warm reality, and the merit of the verses we speak of is that they are coloured from the same source.

In "Stradivarius," the famous old violin-maker affirms in every pregnant phrase the supreme duty of being perfect in one's labour, and lays down the dictum, which should be the first article in every artist's faith:—

> "'Tis God gives skill,
>
> But not without men's hands: He could not make
>
> Antonio Stradivari's violins
>
> Without Antonio."

This is the only really inspiring working-creed, and our author's utterance of it justifies her claim to having the distinctively artistic mind, more forcibly than her not infrequent shortcomings in the direction of an artistic *ensemble*.

Many persons will probably pronounce "A Minor Prophet" the gem of this little collection, and it is certainly interesting, for a great many reasons. It may seem to characterise the author on a number of sides. It illustrates vividly, in the extraordinary ingenuity and flexibility of its diction, her extreme provocation to indulge in the verbal licence of verse. It reads almost like a close imitation of Browning, the great master of the poetical grotesque, except that it observes a discretion which the poet of *Red-Cotton Night-caps* long ago threw overboard. When one can say neat things with such rhythmic felicity, why not attempt it, even if one has at one's command the magnificent vehicle of the style of *Middlemarch*?

The poem is a kindly satire upon the views and the person of an American vegetarian, a certain Elias Baptist Butterworth,—a gentleman, presumably, who under another name, as an evening caller, has not a little retarded the flight of time for the author. Mr. Browning has written nothing better than the account of the Butterworthian "Thought Atmosphere":—

"And when all earth is vegetarian,

When, lacking butchers, quadrupeds die out,

And less Thought-atmosphere is re-absorbed

By nerves of insects parasitical,

Those higher truths, seized now by higher minds,

But not expressed (the insects hindering),

Will either flash out into eloquence,

Or, better still, be comprehensible,

By rappings simply, without need of roots."

The author proceeds to give a sketch of the beatific state of things under the vegetarian *régime* prophesied by her friend in

> "Mildly nasal tones,
>
> And vowels stretched to suit the widest views."

How, for instance,

> "Sahara will be populous
>
> With families of gentlemen retired
>
> From commerce in more Central Africa,
>
> Who order coolness, as we order coal,
>
> And have a lobe anterior strong enough
>
> To think away the sand-storms."

Or how, as water is probably a non-conductor of the Thought-atmosphere,

> "Fishes may lead carnivorous lives obscure,
>
> But must not dream of culinary rank
>
> Or being dished in good society."

Then follows the author's own melancholy head-shake and her reflections on the theme that there can be no easy millennium, and that

"Bitterly

I feel that every change upon this earth

Is bought with sacrifice";

and that, even if Mr. Butterworth's axioms were not too good to be true, one might deprecate them in the interest of that happiness which is associated with error that is deeply familiar. Human improvement, she concludes, is something both larger and smaller than the vegetarian bliss, and consists less in a realised perfection than in the sublime dissatisfaction of generous souls with the shortcomings of the actual. All this is unfolded in verse which, if without the absolute pulse of spontaneity, has at least something that closely resembles it. It has very fine passages.

Very fine, too, both in passages and as a whole, is "The Legend of Jubal." It is noteworthy, by the way, that three of these poems are on themes connected with music; and yet we remember no representation of a musician among the multitudinous figures which people the author's novels. But George Eliot, we take it, has the musical sense in no small degree, and the origin of melody and harmony is here described in some very picturesque and sustained poetry.

Jubal invents the lyre and teaches his companions and his tribe how to use it, and then goes forth to wander in quest of new musical inspiration. In this pursuit he grows patriarchally old, and at last makes his way back to his own people. He finds them, greatly advanced in civilisation, celebrating what we should call nowadays his centennial, and making his name the refrain of their songs. He goes in among them and declares himself, but they receive him as a lunatic, and buffet him, and thrust him out into the wilderness again, where he succumbs to their unconscious ingratitude.

"The immortal name of Jubal filled the sky,

While Jubal, lonely, laid him down to die."

In his last hour he has a kind of metaphysical vision which consoles him, and enables him to die contented. A mystic voice assures him that he has no cause for complaint; that his use to mankind was everything, and his credit and glory nothing; that being rich in his genius, it was his part to give, gratuitously, to unendowed humanity; and that the knowledge of his having become a part of man's joy, and an image in man's soul, should reconcile him to the prospect of lying senseless in the tomb. Jubal assents, and expires.

> "A quenched sun-wave,
>
> The all-creating Presence for his grave."

This is very noble and heroic doctrine, and is enforced in verse not unworthy of it for having a certain air of strain and effort; for surely it is not doctrine that the egoistic heart rises to without some experimental flutter of the wings. It is the expression of a pessimistic philosophy which pivots upon itself only in the face of a really formidable ultimatum. We cordially accept it, however, and are tolerably confident that the artist in general, in his death-throes, will find less repose in the idea of a heavenly compensation for earthly neglect than in the certainty that humanity is really assimilating his productions.

"Agatha" is slighter in sentiment than its companions, and has the vague aroma of an idea rather than the positive weight of thought. It is very graceful. "How Lisa loved the King" seems to us to have, more than its companions, the easy flow and abundance of prime poetry; it wears a reflection of the incomparable naturalness of its model in the *Decameron*. "Armgart" we have found extremely interesting, although perhaps it offers plainest proof of what the author sacrifices in renouncing prose. The drama, in prose, would have been vividly dramatic, while, as it stands, we have merely a situation contemplated, rather than unfolded, in a dramatic light. A great singer loses her voice, and a patronising nobleman, who, before the calamity, had wished her to become his wife, retire from the stage, and employ her genius for the beguilement of private life, finds that he has urgent business in another neighbourhood, and that he has not the mission to espouse her misfortune. Armgart rails tremendously at fate, often in very striking phrase. The Count of course, in bidding her farewell, has hoped that time will soften her disappointment:—

"That empty cup so neatly ciphered, 'Time,'

Handed me as a cordial for despair.

Time—what a word to fling in charity!

Bland, neutral word for slow, dull-beating pain,—

Days, months, and years!"

We must refer the reader to the poem itself for knowledge how resignation comes to so bitter a pain as the mutilation of conscious genius. It comes to Armgart because she is a very superior girl; and though her outline, here, is at once rather sketchy and rather rigid, she may be added to that group of magnificently generous women,—the Dinahs, the Maggies, the Romolas, the Dorotheas,—the representation of whom is our author's chief title to our gratitude. But in spite of Armgart's resignation, the moral atmosphere of the poem, like that of most of the others and like that of most of George Eliot's writings, is an almost gratuitously sad one.

It would take more space than we can command to say how it is that at this and at other points our author strikes us as a spirit mysteriously perverted from her natural temper. We have a feeling that, both intellectually and morally, her genius is essentially of a simpler order than most of her recent manifestations of it. Intellectually, it has run to epigram and polished cleverness, and morally to a sort of conscious and ambitious scepticism, with which it only half commingles. The interesting thing would be to trace the moral divergence from the characteristic type. At bottom, according to this notion, the author of *Romola* and *Middlemarch* has an ardent desire and faculty for positive, active, constructive belief of the old-fashioned kind, but she has fallen upon a critical age and felt its contagion and dominion. If, with her magnificent gifts, she had been borne by the mighty general current in the direction of passionate faith, we often think that she would have achieved something incalculably great.

THE LIMITATIONS OF DICKENS

OUR *Mutual Friend* is, to our perception, the poorest of Mr. Dickens's works. And it is poor with the poverty not of momentary embarrassment, but of permanent exhaustion. It is wanting in inspiration. For the last ten years it has seemed to us that Mr. Dickens has been unmistakeably forcing himself. *Bleak House* was forced; *Little Dorrit* was laboured; the present work is dug out as with a spade and pickaxe.

Of course—to anticipate the usual argument—who but Dickens could have written it? Who, indeed? Who else would have established a lady in business in a novel on the admirably solid basis of her always putting on gloves and tying a handkerchief around her head in moments of grief, and of her habitually addressing her family with "Peace! hold!" It is needless to say that Mrs. Reginald Wilfer is first and last the occasion of considerable true humour. When, after conducting her daughter to Mrs. Boffin's carriage, in sight of all the envious neighbours, she is described as enjoying her triumph during the next quarter of an hour by airing herself on the doorstep "in a kind of splendidly serene trance," we laugh with as uncritical a laugh as could be desired of us. We pay the same tribute to her assertions, as she narrates the glories of the society she enjoyed at her father's table, that she has known as many as three copper-plate engravers exchanging the most exquisite sallies and retorts there at one time. But when to these we have added a dozen more happy examples of the humour which was exhaled from every line of Mr. Dickens's earlier writings, we shall have closed the list of the merits of the work before us.

To say that the conduct of the story, with all its complications, betrays a long-practised hand, is to pay no compliment worthy the author. If this were, indeed, a compliment, we should be inclined to carry it further, and congratulate him on his success in what we should call the manufacture of fiction; for in so doing we should express a feeling that has attended us throughout the book. Seldom, we reflected, had we read a book so intensely *written*, so little seen, known, or felt.

In all Mr. Dickens's works the fantastic has been his great resource; and while his fancy was lively and vigorous it accomplished great things. But the fantastic, when the fancy is dead, is a very poor business. The movement of Mr. Dickens's fancy in Mr. Wilfer and Mr. Boffin and Lady Tippins, and the Lammles and Miss Wren, and even in Eugene Wrayburn, is, to our mind, a movement lifeless, forced, mechanical. It is the letter of his old humour without the spirit. It is hardly too much to say that every character here put before us is a mere bundle of eccentricities, animated by no principle of nature whatever.

In former days there reigned in Mr. Dickens's extravagances a comparative consistency; they were exaggerated statements of types that really existed. We had, perhaps, never known a Newman Noggs, nor a Pecksniff, nor a Micawber; but we had known persons of whom these figures were but the strictly logical consummation. But among the grotesque creatures who occupy the pages before us, there is not one whom we can refer to as an existing type. In all Mr. Dickens's stories, indeed, the reader has been called upon, and has willingly consented, to accept a certain number of figures or creatures of pure fancy, for this was the author's poetry. He was, moreover, always repaid for his concession by a peculiar beauty or power in these exceptional characters. But he is now expected to make the same concession, with a very inadequate reward.

What do we get in return for accepting Miss Jenny Wren as a possible person? This young lady is the type of a certain class of characters of which Mr. Dickens has made a specialty, and with which he has been accustomed to draw alternate smiles and tears, according as he pressed one spring or another. But this is very cheap merriment and very cheap pathos. Miss Jenny Wren is a poor little dwarf, afflicted as she constantly reiterates, with a "bad back" and "queer legs," who makes doll's dresses, and is for ever pricking at those with whom she converses in the air, with her needle, and assuring them that she knows their "tricks and their manners." Like all Mr. Dickens's pathetic characters, she is a little monster; she is deformed, unhealthy, unnatural; she belongs to the troop of hunchbacks, imbeciles, and precocious children who have carried on the sentimental business in all Mr. Dickens's novels; the little Nells, the Smikes, the Paul Dombeys.

Mr. Dickens goes as far out of the way for his wicked people as he does for his good ones. Rogue Riderhood, indeed, in the present story, is villainous with a sufficiently natural villainy; he belongs to that quarter of society in which the author is most at his ease. But was there ever such wickedness as that of the Lammles and Mr. Fledgeby? Not that people have not been as mischievous as they; but was any one ever mischievous in that singular fashion? Did a couple of elegant swindlers ever take such particular pains to be aggressively inhuman?—for we can find no other word for the gratuitous distortions to which they are subjected. The word *humanity* strikes us as strangely discordant, in the midst of these pages; for, let us boldly declare it, there is no humanity here.

Humanity is nearer home than the Boffins, and the Lammles, and the Wilfers, and the Veneerings. It is in what men have in common with each other, and not what they have in distinction. The people just named have nothing in common with each other, except the fact that they have nothing in common with mankind at large. What a world were this world if the world of *Our Mutual Friend* were an honest reflection of it! But a community of eccentrics is impossible. Rules alone are consistent with each other; exceptions are inconsistent. Society is maintained by natural sense and natural feeling. We cannot conceive a society in which these principles are not in some manner represented. Where in these pages are the depositaries of that intelligence without which the movement of life would cease? Who represents nature?

Accepting half of Mr. Dickens's persons as intentionally grotesque, where are those examplars of sound humanity who should afford us the proper measure of their companions' variations? We ought not, in justice to the author, to seek them among his weaker—that is, his mere conventional—characters; in John Harmon, Lizzie Hexam, or Mortimer Lightwood; but we assuredly cannot find them among his stronger—that is, his artificial creations.

Suppose we take Eugene Wrayburn and Bradley Headstone. They occupy a half-way position between the habitual probable of nature and the habitual impossible of Mr. Dickens. A large portion of the story rests upon the enmity borne by Headstone to Wrayburn, both being in love with the same woman. Wrayburn is a gentleman, and Headstone is one of the people. Wrayburn is well-bred, careless, elegant, sceptical, and idle: Headstone is a high-tempered, hard-working, ambitious young schoolmaster. There lay in the opposition of these two characters a very good story. But the prime requisite was that they should *be* characters: Mr. Dickens, according to his usual plan, has made them simply figures, and between them the story that was to be, the story that should have been, has evaporated. Wrayburn lounges about with his hands in his pockets, smoking a cigar, and talking nonsense. Headstone strides about, clenching his fists and biting his lips and grasping his stick.

There is one scene in which Wrayburn chaffs the schoolmaster with easy insolence, while the latter writhes impotently under his well-bred sarcasm. This scene is very clever, but it is very insufficient. If the majority of readers were not so very timid in the use of words we should call it vulgar. By this we do not mean to indicate the conventional impropriety of two gentlemen exchanging lively personalities; we mean to emphasise the essentially small character of these personalities. In other words, the moment, dramatically, is great, while the author's conception is weak. The friction of two *men*, of two characters, of two passions, produces stronger sparks than Wrayburn's boyish repartees and Headstone's melodramatic commonplaces.

Such scenes as this are useful in fixing the limits of Mr. Dickens's insight. Insight is, perhaps, too strong a word; for we are convinced that it is one of the chief conditions of his genius not to see beneath the surface of things. If we might hazard a definition of his literary character, we should, accordingly, call him the greatest of superficial novelists. We are aware that this definition confines him to an inferior rank in the department of letters which he adorns; but we accept this consequence of our proposition. It were, in our opinion, an offence against humanity to place Mr. Dickens among the greatest novelists. For, to repeat what we have already intimated, he has created nothing but figure. He has added nothing to our understanding of human character. He is master of but two alternatives: he reconciles us to what is commonplace, and he reconciles us to what is odd. The value of the former service is questionable; and the manner in which Mr. Dickens performs it sometimes conveys a certain impression of charlatanism. The value of the latter service is incontestable, and here Mr. Dickens is an honest, an admirable artist.

But what is the condition of the truly great novelist? For him there are no alternatives, for him there are no oddities, for him there is nothing outside of humanity. He cannot shirk it; it imposes itself upon him. For him alone, therefore, there is a true and a false; for him alone, it is possible to be right, because it is possible to be wrong. Mr. Dickens is a great observer and a great humourist, but he is nothing of a philosopher.

Some people may hereupon say, so much the better; we say, so much the worse. For a novelist very soon has need of a little philosophy. In treating of Micawber, and Boffin, and Pickwick, *et hoc genus omne*, he can, indeed, dispense with it, for this—we say it with all deference—is not serious writing. But when he comes to tell the story of a passion, a story like that of Headstone and Wrayburn, he becomes a moralist as well as an artist. He must know *man* as well as *men*, and to know man is to be a philosopher.

The writer who knows men alone, if he have Mr. Dickens's humour and fancy, will give us figures and pictures for which we cannot be too grateful, for he will enlarge our knowledge of the world. But when he introduces men and women whose interest is preconceived to lie not in the poverty, the weakness, the drollery of their natures, but in their complete and unconscious subjection to ordinary and healthy human emotions, all his humour, all his fancy, will avail him nothing if, out of the fullness of his sympathy, he is unable to prosecute those generalisations in which alone consists the real greatness of a work of art.

This may sound like very subtle talk about a very simple matter. It is rather very simple talk about a very subtle matter. A story based upon those elementary passions in which alone we seek the true and final manifestation of character must be told in a spirit of intellectual superiority to those passions. That is, the author must understand what he is talking about. The perusal of a story so told is one of the most elevating experiences within the reach of the human mind. The perusal of a story which is not so told is infinitely depressing and unprofitable.

TENNYSON'S DRAMA

I. QUEEN MARY

ANEW poem by Mr. Tennyson is certain to be largely criticised, and if the new poem is a drama, the performance must be a great event for criticism as well as for poetry. Great surprise, great hopes, and great fears had been called into being by the announcement that the author of so many finely musical lyrics and finished, chiselled specimens of narrative verse, had tempted fortune in the perilous field of the drama.

Few poets seemed less dramatic than Tennyson, even in his most dramatic attempts—in "Maud," in "Enoch Arden," or in certain of the *Idyls of the King*. He had never used the dramatic form, even by snatches; and though no critic was qualified to affirm that he had no slumbering ambition in that direction, it seemed likely that a poet who had apparently passed the meridian of his power had nothing absolutely new to show us. On the other hand, if he had for years been keeping a gift in reserve, and suffering it to ripen and mellow in some deep corner of his genius, while shallower tendencies waxed and waned above it, it was not unjust to expect that the consummate fruit would prove magnificent.

On the whole, we think that doubt was uppermost in the minds of those persons who to a lively appreciation of the author of "Maud" added a vivid conception of the exigencies of the drama. But at last *Queen Mary* appeared, and conjecture was able to merge itself in knowledge. There was a momentary interval, during which we all read, among the cable telegrams in the newspapers, that the London *Times* affirmed the new drama to contain more "true fire" than anything since Shakespeare had laid down the pen. This gave an edge to our impatience; for "fire," true or false, was not what the Laureate's admirers had hitherto claimed for him. In a day or two, however, most people had the work in their hands.

Every one, it seems to us, has been justified—those who hoped (that is, expected), those who feared, and those who were mainly surprised. *Queen Mary* is both better and less good than was to have been supposed, and both in its merits and its defects it is extremely singular. It is the least Tennysonian of all the author's productions; and we may say that he has not so much refuted as evaded the charge that he is not a dramatic poet. To produce his drama he has had to cease to be himself. Even if *Queen Mary*, as a drama, had many more than its actual faults, this fact alone—this extraordinary defeasance by the poet of his familiar identity—would make it a remarkable work.

We know of few similar phenomena in the history of literature—few such examples of rupture with a consecrated past. Poets in their prime have groped and experimented, tried this and that, and finally made a great success in a very different vein from that in which they had found their early successes. But the writers in prose or in verse are few who, after a lifetime spent in elaborating and perfecting a certain definite and extremely characteristic manner, have at Mr. Tennyson's age suddenly dismissed it from use and stood forth clad from head to foot in a disguise without a flaw. We are sure that the other great English poet—the author of "The Ring and the Book,"—would be quite incapable of any such feat. The more's the pity, as many of his readers will say!

Queen Mary is upward of three hundred pages long; and yet in all these three hundred pages there is hardly a trace of the Tennyson we know. Of course the reader is on the watch for reminders of the writer he has greatly loved; and of course, vivid signs being absent, he finds a certain eloquence in the slightest intimations. When he reads that

————"that same tide

Which, coming with our coming, seemed to smile

And sparkle like our fortune as thou saidest,

Ran sunless down and moaned against the piers,"

he seems for a moment to detect the peculiar note and rhythm of "Enoch Arden" or "The Princess." Just preceding these, indeed, is a line which seems Tennysonian because it is in a poem by Tennyson:

"Last night I climbed into the gate-house, Brett,

And scared the gray old porter and his wife."

In such touches as these the Tennysonian note is faintly struck; but if the poem were unsigned, they would not do much toward pointing out the author. On the other hand, the fine passages in *Queen Mary* are conspicuously deficient in those peculiar cadences—that exquisite perfume of diction— which every young poet of the day has had his hour of imitating. We may give as an example Pole's striking denial of the charge that the Church of Rome has ever known trepidation:

"What, my Lord!

The Church on Petra's rock? Never! I have seen

A pine in Italy that cast its shadow

Athwart a cataract; firm stood the pine—

The cataract shook the shadow. To my mind

The cataract typed the headlong plunge and fall

Of heresy to the pit: the pine was Rome.

You see, my Lords,

It was the shadow of the Church that trembled."

This reads like Tennyson doing his best not to be Tennyson, and very fairly succeeding. Well as he succeeds, however, and admirably skilful and clever as is his attempt throughout to play tricks with his old habits of language, and prove that he was not the slave but the master of the classic Tennysonian rhythm, I think that few readers can fail to ask themselves whether the new gift is of equal value with the old. The question will perhaps set them to fingering over the nearest volume of the poet at hand, to refresh their memory of his ancient magic. It has rendered the present writer this service, and he feels as if it were a considerable one. Every great poet has something that he does supremely well, and when you come upon Tennyson at his best you feel that you are dealing with poetry at its highest. One of the best passages in *Queen Mary*—the only one, it seems to me, very sensibly warmed by the "fire" commemorated by the London *Times*—is the passionate monologue of Mary when she feels what she supposes to be the intimations of maternity:

"He hath awaked, he hath awaked!

He stirs within the darkness!

Oh Philip, husband! how thy love to mine

Will cling more close, and those bleak manners thaw,

That make me shamed and tongue-tied in my love.

The second Prince of Peace—

The great unborn defender of the Faith,

Who will avenge me of mine enemies—

He comes, and my star rises.

The stormy Wyatts and Northumberlands

And proud ambitions of Elizabeth,

And all her fiercest partisans, are pale

Before my star!

His sceptre shall go forth from Ind to Ind!

His sword shall hew the heretic peoples down!

His faith shall clothe the world that will be his,

Like universal air and sunshine! Open,

Ye everlasting gates! The King is here!—

My star, my son!"

That is very fine, and its broken verses and uneven movement have great felicity and suggestiveness. But their magic is as nothing, surely, to the magic of such a passage as this:

"Yet hold me not for ever in thine East;

How can my nature longer mix with thine?

Coldly thy rosy shadows bathe me, cold

Are all thy lights, and cold my wrinkled feet

Upon thy glimmering thresholds, where the stream

Floats up from those dim fields about the homes

Of happy men that have the power to die,

And grassy barrows of the happier dead.

Release me and restore me to the ground;

Thou seëst all things, thou wilt see my grave;

Thou wilt renew thy beauty morn by morn;

I, earth in earth, forget these empty courts,

And thee returning on thy silver wheels."

In these beautiful lines from "Tithonus" there is a purity of tone, an inspiration, a something sublime and exquisite, which is easily within the compass of Mr. Tennyson's usual manner at its highest, but which is not easily achieved by any really dramatic verse. It is poised and stationary, like a bird whose wings have borne him high, but the beauty of whose movement is less in great ethereal sweeps and circles than in the way he hangs motionless in the blue air, with only a vague tremor of his pinions. Even if the idea with Tennyson were more largely dramatic than it usually is, the immobility, as we must call it, of his phrase would always defeat the dramatic intention. When he wishes to represent movement, the phrase always seems to me to pause and slowly pivot upon itself, or at most to move backward. I do not know whether the reader recognizes the peculiarity to which I allude; one has only to open Tennyson almost at random to find an example of it:

"For once when Arthur, walking all alone,

Vext at a rumour rife about the Queen,

Had met her, Vivien being greeted fair,

Would fain have wrought upon his cloudy mood

With reverent eyes mock-loyal, shaken voice,

And fluttered adoration."

That perhaps is a subtle illustration; the allusion to Teolin's dog in "Aylmer's Field" is a franker one:

——"his old Newfoundlands, when they ran

To lose him at the stables; for he rose,

Two-footed, at the limit of his chain,

Roaring to make a third."

What these pictures present is not the action itself, but the poet's complex perception of it; it seems hardly more vivid and genuine than the sustained posturings of brilliant *tableaux vivants*. With the poets who are natural chroniclers of movement, the words fall into their places as with some throw of the dice, which fortune should always favour. With Scott and Byron they leap into the verse *à pieds joints*, and shake it with their coming; with Tennyson they arrive slowly and settle cautiously into their attitudes, after having well scanned the locality. In consequence they are generally exquisite, and make exquisite combinations; but the result is intellectual poetry and not passionate—poetry which, if the term is not too pedantic, one may qualify as static poetry. Any scene of violence represented by Tennyson is always singularly limited and compressed; it is reduced to a few elements—refined to a single statuesque episode. There are, for example, several descriptions of tournaments and combats in the *Idyls of the King*. They are all most beautiful, but they are all curiously delicate. One gets no sense of the din and shock of battle; one seems to be looking at a bas relief of two contesting knights in chiselled silver, on a priceless piece of plate. They belong to the same family as that charming description, in Hawthorne's *Marble Faun*, of the sylvan dance of Donatello and Miriam in the Borghese gardens. Hawthorne talks of the freedom and frankness of their mirth and revelry; what we seem to see is a solemn frieze in stone along the base of a monument. These are the natural fruits of geniuses who are of the brooding rather than the impulsive order. I do not mean to say that here and there Tennyson does not give us a couplet in which motion seems reflected without being made to tarry. I open "Enoch Arden" at hazard, and I read of Enoch's ship that

——"at first indeed

Thro' many a fair sea-circle, day by day,

114

Scarce rocking, her full-busted figure-head

Stared o'er the ripple feathering from her bows."

I turn the page and read of

"The myriad shriek of wheeling ocean fowl,

The league-long roller thundering on the reef,

The moving whisper of huge trees that branched

And blossomed in the zenith";

of

"The sunrise broken into scarlet shafts

Among the palms and ferns and precipices;

The blaze upon the waters to the east;

The blaze upon his island overhead;

The blaze upon the waters to the west;

Then the great stars that globed themselves in Heaven,

The hollower-bellowing Ocean, and again

The scarlet shafts of sunrise."

These lines represent movement on the grand natural scale—taking place in that measured, majestic fashion which, at any given moment, seems identical with permanence. One is almost ashamed to quote Tennyson;

115

one can hardly lay one's hand on a passage that does not form part of the common stock of reference and recitation. Passages of the more impulsive and spontaneous kind will of course chiefly be found in his lyrics and rhymed verses (though rhyme would at first seem but another check upon his freedom); and passages of the kind to which I have been calling attention, chiefly in his narrative poems, in the *Idyls* generally, and especially in the later ones, while the words strike one as having been pondered and collated with an almost miserly care.

But a man has always the qualities of his defects, and if Tennyson is what I have called a static poet, he at least represents repose and stillness and the fixedness of things, with a splendour that no poet has surpassed. We all of this generation have lived in such intimacy with him, and made him so much part of our regular intellectual meat and drink, that it requires a certain effort to hold him off at the proper distance for scanning him. We need to cease mechanically murmuring his lines, so that we may hear them speak for themselves.

Few persons who have grown up within the last forty years but have passed through the regular Tennysonian phase; happy few who have paid it a merely passive tribute, and not been moved to commit their emotions to philosophic verse, in the metre of "In Memoriam"! The phase has lasted longer with some persons than with others; but it will not be denied that with the generation at large it has visibly declined. The young persons of twenty now read Tennyson (though, as we imagine, with a fervour less intense than that which prevailed twenty years ago); but the young persons of thirty read Browning and Dante Rossetti, and Omar Kheyam—and are also sometimes heard to complain that poetry is dead and that there is nothing nowadays to read.

We have heard Tennyson called "dainty" so often, we have seen so many allusions to the "Tennysonian trick," we have been so struck, in a certain way, with M. Taine's remarkable portrait of the poet, in contrast to that of Alfred de Musset, that every one who has anything of a notion of keeping abreast of what is called the "culture of the time" is rather shy of making an explicit, or even a serious profession of admiration for his earlier idol. It has long been the fashion to praise Byron, if one praises him at all, with an apologetic smile; and Tennyson has been, I think, in a measure, tacitly classed with the author of "Childe Harold" as a poet whom one thinks most of while one's taste is immature.

This is natural enough, I suppose, and the taste of the day must travel to its opportunity's end. But I do not believe that Byron has passed, by any means, and I do not think that Tennyson has been proved to be a secondary or a tertiary poet. If he is not in the front rank, it is hard to see what it is that constitutes exquisite quality. There are poets of a larger compass; he has not the passion of Shelley nor the transcendent meditation of Wordsworth; but his inspiration, in its own current, is surely as pure as theirs. He depicts the assured beauties of life, the things that civilisation has gained and permeated, and he does it with an ineffable delicacy of imagination. Only once, as it seems to me (at the close of "Maud"), has he struck the note of irrepressible emotion, and appeared to say the thing that must be said at the moment, at any cost. For the rest, his verse is the verse of leisure, of luxury, of contemplation, of a faculty that circumstances have helped to become fastidious; but this leaves it a wide province—a province that it fills with a sovereign splendour.

When a poet is such an artist as Tennyson, such an unfaltering, consummate master, it is no shame to surrender one's self to his spell. Reading him over here and there, as I have been doing, I have received an extraordinary impression of talent—talent ripened and refined, and passed, with a hundred incantations, through the crucible of taste. The reader is in thoroughly good company, and if the language is to a certain extent that of a coterie, the coterie can offer convincing evidence of its right to be exclusive. Its own tone is exquisite; listen to it, and you will desire nothing more.

Tennyson's various *Idyls* have been in some degree discredited by insincere imitations, and in some degree, perhaps, by an inevitable lapse of sympathy on the part of some people from what appears their falsetto pitch. That King Arthur, in the great ones of the series, is rather a prig, and that he couldn't have been all the poet represents him without being a good deal of a hypocrite; that the poet himself is too monotonously unctuous, and that in relating the misdeeds of Launcelot and Guinevere he seems, like the lady in the play in "Hamlet," to "protest too much" for wholesomeness—all this has been often said, and said with abundant force. But there is a way of reading the *Idyls*, one and all, and simply enjoying them. It has been, just now, the way of the writer of these lines; he does not exactly know what may be gained by taking the other way, but he feels as if there were a pitiful loss in not taking this one. If one surrenders one's sense to their perfect picturesqueness, it is the most charming poetry in the world. The prolonged, delicate, exquisite sustentation of the pictorial tone seems to me a marvel of ingenuity and fancy. It appeals to a highly cultivated sense, but what enjoyment is so keen as that of the cultivated sense when its finer nerve is really touched? The *Idyls* all belong to the poetry of association; but before they were written we had yet to learn how finely association could be analysed, and how softly its chords could be played upon. When Enoch Arden came back from his desert island,

"He like a lover down through all his blood

Drew in the dewy, meadowy morning breath

Of England, blown across her ghostly wall."

Tennyson's solid verbal felicities, his unerring sense of the romantic, his acute perception of everything in nature that may contribute to his fund of exquisite imagery, his refinement, his literary tone, his aroma of English lawns and English libraries, the whole happy chance of his selection of the Arthurian legends—all this, and a dozen minor graces which it would take almost his own "daintiness" to formulate, make him, it seems to me, the most charming of the *entertaining* poets. It is as an entertaining poet I chiefly think of him; his morality, at moments, is certainly importunate enough, but elevated as it is, it never seems to me of so fine a distillation as his imagery. As a didactic creation I do not greatly care for King Arthur; but as a fantastic one he is infinitely remunerative. He is doubtless not, as an intellectual conception, massive enough to be called a great figure; but he is, picturesquely, so admirably self-consistent, that the reader's imagination is quite willing to turn its back, if need be, on his judgment, and give itself up to idle enjoyment.

As regards Tennyson's imagery, anything that one quotes in illustration is, as I have said, certain to be extremely familiar; but even familiarity can hardly dull the beauty of such a touch as that about Merlin's musings:

"So dark a forethought rolled about his brain,

As on a dull day in an Ocean cave

The blind wave feeling round his long sea-hall

In silence."

Or of that which puts in vivid form the estrangement of Enid and Geraint:

"The two remained

Apart by all the chamber's width, and mute

As creatures voiceless through the fault of birth,

Or two wild men, supporters of a shield,

Painted, who stare at open space, nor glance

The one at other, parted by the shield."

Happy, in short, the poet who can offer his heroine for her dress

——"a splendid silk of foreign loom,

Where, like a shoaling sea, the lovely blue

Played into green."

I have touched here only upon Tennyson's narrative poems, because they seemed most in order in any discussion of the author's dramatic faculty. They cannot be said to place it in an eminent light, and they remind one more of the courage than of the discretion embodied in *Queen Mary*. Lovely pictures of things standing, with a sort of conscious stillness, for their poetic likeness, measured speeches, full of delicate harmonies and curious cadences—these things they contain in plenty, but little of that liberal handling of cross-speaking passion and humour which, with a strong constructive faculty, we regard as the sign of a genuine dramatist.

The dramatic form seems to me of all literary forms the very noblest, I have so extreme a relish for it that I am half afraid to trust myself to praise it, lest I should seem to be merely rhapsodizing. But to be really noble it must be quite itself, and between a poor drama and a fine one there is, I think, a wider interval than anywhere else in the scale of success. A sequence of speeches headed by proper names—a string of dialogues broken into acts and scenes—does not constitute a drama; not even when the speeches are very clever and the dialogue bristles with "points."

The fine thing in a real drama, generally speaking, is that, more than any other work of literary art, it needs a masterly structure. It needs to be shaped and fashioned and laid together, and this process makes a demand upon an artist's rarest gifts. He must combine and arrange, interpolate and eliminate, play the joiner with the most attentive skill; and yet at the end effectually bury his tools and his sawdust, and invest his elaborate skeleton with the smoothest and most polished integument. The five-act drama—serious or humourous, poetic or prosaic—is like a box of fixed dimensions and inelastic material, into which a mass of precious things are to be packed away. It is a problem in ingenuity and a problem of the most interesting kind. The precious things in question seem out of all proportion to the compass of the receptacle; but the artist has an assurance that with patience and skill a place may be made for each, and that nothing need be clipped or crumpled, squeezed or damaged. The false dramatist either knocks out the sides of his box, or plays the deuce with the contents; the real one gets down on his knees, disposes of his goods tentatively, this, that, and the other way, loses his temper but keeps his ideal, and at last rises in triumph, having packed his coffer in the one way that is mathematically right. It closes perfectly, and the lock turns with a click; between one object and another you cannot insert the point of a penknife.

To work successfully beneath a few grave, rigid laws, is always a strong man's highest ideal of success. The reader cannot be sure how deeply conscious Mr. Tennyson has been of the laws of the drama, but it would seem as if he had not very attentively pondered them. In a play, certainly, the subject is of more importance than in any other work of art. Infelicity, triviality, vagueness of subject, may be outweighed in a poem, a novel, or a picture, by charm of manner, by ingenuity of execution; but in a drama the subject is of the essence of the work—it *is* the work. If it is feeble, the work can have no force; if it is shapeless, the work must be amorphous.

Queen Mary, I think, has this fundamental weakness; it would be very hard to say what its subject is. Strictly speaking, the drama has none. To the statement, "It is the reign of the elder daughter of Henry VIII.," it seems to me very nearly fair to reply that that is not a subject. I do not mean to say that a consummate dramatist could not resolve it into one, but the presumption is altogether against it. It cannot be called an intrigue, nor treated as one; it tends altogether to expansion; whereas a genuine dramatic subject should tend to concentration.

Madame Ristori, that accomplished tragédienne, has for some years been carrying about the world with her a piece of writing, punctured here and there with curtain-falls, which she presents to numerous audiences as a tragedy embodying the history of Queen Elizabeth. The thing is worth mentioning only as an illustration; it is from the hand of a prolific Italian purveyor of such wares, and is as bad as need be. Many of the persons who read these lines will have seen it, and will remember it as a mere bald sequence of anecdotes, roughly cast into dialogue. It is not incorrect to say that, as regards form, Mr. Tennyson's drama is of the same family as the historical tragedies of Signor Giacometti. It is simply a dramatised chronicle, without an internal structure, taking its material in pieces, as history hands them over, and working each one up into an independent scene—usually with rich ability. It has no shape; it is cast into no mould; it has neither beginning, middle, nor end, save the chronological ones.

A work of this sort may have a great many merits (those of *Queen Mary* are numerous), but it cannot have the merit of being a drama. We have, indeed, only to turn to Shakespeare to see how much of pure dramatic interest may be infused into an imperfect dramatic form. *Henry IV.* and the others of its group, *Richard III.*, *Henry VIII.*, *Antony and Cleopatra*, *Julius Cæsar*, are all chronicles in dialogue, are all simply Holinshed and Plutarch transferred into immortal verse. They are magnificent because Shakespeare could do nothing weak; but all Shakespearian as they are, they are not models; the models are *Hamlet* and *Othello*, *Macbeth* and *Lear*. Tennyson is not Shakespeare, but in everything he had done hitherto there had been an essential perfection, and we are sorry that, in the complete maturity of his talent, proposing to write a drama, he should have chosen the easy way rather than the hard.

He chose, however, a period out of which a compact dramatic subject of the richest interest might well have been wrought. For this, of course, considerable invention would have been needed, and Mr. Tennyson had apparently no invention to bring to his task. He has embroidered cunningly the groundwork offered him by Mr. Froude, but he has contributed no new material. The field offers a great stock of dramatic figures, and one's imagination kindles as one thinks of the multifarious combinations into which they might have been cast. We do not pretend of course to say in detail what Mr. Tennyson might have done; we simply risk the affirmation that he might have wrought a somewhat denser tissue. History certainly would have suffered, but poetry would have gained, and he is writing poetry and not history. As his drama stands, we take it that he does not pretend to have deepened our historic light.

Psychologically, picturesquely, the persons in the foreground of Mary's reign constitute a most impressive and interesting group. The imagination plays over it importunately, and wearies itself with scanning the outlines and unlighted corners. Mary herself unites a dozen strong dramatic elements— in her dark religious passion, her unrequited conjugal passion, her mixture of the Spanish and English natures, her cruelty and her conscience, her high-handed rule and her constant insecurity. With her dark figure lighted luridly by perpetual martyr-fires, and made darker still by the presence of her younger sister, radiant with the promise of England's coming greatness; with Lady Jane Grey groping for the block behind her; her cold fanatic of a husband beside her, as we know him by Velasquez (with not a grain of fanaticism to spare for her); with her subtle ecclesiastical cousin Pole on the other side, with evil counsellors and dogged martyrs and a threatening people all around her, and with a lonely, dreary, disappointed and unlamented death before her, she is a subject made to the hand of a poet who should know how to mingle cunningly his darker shades. Tennyson has elaborated her figure in a way that is often masterly; it is a success—the greatest success of the poem. It is compounded in his hands of very subtle elements, and he keeps them from ever becoming gross.

The Mary of his pages is a complex personage, and not what she might so easily become—a mere picturesque stalking-horse of melodrama. The art with which he has still kept her sympathetic and human, at the same time that he has darkened the shadows in her portrait to the deepest tone that he had warrant for, is especially noticeable. It is not in Mr. Tennyson's pages that Mary appears for the first time in the drama; she gives her name to a play of Victor Hugo's dating from the year 1833—the prime of the author's career. I have just been reading over *Marie Tudor*, and it has suggested a good many reflections. I think it probable that many of the readers of *Queen Mary* would be quite unable to peruse Victor Hugo's consummately unpleasant production to the end; but they would admit, I suppose, that a person who had had the stomach to do so might have something particular to say about it.

If one had an eye for contrasts, the contrast between these two works is extremely curious. I said just now that Tennyson had brought no invention to his task; but it may be said, on the other side, that Victor Hugo has brought altogether too much. If Tennyson has been unduly afraid of remodelling history, the author of *Marie Tudor* has known no such scruples; he has slashed into the sacred chart with the shears of a *romantique* of 1830. Although Tennyson, in a general way, is an essentially picturesque poet, his picturesqueness is of an infinitely milder type than that of Victor Hugo; the one ends where the other begins. With Victor Hugo the horrible is always the main element of the picturesque, and the beautiful and the tender are rarely introduced save to give it relief. In *Marie Tudor* they cannot be said to be introduced at all; the drama is one masterly compound of abominable horror; horror for horror's sake—for the sake of chiaroscuro, of colour, of the footlights, of the actors; not in the least in any visible interest of human nature, of moral verity, of the discrimination of character.

What Victor Hugo has here made of the rigid, strenuous, pitiable English queen seems to me a good example of how little the handling of sinister passions sometimes costs a genius of his type—how little conviction or deep reflection goes with it. There was a Mary of a far keener tragic interest than the epigrammatic Messalina whom he has portrayed; but her image was established in graver and finer colours, and he passes jauntily beside it, without suspecting its capacity. Marie Tudor is a lascivious termagant who amuses herself, first, with caressing an Italian adventurer, then with slapping his face, and then with dabbling in his blood; but we do not really see why the author should have given his heroine a name which history held in her more or less sacred keeping; one's interest in the drama would have been more comfortable if the persons, in their impossible travesty, did not present themselves as old friends. It is true that the "Baron of Dinasmonddy" can hardly be called an old friend; but he is at least as familiar as the Earl of Clanbrassil, the Baron of Darmouth in Devonshire, and Lord South-Repps.

Marie Tudor, then has little to do with nature and nothing with either history or morality; and yet, without a paradox, it has some very strong qualities. It is at any rate a genuine drama, and it succeeds thoroughly well in what it attempts. It is moulded and proportioned to a definite scenic end, and never falters in its course. To read it just after you have read *Queen Mary* brings out its merits, as well as its defects; and if the contrast makes you inhale with a double satisfaction the clearer moral atmosphere of the English work, it leads you also to reflect with some gratitude that dramatic tradition, in our modern era, has not remained solely in English hands.

Mr. Tennyson has very frankly fashioned his play upon the model of the Shakespearian "histories." He has given us the same voluminous list of characters; he has made the division into acts merely arbitrary; he has introduced low-life interlocutors, talking in archaic prose; and whenever the fancy has taken him, he has culled his idioms and epithets from the Shakespearian vocabulary. As regards this last point, he has shown all the tact and skill that were to be expected from so approved a master of language. The prose scenes are all of a quasi-humourous description, and they emulate the queer jocosities of Shakespeare more successfully than seemed probable; though it was not to be forgotten that the author of the "Palace of Art" was also the author of the "Northern Farmer." These few lines might have been taken straight from *Henry IV.* or *Henry VIII.*:

"No; we know that you be come to kill the Queen, and we'll pray for you all on our bended knees. But o' God's mercy, don't you kill the Queen here, Sir Thomas; look ye, here's little Dickon, and little Robin, and little Jenny—though she's but a side cousin—and all, on our knees, we pray you to kill the Queen farther off, Sir Thomas."

The poet, however, is modern when he chooses to be:

"Action and reaction,

The miserable see-saw of our child-world,

Make us despise it at odd hours, my Lord."

That reminds one less of the Elizabethan than of the Victorian era. Mr. Tennyson has desired to give a general picture of the time, to reflect all its leading elements and commemorate its salient episodes. From this point of view England herself—England struggling and bleeding in the clutches of the Romish wolf, as he would say—is the heroine of the drama. This heroine is very nobly and vividly imaged, and we feel the poet to be full of a retroactive as well as a present patriotism. It is a plain Protestant attitude that he takes; there is no attempt at analysis of the Catholic sense of the situation; it is quite the old story that we learned in our school-histories as children. We do not mean that this is not the veracious way of presenting it; but we notice the absence of that tendency to place it in different lights, accumulate *pros* and *cons*, and plead opposed causes in the interest of ideal truth, which would have been so obvious if Mr. Browning had handled the theme. And yet Mr. Tennyson has been large and liberal, and some of the finest passages in the poem are uttered by independent Catholics. The author has wished to give a hint of everything, and he has admirably divined the anguish of mind of many men who were unprepared to go with the new way of thinking, and yet were scandalised at the license of the old—who were willing to be Catholics, and yet not willing to be delivered over to Spain.

Where so many episodes are sketched, few of course can be fully developed; but there is a vivid manliness of the classic English type in such portraits as Lord William Howard and Sir Ralph Bagenhall—poor Sir Ralph, who declares that

> "Far liefer had I in my country hall
>
> Been reading some old book, with mine old hound
>
> Couch'd at my hearth, and mine old flask of wine
>
> Beside me,"

than stand as he does in the thick of the trouble of the time; and who finally is brought to his account for not having knelt with the commons to the legate of Charles V. We have a glimpse of Sir Thomas Wyatt's insurrection, and a portrait of that robust rebel, who was at the same time an editor of paternal sonnets—sonnets of a father who loved

> "To read and rhyme in solitary fields,
>
> The lark above, the nightingale below,
>
> And answer them in song."

We have a very touching report of Lady Jane Grey's execution, and we assist almost directly at the sad perplexities of poor Cranmer's eclipse. We appreciate the contrast between the fine nerves and many-sided conscience of that wavering martyr, and the more comfortable religious temperament of Bonner and Gardiner—Bonner, apt "to gorge a heretic whole, roasted, or raw;" and Gardiner, who can say,

> "I've gulpt it down; I'm wholly for the Pope,
>
> Utterly and altogether for the Pope,
>
> The Eternal Peter of the changeless chair,
>
> Crowned slave of slaves and mitred king of kings.
>
> God upon earth! What more? What would you have?"

Elizabeth makes several appearances, and though they are brief, the poet has evidently had a definite figure in his mind's eye. On a second reading it betrays a number of fine intentions. The circumspection of the young princess, her high mettle, her coquetry, her frankness, her coarseness, are all rapidly glanced at. Her exclamation—

> "I would I were a milkmaid,
>
> To sing, love, marry, churn, brew, bake, and die,
>
> And have my simple headstone by the church,
>
> And all things lived and ended honestly"—

marks one limit of the sketch; and the other is indicated by her reply to Cecil at the end of the drama, on his declaring, in allusion to Mary, that "never English monarch dying left England so little":

127

"But with Cecil's aid

And others', if our person be secured

From traitor stabs, we will make England great!"

The middle term is perhaps marked by her reception of the functionary who comes to inform her that her sister bids her know that the King of Spain desires her to marry Prince Philibert of Savoy:

"I thank you heartily, sir,

But I am royal, tho' your prisoner,

And God hath blessed or cursed me with a nose—

Your boots are from the horses."

The drama is deficient in male characters of salient interest. Philip is vague and blank, as he is evidently meant to be, and Cardinal Pole is a portrait of a character constitutionally inapt for breadth of action. The portrait is a skilful one, however, and expresses forcibly the pangs of a sensitive nature entangled in trenchant machinery. There is a fine scene near the close of the drama in which Pole and the Queen—cousins, old friends, and for a moment betrothed (Victor Hugo characteristically assumes Mary to have been her cousin's mistress)—confide to each other their weariness and disappointment. Mary endeavours to console the Cardinal, but he has only grim answers for her:

"Our altar is a mound of dead men's clay,

Dug from the grave that yawns for us beyond;

And there is one Death stands beside the Groom,

And there is one Death stands beside the Bride."

Queen Mary, I believe, is to be put upon the stage next winter in London. I do not pretend to forecast its success in representation; but it is not indiscrete to say that it will suffer from the absence of a man's part capable of being made striking. The very clever Mr. Henry Irving has, we are told, offered his services, presumably to play either Philip or Pole. If he imparts any great relief to either figure, it will be a signal proof of talent. The actress, however, to whom the part of the Queen is allotted will have every reason to be grateful. The character is full of colour and made to utter a number of really dramatic speeches. When Renard assures her that Philip is only waiting for leave of the Parliament to land on English shores she has an admirable outbreak:

"God change the pebble which his kingly foot

First presses into some more costly stone

Than ever blinded eye. I'll have one mark it

And bring it me. I'll have it burnished firelike;

I'll set it round with gold, with pearl, with diamond.

Let the great angel of the Church come with him,

Stand on the deck and spread his wings for sail!"

Mary is not only vividly conceived from within, but her physiognomy, as seen from without, is indicated with much pictorial force:

"Did you mark our Queen?

The colour freely played into her face,

129

And the half sight which makes her look so stern

Seemed, through that dim, dilated world of hers,

To read our faces."

In the desolation of her last days, when she bids her attendants go to her sister and

"Tell her to come and close my dying eyes

And wear my crown and dance upon my grave,"

Mary, to attest her misery, seats herself on the ground, like Constance in "King John"; and the comment of one of her women hereupon is strikingly picturesque:

"Good Lord! how grim and ghastly looks her Grace,

With both her knees drawn upward to her chin.

There was an old-world tomb beside my father's,

And this was opened, and the dead were found

Sitting, and in this fashion; she looks a corpse."

The great merit of Mr. Tennyson's drama, however, is not in the quotableness of certain passages, but in the thoroughly elevated spirit of the whole. He desired to make us feel of what sound manly stuff the Englishmen of that Tudor reign of terror needed to be, and his verse is pervaded by the echo of their deep-toned refusal to abdicate their manhood. The temper of the poem, on this line, is so noble that the critic who has indulged in a few strictures as to matters of form feels as if he had been frivolous and niggardly. I nevertheless venture to add in conclusion that *Queen Mary* seems to me a work of rare ability rather than great inspiration; a powerful *tour de force* rather than a labour of love. But though it is not the best of a great poet's achievement, only a great poet could have written it.

II. HAROLD

The author of *Queen Mary* seems disposed to show us that that work was not an accident, but rather, as it may be said, an incident of his literary career. The incident has just been repeated, though *Harold* has come into the world more quietly than its predecessor.

It is singular how soon the public gets used to unfamiliar notions. By the time the reader has finished *Harold* he has almost contracted the habit of thinking of Mr. Tennyson as a writer chiefly known to fame by "dramas" without plots and dialogues without point. This impression it behooves him, of course, to shake off if he wishes to judge the book properly. He must compare the author of "Maud" and the earlier *Idyls* with the great poets, and not with the small. *Harold* would be a respectable production for a writer who had spent his career in producing the same sort of thing, but it is a somewhat graceless anomaly in the record of a poet whose verse has, in a large degree, become part of the civilisation of his day.

Queen Mary was not, on the whole, pronounced a success, and *Harold*, roughly speaking, is to *Queen Mary* what that work is to the author's earlier masterpieces. *Harold* is not in the least bad: it contains nothing ridiculous, unreasonable, or disagreeable; it is only decidedly weak, decidedly colourless, and tame. The author's inspiration is like a fire which is quietly and contentedly burning low. The analogy is perfectly complete. The hearth is clean swept and the chimney-side is garnished with its habitual furniture; but the room is getting colder and colder, and the occasional little flickers emitted by the mild embers are not sufficient to combat the testimony of the poetical thermometer. There is nothing necessarily harsh in this judgment. Few fires are always at a blaze, and the imagination, which is the most delicate machine in the world, cannot be expected to serve longer than a good gold repeater. We must take what it gives us, in every case, and be thankful. Mr. Tennyson is perfectly welcome to amuse himself with listening to the fainter tick of his honoured time-piece; it is going still, unquestionably; it has not stopped. Only we may without rudeness abstain from regulating our engagements by the indications of the instrument.

Harold seems at first to have little, in form, that is characteristic of the author—little of the thoroughly familiar Tennysonian quality. Nevertheless, there is every now and then a line which arrests the ear by the rhythm and cadence which have always formed the chief mystery in the art of imitating the Laureate.

Meeting in the early pages such a line as

"What, with this flaming horror overhead?"

we should suspect we were reading Tennyson if we did not know it; and our suspicion would he amply confirmed by half a dozen other lines:

"Taken the rifted pillars of the wood."

"My greyhounds fleeting like a beam of light."

"Suffer a stormless shipwreck in the pools."

"That scared the dying conscience of the king."

Harold is interesting as illustrating, in addition to *Queen Mary*, Mr. Tennyson's idea of what makes a drama. A succession of short scenes, detached from the biography of a historical character, is, apparently, to his sense sufficient; the constructive side of the work is thereby reduced to a primitive simplicity. It is even more difficult to imagine acting *Harold* than it was to imagine acting *Queen Mary*; and it is probable that in this case the experiment will not be tried. And yet the story, or rather the historical episode, upon which Mr. Tennyson has here laid his hand is eminently interesting.

Harold, the last of the "English," as people of a certain way of feeling are fond of calling him—the son of Godwin, masterful minister of Edward the Confessor, the wearer for a short and hurried hour of the English crown, and the opponent and victim of William of Normandy on the field of Hastings— is a figure which combines many of the elements of romance and of heroism. The author has very characteristically tried to accentuate the moral character of his hero by making him a sort of distant relation of the family of Galahad and Arthur and the other moralising gallants to whom his pages have introduced us. Mr. Tennyson's Harold is a warrior who talks about his "better self," and who alludes to

"Waltham, my foundation

For men who serve their neighbour, not themselves,"

—a touch which transports us instantly into the atmosphere of the Arthurian Idyls. But Harold's history may be very easily and properly associated with a moral problem, inasmuch as it was his unhappy fortune to have to solve, practically, a knotty point which might have been more comfortably left to the casuists. Shipwrecked during Edward's life upon the coast of Normandy, he is betrayed into the hands of Duke William, who already retains as hostage one of his brothers (the sons of Godwin were very numerous, and they all figure briefly, but with a certain attempt at individual characterisation, in the drama). To purchase his release and that of his brother, who passionately entreats him, he consents to swear by certain unseen symbols, which prove afterwards to be the bones of certain august Norman saints, that if William will suffer him to return to England, he will, on the Confessor's death, abstain from urging the claim of the latter's presumptive heir and do his utmost to help the Norman duke himself to the crown.

This scene is presented in the volume before us. Harold departs and regains England, and there, on the king's death, overborne by circumstances, but with much tribulation of mind, violates his oath, and himself takes possession of the throne. The interest of the drama is in a great measure the picture of his temptation and remorse, his sense of his treachery and of the inevitableness of his chastisement. With this other matters are mingled: Harold's conflict with his disloyal brother Tostig, Earl of Northumberland, who brings in the King of Norway to claim the crown, and who, with his Norwegian backers, is defeated by Harold in battle just before William comes down upon him. Then there is his love-affair with Edith, ward of the Confessor, whom the latter, piously refusing to hear of his violation of his oath, condemns him to put away, as penance for the very thought. There is also his marriage with Aldwyth, a designing person, widow of a Welsh king whom Harold has defeated, and who, having herself through her parentage, strong English interests, inveigles Harold into a union which may consolidate their forces.

Altogether, Harold is, for a hero, rather inclined to falter and succumb. It is to his conscience, however, that he finally succumbs; he loses heart and goes to meet William at Hastings with a depressing presentiment of defeat. Mr. Tennyson, however, as we gather from a prefatory sonnet, which is perhaps finer than anything in the drama itself, holds that much can be said for the "Norman-slandered hero," and declares that he has nothing to envy William if

"Each stands full face with all he did below."

Edith, Harold's repudiated lady-love, is, we suppose, the heroine of the story, inasmuch as she has the privilege of expiring upon the corpse of the hero. Harold's defeat is portrayed through a conversation between Edith and Stigand, the English and anti-papal Archbishop of Canterbury, who watches the fight at Senlac from a tent near the field, while the monks of Waltham, outside, intone a Latin invocation to the God of Battles to sweep away the Normans.

The drama closes with a scene on the field, after the fight, in which Edith and Aldwyth wander about, trying to identify Harold among the slain. On discovering him they indulge in a few natural recriminations, then Edith loses her head and expires by his side. William comes in, rubbing his hands over his work, and intimates to Aldwyth that she may now make herself agreeable to *him*. She replies, hypocritically, "My punishment is more than I can bear"; and with this, the most dramatic speech, perhaps in the volume, the play terminates. Edith, we should say, is a heroine of the didactic order. She has a bad conscience about Harold's conduct, and about her having continued on affectionate terms with him after his diplomatic marriage with Aldwyth. When she prays for Harold's success she adds that she hopes heaven will not refuse to listen to her because she loves "the husband of another"; and after he is defeated she reproaches herself with having injured his prospects—

"For there was more than sister in my kiss."

Though there are many persons in the poem it cannot be said that any of them attains a very vivid individuality. Indeed, their great number, the drama being of moderate length, hinders the unfolding of any one of them.

Mr. Tennyson, moreover, has not the dramatic touch; he rarely finds the phrase or the movement that illuminates a character, rarely makes the dialogue strike sparks. This is generally mild and colourless, and the passages that arrest us, relatively, owe their relief to juxtaposition rather than to any especial possession of the old Tennysonian energy. Now and then we come upon a few lines together in which we seem to catch an echo of the author's earlier magic, or sometimes simply of his earlier manner. When we do, we make the most of them and are grateful. Such, for instance, is the phrase of one of the characters describing his rescue from shipwreck. He dug his hands, he says, into

135

"My old fast friend the shore, and clinging thus

Felt the remorseless outdraught of the deep

Haul like a great strong fellow at my legs."

Such are the words in which Wulfnoth, Harold's young brother, detained in Normandy, laments his situation:

"Yea, and I

Shall see the dewy kiss of dawn no more

Make blush the maiden-white of our tall cliffs,

Nor mark the sea-bird rouse himself and hover

Above the windy ripple, and fill the sky

With free sea-laughter."

In two or three places the author makes, in a few words, a picture, an image, of considerable felicity. Harold wishes that he were like Edward the Confessor,

"As holy and as passionless as he!

That I might rest as calmly! Look at him—

The rosy face, and long, down-silvering beard,

The brows unwrinkled as a summer mere."

We may add that in the few speeches allotted to this monarch of virtuous complexion this portrait is agreeably sustained. "Holy, is he?" says the Archbishop, Stigand, of him to Harold—

"A conscience for his own soul, not his realm;

A twilight conscience lighted thro' a chink;

Thine by the sun."

And the same character hits upon a really vigorous image in describing, as he watches them, Harold's exploits on the battle-fields:

"Yea, yea, for how their lances snap and shiver,

Against the shifting blaze of Harold's axe!

War-woodman of old Woden, how he fells

The mortal copse of faces!"

We feel, after all, in Mr. Tennyson, even in the decidedly minor key in which this volume is pitched, that he has once known how to turn our English poetic phrase as skilfully as any one, and that he has not altogether forgotten the art.

CONTEMPORARY NOTES ON WHISTLER VS. RUSKIN

I. THE SUIT FOR LIBEL

THE London public is never left for many days without a *cause célèbre* of some kind. The latest novelty in this line has been the suit for damages brought against Mr. Ruskin by Mr. James Whistler, the American painter, and decided last week. Mr. Whistler is very well known in the London world, and his conspicuity, combined with the renown of the defendant and the nature of the case, made the affair the talk of the moment. All the newspapers have had leading articles upon it, and people have differed for a few hours more positively than it had come to be supposed that they could differ about anything save the character of the statesmanship of Lord Beaconsfield. The injury suffered by Mr. Whistler resides in a paragraph published more than a year ago in that strange monthly manifesto called *Fors Clavigera*, which Mr. Ruskin had for a long time addressed to a partly edified, partly irritated, and greatly amused public. Mr. Ruskin spoke at some length of the pictures at the Grosvenor Gallery, and, falling foul of Mr. Whistler, he alluded to him in these terms:

"For Mr. Whistler's own sake, no less than for the protection of the purchaser, Sir Coutts Lindsay ought not to have admitted works into the gallery in which the ill-educated conceit of the artist so nearly approached the aspect of wilful imposture. I have seen and heard much of cockney impudence before now, but never expected to hear a coxcomb ask 200 guineas for flinging a pot of paint in the public's face."

Mr. Whistler alleged that these words were libellous, and that, coming from a critic of Mr. Ruskin's eminence, they had done him, professionally, serious injury; and he asked for £1,000 damage. The case had a two days' hearing, and it was a singular and most regrettable exhibition. If it had taken place in some Western American town, it would have been called provincial and barbarous; it would have been cited as an incident of a low civilisation. Beneath the stately towers of Westminster it hardly wore a higher aspect.

A British jury of ordinary tax-payers was appealed to decide whether Mr. Whistler's pictures belonged to a high order of art, and what degree of "finish" was required to render a picture satisfactory. The painter's singular canvases were handed about in court, and the counsel for the defence, holding one of them up, called upon the jury to pronounce whether it was an "accurate representation" of Battersea Bridge. Witnesses were summoned on either side to testify to the value of Mr. Whistler's productions, and Mr. Ruskin had the honour of having his estimate of them substantiated by Mr. Frith. The weightiest testimony, the most intelligently, and apparently the most reluctantly delivered, was that of Mr. Burne Jones, who appeared to appreciate the ridiculous character of the process to which he had been summoned (by the defence) to contribute, and who spoke of Mr. Whistler's performance as only in a partial sense of the word pictures—as being beautiful in colour, and indicating an extraordinary power of representing the atmosphere, but as being also hardly more than beginnings, and fatally deficient in finish. For the rest the crudity and levity of the whole affair were decidedly painful, and few things, I think, have lately done more to vulgarise the public sense of the character of artistic production.

The jury gave Mr. Whistler nominal damages. The opinion of the newspapers seems to be that he has got at least all he deserved—that anything more would have been a blow at the liberty of criticism. I confess to thinking it hard to decide what Mr. Whistler ought properly to have done, while—putting aside the degree of one's appreciation of his works—I quite understand his resentment. Mr. Ruskin's language quite transgresses the decencies of criticism, and he has been laying about him for some years past with such promiscuous violence that it gratifies one's sense of justice to see him brought up as a disorderly character. On the other hand, he is a chartered libertine—he has possessed himself by prescription of the function of a general scold. His literary bad manners are recognised, and many of his contemporaries have suffered from them without complaining. It would very possibly, therefore, have been much wiser on Mr. Whistler's part to feign indifference.

Unfortunately, Mr. Whistler's productions are so very eccentric and imperfect (I speak here of his paintings only; his etchings are quite another affair, and altogether admirable) that his critic's denunciation could by no means fall to the ground of itself. I wonder that before a British jury they had any chance whatever; they must have been a terrible puzzle.

The verdict, of course, satisfies neither party; Mr. Ruskin is formally condemned, but the plaintiff is not compensated. Mr. Ruskin too, doubtless, is not gratified at finding that the fullest weight of his disapproval is thought to be represented by the sum of one farthing.

II. MR. WHISTLER'S REJOINDER

I may mention as a sequel to the brief account of the suit Whistler v. Ruskin, which I sent you a short time since, that the plaintiff has lately published a little pamphlet in which he delivers himself on the subject of art-criticism.

This little pamphlet, issued by Chatto & Windus, is an affair of seventeen very prettily-printed small pages; it is now in its sixth edition, it sells for a shilling, and is to be seen in most of the shop-windows. It is very characteristic of the painter, and highly entertaining; but I am not sure that it will have rendered appreciable service to the cause, which he has at heart. The cause that Mr. Whistler has at heart is the absolute suppression and extinction of the art-critic and his function. According to Mr. Whistler the art-critic is an impertinence, a nuisance, a monstrosity—and usually, into the bargain, an arrant fool.

Mr. Whistler writes in an off-hand, colloquial style, much besprinkled with French—a style which might be called familiar if one often encountered anything like it. He writes by no means as well as he paints; but his little diatribe against the critics is suggestive, apart from the force of anything that he specifically urges. The painter's irritated feeling is interesting, for it suggests the state of mind of many of his brothers of the brush in the presence of the bungling and incompetent disquisitions of certain members of the fraternity who sit in judgment upon their works.

"Let work be received in silence," says Mr. Whistler, "as it was in the days to which the penman still points as an era when art was at its apogee." He is very scornful of the "penman," and it is on the general ground of his being a penman that he deprecates the existence of his late adversary, Mr. Ruskin. He does not attempt to make out a case in detail against the great commentator of pictures; it is enough for Mr. Whistler that he is a "littérateur," and that a littérateur should concern himself with his own business. The author also falls foul of Mr. Tom Taylor, who does the reports of the exhibitions in the *Times*, and who had the misfortune, fifteen years ago, to express himself rather unintelligently about Velasquez.

"The Observatory at Greenwich under the direction of an apothecary," says Mr. Whistler, "the College of Physicians with Tennyson as president, and we know what madness is about! But a school of art with an accomplished littérateur at its head disturbs no one, and is actually what the world receives as rational, while Ruskin writes for pupils and Colvin holds forth at Cambridge! Still, quite alone stands Ruskin, whose writing is art and whose art is unworthy his writing. To him and his example do we owe the outrage of proffered assistance from the unscientific—the meddling of the immodest—the intrusion of the garrulous. Art, that for ages has hewn its own history in marble and written its own comments on canvas, shall it suddenly stand still and stammer and wait for wisdom from the passer-by?—for guidance from the hand that holds neither brush nor chisel? Out upon the shallow conceit! What greater sarcasm can Mr. Ruskin pass upon himself than that he preaches to young men what he cannot perform? Why, unsatisfied with his conscious power, should he choose to become the type of incompetency by talking for forty years of what he has never done?"

Mr. Whistler winds up by pronouncing Mr. Ruskin, of whose writings he has perused, I suspect, an infinitesimally small number of pages, "the Peter Parley of Painting." This is very far, as I say, from exhausting the question; but it is easy to understand the state of mind of a London artist (to go no further) who skims through the critiques in the local journals. There is no scurrility in saying that these are for the most part almost incredibly weak and unskilled; to turn from one of them to a critical *feuilleton* in one of the Parisian journals is like passing from a primitive to a very high civilisation. Even, however, if the reviews of pictures were very much better, the protest of the producer as against the critic would still have a considerable validity.

Few people will deny that the development of criticism in our day has become inordinate, disproportionate, and that much of what is written under that exalted name is very idle and superficial. Mr. Whistler's complaint belongs to the general question, and I am afraid it will never obtain a serious hearing, on special and exceptional grounds. The whole artistic fraternity is in the same boat—the painters, the architects, the poets, the novelists, the dramatists, the actors, the musicians, the singers. They have a standing, and in many ways a very just, quarrel with criticism; but perhaps many of them would admit that, on the whole, so long as they appeal to a public laden with many cares and a great variety of interests, it gratifies as much as it displeases them. Art is one of the necessities of life; but even the critics themselves would probably not assert that criticism is anything more than an agreeable luxury—something like printed talk. If it be said that they claim too much in calling it "agreeable" to the criticised, it may be added in their behalf that they probably mean agreeable in the long run.

A NOTE ON JOHN BURROUGHS

THIS is a very charming little book. We had noticed, on their appearance in various periodicals, some of the articles of which it is composed, and we find that, read continuously, they have given us even more pleasure. We have, indeed, enjoyed them more perhaps than we can show sufficient cause for. They are slender and light, but they have a real savour of their own.

Mr. Burroughs is known as an out-of-door observer—a devotee of birds and trees and fields and aspects of weather and humble wayside incidents. The minuteness of his observation, the keenness of his perception of all these things, give him a real originality which is confirmed by a style sometimes indeed idiomatic and unfinished to a fault, but capable of remarkable felicity and vividness. Mr. Burroughs is also, fortunately for his literary prosperity in these days, a decided "humourist"; he is essentially and genially an American, without at all posing as one, and his sketches have a delightful oddity, vivacity, and freshness.

The first half of his volume, and the least substantial, treats of certain rambles taken in the winter and spring in the country around Washington; the author is an apostle of pedestrianism, and these pages form a prolonged rhapsody upon the pleasures within the reach of any one who will take the trouble to stretch his legs. They are full of charming touches, and indicate a real genius for the observation of natural things. Mr. Burroughs is a sort of reduced, but also more humourous, more available, and more sociable Thoreau. He is especially intimate with the birds, and he gives his reader an acute sense of how sociable an affair, during six months of the year, this feathery lore may make a lonely walk. He is also intimate with the question of apples, and he treats of it in a succulent disquisition which imparts to the somewhat trivial theme a kind of lyrical dignity. He remarks, justly, that women are poor apple-eaters.

But the best pages in his book are those which commemorate a short visit to England and the rapture of his first impressions. This little sketch, in spite of its extreme slightness, really deserves to become classical. We have read far solider treatises which contained less of the essence of the matter; or at least, if it is not upon the subject itself that Mr. Burroughs throws particularly powerful light, it is the essence of the ideal traveller's spirit that he gives us, the freshness and intensity of impression, the genial bewilderment, the universal appreciativeness. All this is delightfully *naïf*, frank, and natural.

"All this had been told, and it pleased me so in the seeing that I must tell it again," the author says; and this is the constant spirit of his talk. He appears to have been "pleased" as no man was ever pleased before; so much so that his reflections upon his own country sometimes become unduly invidious. But if to be appreciative is the traveller's prime duty, Mr. Burroughs is a prince of travellers.

"Then to remember that it was a new sky and a new earth I was beholding, that it was England, the old mother at last, no longer a faith or a fable but an actual fact, there before my eyes and under my feet—why should I not exult? Go to! I will be indulged. These trees, those fields, that bird darting along the hedge-rows, those men and boys picking blackberries in October, those English flowers by the roadside (stop the carriage while I leap out and pluck them), the homely domestic look of things, those houses, those queer vehicles, those thick-coated horses, those big-footed, coarsely-clad, clear-skinned men and women; this massive, homely, compact architecture—let me have a good look, for this is my first hour in England, and I am drunk with the joy of seeing! This house-fly let me inspect it, and that swallow skimming along so familiarly."

One envies Mr. Burroughs his acute relish of the foreign spectacle even more than one enjoys his expression of it. He is not afraid to start and stare; his state of mind is exactly opposed to the high dignity of the *nil admirari*. When he goes into St. Paul's, "my companions rushed about," he says, "as if each one had a search-warrant in his pocket; but I was content to uncover my head and drop into a seat, and busy my mind with some simple object near at hand, while the sublimity that soared about me stole into my soul." He meets a little girl carrying a pail in a meadow near Stratford, stops her and talks with her, and finds an ineffable delight in "the sweet and novel twang of her words.

Her family had emigrated to America, failed to prosper, and come back; but I hardly recognise even the name of my own country in her innocent prattle; it seemed like a land of fable—all had a remote mythological air, and I pressed my enquiries as if I was hearing of this strange land for the first time."

Mr. Burroughs is unfailingly complimentary; he sees sermons in stones and good in everything; the somewhat dusky British world was never steeped in so intense a glow of rose-colour. Sometimes his optimism rather interferes with his accuracy—as when he detects "forests and lakes" in Hyde Park, and affirms that the English rural landscape does not, in comparison with the American, appear highly populated. This latter statement is apparently made apropos of that long stretch of suburban scenery, pure and simple, which extends from Liverpool to London. It does not strike us as felicitous, either, to say that women are more kindly treated in England than in the United States, and especially that they are less "leered at." "Leering" at women is happily less common all the world over than it is sometimes made to appear for picturesque purposes in the magazines; but we should say that if there is a country where the art has not reached a high stage of development, it is our own.

It must be added that although Mr. Burroughs is shrewd as well as *naïf,* the latter quality sometimes distances the former. He runs over for a week to France. "At Dieppe I first saw the wooden shoe, and heard its dry, senseless clatter upon the pavement. How suggestive of the cramped and inflexible conditions with which human nature has borne so long in these lands!" But in Paris also he is appreciative—singularly so for so complete an outsider as he confesses himself to be—and throughout he is very well worth reading. We heartily commend his little volume for its honesty, its individuality, and, in places, its really blooming freshness.

MR. KIPLING'S EARLY STORIES

IT would be difficult to answer the general question whether the books of the world grow, as they multiply, as much better as one might suppose they ought, with such a lesson of wasteful experiment spread perpetually behind them. There is no doubt, however, that in one direction we profit largely by this education: whether or not we have become wiser to fashion, we have certainly become keener to enjoy. We have acquired the sense of a particular quality which is precious beyond all others—so precious as to make us wonder where, at such a rate, our posterity will look for it, and how they will pay for it. After tasting many essences we find freshness the sweetest of all. We yearn for it, we watch for it and lie in wait for it, and when we catch it on the wing (it flits by so fast) we celebrate our capture with extravagance. We feel that after so much has come and gone it is more and more of a feat and a *tour de force* to be fresh. The tormenting part of the phenomenon is that, in any particular key, it can happen but once—by a sad failure of the law that inculcates the repetition of goodness. It is terribly a matter of accident; emulation and imitation have a fatal effect upon it. It is easy to see, therefore, what importance the epicure may attach to the brief moment of its bloom. While that lasts we all are epicures.

This helps to explain, I think, the unmistakeable intensity of the general relish for Mr. Rudyard Kipling. His bloom lasts, from month to month, almost surprisingly—by which I mean that he has not worn out even by active exercise the particular property that made us all, more than a year ago, so precipitately drop everything else to attend to him. He has many others which he will doubtless always keep; but a part of the potency attaching to his freshness, what makes it as exciting as a drawing of lots, is our instinctive conviction that he cannot, in the nature of things, keep that; so that our enjoyment of him, so long as the miracle is still wrought, has both the charm of confidence and the charm of suspense. And then there is the further charm, with Mr. Kipling, that this same freshness is such a very strange affair of its kind—so mixed and various and cynical, and, in certain lights, so contradictory of itself. The extreme recentness of his inspiration is as enviable as the tale is startling that his productions tell of his being at home, domesticated and initiated, in this wicked and weary world. At times he strikes us as shockingly precocious, at others as serenely wise. On the whole, he presents himself as a strangely clever youth who has stolen the formidable mask of maturity and rushes about, making people jump with the deep sounds, and sportive exaggerations of tone, that issue from its painted lips. He has this mark of a real vocation, that different spectators may like him—must like him, I should almost say—for different things; and this refinement of attraction, that to those who reflect even upon their pleasures he has as much to say as to those who never reflect upon anything. Indeed there is a certain amount of room for surprise in the fact that, being so much the sort of figure that the hardened critic likes to meet, he should also be the sort of figure that inspires the multitude with confidence—for a complicated air is, in general, the last thing that does this.

By the critic who likes to meet such a bristling adventurer as Mr. Kipling I mean, of course, the critic for whom the happy accident of character, whatever form it may take, is more of a bribe to interest than the promise of some character cherished in theory—the appearance of justifying some foregone conclusion as to what a writer or a book "ought," in the Ruskinian sense, to be; the critic, in a word, who has, *à priori*, no rule for a literary production but that it shall have genuine life. Such a critic (he gets much more out of his opportunities, I think, than the other sort) likes a writer exactly in proportion as he is a challenge, an appeal to interpretation, intelligence, ingenuity, to what is elastic in the critical mind—in proportion indeed as he may be a negation of things familiar and taken for granted. He feels in this case how much more play and sensation there is for himself.

Mr. Kipling, then, has the character that furnishes plenty of play and of vicarious experience—that makes any perceptive reader foresee a rare luxury. He has the great merit of being a compact and convenient illustration of the surest source of interest in any painter of life—that of having an identity as marked as a window-frame. He is one of the illustrations, taken near at hand, that help to clear up the vexed question in the novel or the tale, of kinds, camps, schools, distinctions, the right way and the wrong way; so very positively does he contribute to the showing that there are just as many kinds, as many ways, as many forms and degrees of the "right," as there are personal points in view. It is the blessing of the art he practises that it is made up of experience conditioned, infinitely, in this personal way—the sum of the feeling of life as reproduced by innumerable natures; natures that feel through all their differences, testify through their diversities. These differences, which make the identity, are of the individual; they form the channel by which life flows through him, and how much he is able to give us of life—in other words, how much he appeals to us—depends on whether they form it solidly.

This hardness of the conduit, cemented with a rare assurance, is perhaps the most striking idiosyncrasy of Mr. Kipling; and what makes it more remarkable is that incident of his extreme youth which, if we talk about him at all, we cannot affect to ignore. I cannot pretend to give a biography or a chronology of the author of "Soldiers Three," but I cannot overlook the general, the importunate fact that, confidently as he has caught the trick and habit of this sophisticated world, he has not been long of it. His extreme youth is indeed what I may call his window-bar—the support on which he somewhat rowdily leans while he looks down at the human scene with his pipe in his teeth; just as his other conditions (to mention only some of them), are his prodigious facility, which is only less remarkable than his stiff selection; his unabashed temperament, his flexible talent, his smoking-room manner, his familiar friendship with India—established so rapidly, and so completely under his control; his delight in battle, his "cheek" about women—and indeed about men and about everything; his determination not to be duped, his "imperial" fibre, his love of the inside view, the private soldier and the primitive man. I must add further to this list of attractions the remarkable way in which he makes us aware that he has been put up to the whole thing directly by life (miraculously, in his teens), and not by the communications of others. These elements, and many more, constitute a singularly robust little literary character (our use of the diminutive is altogether a note of endearment and enjoyment) which, if it has the rattle of high spirits and is in no degree apologetic or shrinking, yet offers a very liberal pledge in the way of good faith and immediate performance. Mr. Kipling's performance comes off before the more circumspect have time to decide whether they like him or not, and if you have seen it once you will be sure to return to the show. He makes us prick up our ears to the good news that in the smoking-room too there may be artists; and indeed to an intimation still more refined—that the latest development of the modern also may be, most successfully, for the canny artist to put his victim off his guard by imitating the amateur (superficially, of course) to the life.

These, then, are some of the reasons why Mr. Kipling may be dear to the analyst as well as, M. Renan says, to the simple. The simple may like him because he is wonderful about India, and India has not been "done"; while there is plenty left for the morbid reader in the surprises of his skill and the *fioriture* of his form, which are so oddly independent of any distinctively literary note in him, any bookish association. It is as one of the morbid that the writer of these remarks (which doubtless only too shamefully betray his character) exposes himself as most consentingly under the spell. The freshness arising from a subject that—by a good fortune I do not mean to underestimate—has never been "done," is after all less of an affair to build upon than the freshness residing in the temper of the artist. Happy indeed is Mr. Kipling, who can command so much of both kinds. It is still as one of the morbid, no doubt—that is, as one of those who are capable of sitting up all night for a new impression of talent, of scouring the trodden field for one little spot of green—that I find our young author quite most curious in his air, and not only in his air, but in his evidently very real sense, of knowing his way about life. Curious in the highest degree and well worth attention is such an idiosyncrasy as this in a young Anglo-Saxon. We meet it with familiar frequency in the budding talents of France, and it startles and haunts us for an hour. After an hour, however, the mystery is apt to fade, for we find that the wondrous initiation is not in the least general, is only exceedingly special, and is, even with this limitation, very often rather conventional. In a word, it is with the ladies that the young Frenchman takes his ease, and more particularly with the ladies selected expressly to make this attitude convincing. When they have let him off, the dimnesses too often encompass him. But for Mr. Kipling there are no dimnesses anywhere, and if the ladies are indeed violently distinct they are not only strong notes in a universal loudness. This loudness fills the ears of Mr. Kipling's admirers (it lacks sweetness, no doubt, for those who are not of the number), and there is really only one strain that is absent from it—the voice, as it were, of the civilised man; in whom I of course also include the civilised woman. But this is an element that for the present one does not miss—every other note is so articulate and direct.

It is a part of the satisfaction the author gives us that he can make us speculate as to whether he will be able to complete his picture altogether (this is as far as we presume to go in meddling with the question of his future) without bringing in the complicated soul. On the day he does so, if he handles it with anything like the cleverness he has already shown, the expectation of his friends will take a great bound. Meanwhile, at any rate, we have Mulvaney, and Mulvaney is after all tolerably complicated. He is only a six-foot saturated Irish private, but he is a considerable pledge of more to come. Hasn't he, for that matter, the tongue of a hoarse siren, and hasn't he also mysteries and infinitudes almost Carlylese? Since I am speaking of him I may as well say that, as an evocation, he has probably led captive those of Mr. Kipling's readers who have most given up resistance. He is a piece of portraiture of the largest, vividest kind, growing and growing on the painter's hands without ever outgrowing them. I can't help regarding him, in a certain sense, as Mr. Kipling's tutelary deity—a landmark in the direction in which it is open to him to look furthest. If the author will only go as far in this direction as Mulvaney is capable of taking him (and the inimitable Irishman is like Voltaire's Habakkuk, *capable de tout*) he may still discover a treasure and find a reward for the services he has rendered the winner of Dinah Shadd. I hasten to add that the truly appreciative reader should surely have no quarrel with the primitive element in Mr. Kipling's subject-matter, or with what, for want of a better name, I may call his love of low life. What is that but essentially a part of his freshness? And for what part of his freshness are we exactly more thankful than for just this smart jostle that he gives the old stupid superstition that the amiability of a story-teller is the amiability of the people he represents—that their vulgarity, or depravity, or gentility, or fatuity are tantamount to the same qualities in the painter itself? A blow from which, apparently, it will not easily recover is dealt this infantine philosophy by Mr. Howells when, with the most distinguished dexterity and all the detachment of a master, he handles some of the clumsiest, crudest, most human things in life—answering surely thereby the play-goers in the sixpenny gallery who howl at the representative of the villain when he comes before the curtain.

Nothing is more refreshing than this active, disinterested sense of the real; it is doubtless the quality for the want of more of which our English and American fiction has turned so wofully stale. We are ridden by the old conventionalities of type and small proprieties of observance—by the foolish baby-formula (to put it sketchily) of the picture and the subject. Mr. Kipling has all the air of being disposed to lift the whole business off the nursery carpet, and of being perhaps even more able than he is disposed. One must hasten of course to parenthesise that there is not, intrinsically, a bit more luminosity in treating of low life and of primitive man than of those whom civilisation has kneaded to a finer paste: the only luminosity in either case is in the intelligence with which the thing is done. But it so happens that, among ourselves, the frank, capable outlook, when turned upon the vulgar majority, the coarse, receding edges of the social perspective, borrows a charm from being new; such a charm as, for instance, repetition has already despoiled it of among the French—the hapless French who pay the penalty as well as enjoy the glow of living intellectually so much faster than we. It is the most inexorable part of our fate that we grow tired of everything, and of course in due time we may grow tired even of what explorers shall come back to tell us about the great grimy condition, or, with unprecedented items and details, about the gray middle state which darkens into it. But the explorers, bless them! may have a long day before that; it is early to trouble about reactions, so that we must give them the benefit of every presumption. We are thankful for any boldness and any sharp curiosity, and that is why we are thankful for Mr. Kipling's general spirit and for most of his excursions.

Many of these, certainly, are into a region not to be designated as superficially dim, though indeed the author always reminds us that India is above all the land of mystery. A large part of his high spirits, and of ours, comes doubtless from the amusement of such vivid, heterogeneous material, from the irresistible magic of scorching suns, subject empires, uncanny religions, uneasy garrisons and smothered-up women—from heat and colour and danger and dust. India is a portentous image, and we are duly awed by the familiarities it undergoes at Mr. Kipling's hand and by the fine impunity, the sort of fortune that favours the brave, of *his* want of awe. An abject humility is not his strong point, but he gives us something instead of it—vividness and drollery, the vision and the thrill of many things, the misery and strangeness of most, the personal sense of a hundred queer contacts and risks. And then in the absence of respect he has plenty of knowledge, and if knowledge should fail him he would have plenty of invention. Moreover, if invention should ever fail him, he would still have the lyric string and the patriotic chord, on which he plays admirably; so that it may be said he is a man of resources. What he gives us, above all, is the feeling of the English manner and the English blood in conditions they have made at once so much and so little their own; with manifestations grotesque enough in some of his satiric sketches and deeply impressive in some of his anecdotes of individual responsibility.

His Indian impressions divide themselves into three groups, one of which, I think, very much outshines the others. First to be mentioned are the tales of native life, curious glimpses of custom and superstition, dusky matters not beholden of the many, for which the author has a remarkable *flair*. Then comes the social, the Anglo-Indian episode, the study of administrative and military types, and of the wonderful rattling, riding ladies who, at Simla and more desperate stations, look out for husbands and lovers; often, it would seem, and husbands and lovers of others. The most brilliant group is devoted wholly to the common soldier, and of this series it appears to me that too much good is hardly to be said. Here Mr. Kipling, with all his off-handedness, is a master; for we are held not so much by the greater or less oddity of the particular yarn—sometimes it is scarcely a yarn at all, but something much less artificial—as by the robust attitude of the narrator, who never arranges or glosses or falsifies, but makes straight for the common and the characteristic. I have mentioned the great esteem in which I hold Mulvaney—surely a charming man and one qualified to adorn a higher sphere. Mulvaney is a creation to be proud of, and his two comrades stand as firm on their legs. In spite of Mulvaney's social possibilities, they are all three finished brutes; but it is precisely in the finish that we delight. Whatever Mr. Kipling may relate about them forever will encounter readers equally fascinated and unable fully to justify their faith.

Are not those literary pleasures after all the most intense which are the most perverse and whimsical, and even indefensible? There is a logic in them somewhere, but it often lies below the plummet of criticism. The spell may be weak in a writer who has every reasonable and regular claim, and it may be irresistible in one who presents himself with a style corresponding to a bad hat. A good hat is better than a bad one, but a conjuror may wear either. Many a reader will never be able to say what secret human force lays its hand upon him when Private Ortheris, having sworn "quietly into the blue sky," goes mad with homesickness by the yellow river and raves for the basest sights and sounds of London. I can scarcely tell why I think "The Courting of Dinah Shadd" a masterpiece (though, indeed, I can make a shrewd guess at one of the reasons), nor would it be worth while perhaps to attempt to defend the same pretension in regard to "On Greenhow Hill"—much less to trouble the tolerant reader of these remarks with a statement of how many more performances in the nature of "The End of the Passage" (quite admitting even that they might not represent Mr. Kipling at his best) I am conscious of a latent relish for. One might as well admit while one is about it that one has wept profusely over "The Drums of the Fore and Aft," the history of the "Dutch courage" of two dreadful dirty little boys, who, in the face of Afghans scarcely more dreadful, saved the reputation of their regiment and perished, the least mawkishly in the world, in a squalor of battle incomparably expressed. People who know how peaceful they are themselves and have no bloodshed to reproach themselves with needn't scruple to mention the glamour that Mr. Kipling's intense militarism has for them, and how astonishing and contagious they find it, in spite of the unromantic complexion of it—the way it bristles with all sorts of ugliness and technicalities. Perhaps that is why I go all the way even with "The Gadsbys"—the Gadsbys were so connected (uncomfortably, it is true) with the army. There is fearful fighting—or a fearful danger of it—in "The Man Who Would be King"; is that the reason we are deeply affected by this extraordinary tale? It is one of them, doubtless, for Mr. Kipling has many reasons, after all, on his side, though they don't equally call aloud to be uttered.

One more of them, at any rate, I must add to these unsystematised remarks—it is the one I spoke of a shrewd guess at in alluding to "The

Courting of Dinah Shadd." The talent that produces such a tale is a talent eminently in harmony with the short story, and the short story is, on our side of the Channel and of the Atlantic, a mine which will take a great deal of working. Admirable is the clearness with which Mr. Kipling perceives this—perceives what innumerable chances it gives, chances of touching life in a thousand different places, taking it up in innumerable pieces, each a specimen and an illustration. In a word, he appreciates the episode, and there are signs to show that this shrewdness will, in general, have long innings. It will find the detachable, compressible "case" an admirable, flexible form; the cultivation of which may well add to the mistrust already entertained by Mr. Kipling, if his manner does not betray him, for what is clumsy and tasteless in the time-honoured practice of the "plot." It will fortify him in the conviction that the vivid picture has a greater communicative value than the Chinese puzzle. There is little enough "plot" in such a perfect little piece of hard representation as "The End of the Passage," to cite again only the most salient of twenty examples.

But I am speaking of our author's future, which is the luxury that I meant to forbid myself—precisely because the subject is so tempting. There is nothing in the world (for the prophet) so charming as to prophesy, and as there is nothing so inconclusive the tendency should be repressed in proportion as the opportunity is good. There is a certain want of courtesy to a peculiarly contemporaneous present even in speculating, with a dozen differential precautions, on the question of what will become in the later hours of the day of a talent that has got up so early. Mr. Kipling's actual performance is like a tremendous walk before breakfast, making one welcome the idea of the meal, but consider with some alarm the hours still to be traversed. Yet if his breakfast is all to come, the indications are that he will be more active than ever after he has had it. Among these indications are the unflagging character of his pace and the excellent form, as they say in athletic circles, in which he gets over the ground. We don't detect him stumbling; on the contrary, he steps out quite as briskly as at first, and still more firmly. There is something zealous and craftsman-like in him which shows that he feels both joy and responsibility. A whimsical, wanton reader, haunted by a recollection of all the good things he has seen spoiled; by a sense of the miserable, or, at any rate, the inferior, in so many continuations and endings, is almost capable of perverting poetic justice to the idea that it would be even positively well for so surprising a producer to remain simply the fortunate, suggestive, unconfirmed and unqualified representative of what he has actually done. We can always refer to that.

WASHINGTON SQUARE

I

DURING a portion of the first half of the present century, and more particularly during the latter part of it, there flourished and practised in the city of New York a physician who enjoyed perhaps an exceptional share of the consideration which, in the United States, has always been bestowed upon distinguished members of the medical profession. This profession in America has constantly been held in honour, and more successfully than elsewhere has put forward a claim to the epithet of "liberal." In a country in which, to play a social part, you must either earn your income or make believe that you earn it, the healing art has appeared in a high degree to combine two recognised sources of credit. It belongs to the realm of the practical, which in the United States is a great recommendation; and it is touched by the light of science—a merit appreciated in a community in which the love of knowledge has not always been accompanied by leisure and opportunity. It was an element in Dr. Sloper's reputation that his learning and his skill were very evenly balanced; he was what you might call a scholarly doctor, and yet there was nothing abstract in his remedies—he always ordered you to take something. Though he was felt to be extremely thorough, he was not uncomfortably theoretic, and if he sometimes explained matters rather more minutely than might seem of use to the patient, he never went so far (like some practitioners one has heard of) as to trust to the explanation alone, but always left behind him an inscrutable prescription. There were some doctors that left the prescription without offering any explanation at all; and he did not belong to that class either, which was, after all, the most vulgar. It will be seen that I am describing a clever man; and this is really the reason why Dr. Sloper had become a local celebrity. At the time at which we are chiefly concerned with him, he was some fifty years of age, and his popularity was at its height. He was very witty, and he passed in the best society of New York for a man of the world—which, indeed, he was, in a very sufficient degree. I hasten to add, to anticipate possible misconception, that he was not the least of a charlatan. He was a thoroughly honest man—honest in a degree of which he had perhaps lacked the opportunity to give the complete measure;

and, putting aside the great good-nature of the circle in which he practised, which was rather fond of boasting that it possessed the "brightest" doctor in the country, he daily justified his claim to the talents attributed to him by the popular voice. He was an observer, even a philosopher, and to be bright was so natural to him, and (as the popular voice said) came so easily, that he never aimed at mere effect, and had none of the little tricks and pretensions of second-rate reputations. It must be confessed that fortune had favoured him, and that he had found the path to prosperity very soft to his tread. He had married at the age of twenty-seven, for love, a very charming girl, Miss Catherine Harrington, of New York, who, in addition to her charms, had brought him a solid dowry. Mrs. Sloper was amiable, graceful, accomplished, elegant, and in 1820 she had been one of the pretty girls of the small but promising capital which clustered about the Battery and overlooked the Bay, and of which the uppermost boundary was indicated by the grassy waysides of Canal Street. Even at the age of twenty-seven Austin Sloper had made his mark sufficiently to mitigate the anomaly of his having been chosen among a dozen suitors by a young woman of high fashion, who had ten thousand dollars of income and the most charming eyes in the island of Manhattan. These eyes, and some of their accompaniments, were for about five years a source of extreme satisfaction to the young physician, who was both a devoted and a very happy husband. The fact of his having married a rich woman made no difference in the line he had traced for himself, and he cultivated his profession with as definite a purpose as if he still had no other resources than his fraction of the modest patrimony which on his father's death he had shared with his brothers and sisters. This purpose had not been preponderantly to make money—it had been rather to learn something and to do something. To learn something interesting, and to do something useful—this was, roughly speaking, the programme he had sketched, and of which the accident of his wife having an income appeared to him in no degree to modify the validity. He was fond of his practice, and of exercising a skill of which he was agreeably conscious, and it was so patent a truth that if he were not a doctor there was nothing else he could be, that a doctor he persisted in being, in the best possible conditions. Of course his easy domestic situation saved him a good deal of drudgery, and his wife's affiliation to the "best people" brought him a good many of those patients whose symptoms are, if not more interesting in themselves than those of the lower orders, at least more consistently displayed. He desired experience, and in the course of twenty years he got a great deal. It must be added that it came to him in some forms which, whatever might have been their intrinsic value, made it the reverse of welcome. His first child, a little boy of extraordinary promise, as the Doctor, who was not addicted to easy enthusiasms, firmly believed, died at three years of age, in spite of everything that the mother's tenderness and the father's science could invent to save him. Two years later Mrs. Sloper gave birth to a second infant—an infant of a sex which rendered the poor child, to the Doctor's sense, an inadequate substitute for his lamented first-born, of whom he had promised himself to make an admirable man. The little girl was a disappointment; but this was not the worst. A week after her birth the young mother, who, as the phrase is, had been doing well, suddenly betrayed alarming symptoms, and before another week had elapsed Austin Sloper was a widower.

For a man whose trade was to keep people alive, he had certainly done poorly in his own family; and a bright doctor who within three years loses his wife and his little boy should perhaps be prepared to see either his skill or his affection impugned. Our friend, however, escaped criticism: that is, he escaped all criticism but his own, which was much the most competent and most formidable. He walked under the weight of this very private censure for the rest of his days, and bore for ever the scars of a castigation to which the strongest hand he knew had treated him on the night that followed his wife's death. The world, which, as I have said, appreciated him, pitied him too much to be ironical; his misfortune made him more interesting, and even helped him to be the fashion. It was observed that even medical families cannot escape the more insidious forms of disease, and that, after all, Dr. Sloper had lost other patients beside the two I have mentioned; which constituted an honourable precedent. His little girl remained to him, and though she was not what he had desired, he proposed to himself to make the best of her. He had on hand a stock of unexpended authority, by which the child, in its early years, profited largely. She had been named, as a matter of course, after her poor mother, and even in her most diminutive babyhood the Doctor never called her anything but Catherine. She grew up a very robust and healthy child, and her father, as he looked at her, often said to himself that, such as she was, he at least need have no fear of losing her. I say "such as she was," because, to tell the truth—But this is a truth of which I will defer the telling.

II

WHEN the child was about ten years old, he invited his sister, Mrs. Penniman, to come and stay with him. The Miss Slopers had been but two in number, and both of them had married early in life. The younger, Mrs. Almond by name, was the wife of a prosperous merchant, and the mother of a blooming family. She bloomed herself, indeed, and was a comely, comfortable, reasonable woman, and a favourite with her clever brother, who, in the matter of women, even when they were nearly related to him, was a man of distinct preferences. He preferred Mrs. Almond to his sister Lavinia, who had married a poor clergyman, of a sickly constitution and a flowery style of eloquence, and then, at the age of thirty-three, had been left a widow, without children, without fortune—with nothing but the memory of Mr. Penniman's flowers of speech, a certain vague aroma of which hovered about her own conversation. Nevertheless he had offered her a home under his own roof, which Lavinia accepted with the alacrity of a woman who had spent the ten years of her married life in the town of Poughkeepsie. The Doctor had not proposed to Mrs. Penniman to come and live with him indefinitely; he had suggested that she should make an asylum of his house while she looked about for unfurnished lodgings. It is uncertain whether Mrs. Penniman ever instituted a search for unfurnished lodgings, but it is beyond dispute that she never found them. She settled herself with her brother and never went away, and when Catherine was twenty years old her Aunt Lavinia was still one of the most striking features of her immediate *entourage*. Mrs. Penniman's own account of the matter was that she had remained to take charge of her niece's education. She had given this account, at least, to every one but the Doctor, who never asked for explanations which he could entertain himself any day with inventing. Mrs. Penniman, moreover, though she had a good deal of a certain sort of artificial assurance, shrank, for indefinable reasons, from presenting herself to her brother as a fountain of instruction. She had not a high sense of humour, but she had enough to prevent her from making this mistake; and her brother, on his side, had enough to excuse her, in her situation, for laying him under contribution during a considerable part of a lifetime. He therefore assented tacitly to the proposition which Mrs. Penniman had tacitly laid down, that it was of importance that the poor motherless girl should have a brilliant woman near her. His assent could only be tacit, for he had never been dazzled by his sister's intellectual lustre. Save when he fell in love with Catherine Harrington, he had never been dazzled, indeed, by any feminine characteristics whatever; and though he was to a certain extent what is called a ladies' doctor, his private opinion of the more complicated sex was not exalted. He regarded its complications as more curious than edifying, and he had an idea of the beauty of *reason*, which was, on the whole, meagrely gratified by what he observed in his female patients. His wife had been a reasonable woman, but she was a bright exception; among several things that he was sure of, this was perhaps the principal. Such a conviction, of course, did little either to mitigate or to abbreviate his widowhood; and it set a limit to his recognition, at the best, of Catherine's possibilities and of Mrs. Penniman's ministrations. He, nevertheless, at the end of six months, accepted his sister's permanent presence as an accomplished fact, and as Catherine grew older perceived that there were in effect good reasons why she should have a companion of her own imperfect sex. He was extremely polite to Lavinia, scrupulously, formally polite; and she had never seen him in anger but once in her life, when he lost his temper in a theological discussion with her late husband. With her he never discussed theology, nor, indeed, discussed anything; he contented himself with making known, very distinctly, in the form of a lucid ultimatum, his wishes with regard to Catherine.

Once, when the girl was about twelve years old, he had said to her:

"Try and make a clever woman of her, Lavinia; I should like her to be a clever woman."

Mrs. Penniman, at this, looked thoughtful a moment. "My dear Austin," she then inquired, "do you think it is better to be clever than to be good?"

"Good for what?" asked the Doctor. "You are good for nothing unless you are clever."

From this assertion Mrs. Penniman saw no reason to dissent; she possibly reflected that her own great use in the world was owing to her aptitude for many things.

"Of course I wish Catherine to be good," the Doctor said next day; "but she won't be any the less virtuous for not being a fool. I am not afraid of her being wicked; she will never have the salt of malice in her character. She is as good as good bread, as the French say; but six years hence I don't want to have to compare her to good bread and butter."

"Are you afraid she will turn insipid? My dear brother, it is I who supply the butter; so you needn't fear!" said Mrs. Penniman, who had taken in hand the child's accomplishments, overlooking her at the piano, where Catherine displayed a certain talent, and going with her to the dancing-class, where it must be confessed that she made but a modest figure.

Mrs. Penniman was a tall, thin, fair, rather faded woman, with a perfectly amiable disposition, a high standard of gentility, a taste for light literature, and a certain foolish indirectness and obliquity of character. She was romantic, she was sentimental, she had a passion for little secrets and mysteries—a very innocent passion, for her secrets had hitherto always been as unpractical as addled eggs. She was not absolutely veracious; but this defect was of no great consequence, for she had never had anything to conceal. She would have liked to have a lover, and to correspond with him under an assumed name in letters left at a shop; I am bound to say that her imagination never carried the intimacy farther than this. Mrs. Penniman had never had a lover, but her brother, who was very shrewd, understood her turn of mind. "When Catherine is about seventeen," he said to himself, "Lavinia will try and persuade her that some young man with a moustache is in love with her. It will be quite untrue; no young man, with a moustache or without, will ever be in love with Catherine. But Lavinia will take it up, and talk to her about it; perhaps, even, if her taste for clandestine operations doesn't prevail with her, she will talk to me about it. Catherine won't see it, and won't believe it, fortunately for her peace of mind; poor Catherine isn't romantic."

165

She was a healthy well-grown child, without a trace of her mother's beauty. She was not ugly; she had simply a plain, dull, gentle countenance. The most that had ever been said for her was that she had a "nice" face, and, though she was an heiress, no one had ever thought of regarding her as a belle. Her father's opinion of her moral purity was abundantly justified; she was excellently, imperturbably good; affectionate, docile, obedient, and much addicted to speaking the truth. In her younger years she was a good deal of a romp, and, though it is an awkward confession to make about one's heroine, I must add that she was something of a glutton. She never, that I know of, stole raisins out of the pantry; but she devoted her pocket-money to the purchase of cream-cakes. As regards this, however, a critical attitude would be inconsistent with a candid reference to the early annals of any biographer. Catherine was decidedly not clever; she was not quick with her book, nor, indeed, with anything else. She was not abnormally deficient, and she mustered learning enough to acquit herself respectably in conversation with her contemporaries, among whom it must be avowed, however, that she occupied a secondary place. It is well known that in New York it is possible for a young girl to occupy a primary one. Catherine, who was extremely modest, had no desire to shine, and on most social occasions, as they are called, you would have found her lurking in the background. She was extremely fond of her father, and very much afraid of him; she thought him the cleverest and handsomest and most celebrated of men. The poor girl found her account so completely in the exercise of her affections that the little tremor of fear that mixed itself with her filial passion gave the thing an extra relish rather than blunted its edge. Her deepest desire was to please him, and her conception of happiness was to know that she had succeeded in pleasing him. She had never succeeded beyond a certain point. Though, on the whole, he was very kind to her, she was perfectly aware of this, and to go beyond the point in question seemed to her really something to live for. What she could not know, of course, was that she disappointed him, though on three or four occasions the Doctor had been almost frank about it. She grew up peacefully and prosperously, but at the age of eighteen Mrs. Penniman had not made a clever woman of her. Dr. Sloper would have liked to be proud of his daughter; but there was nothing to be proud of in poor

Catherine. There was nothing, of course, to be ashamed of; but this was not enough for the Doctor, who was a proud man and would have enjoyed being able to think of his daughter as an unusual girl. There would have been a fitness in her being pretty and graceful, intelligent and distinguished; for her mother had been the most charming woman of her little day, and as regards her father, of course he knew his own value. He had moments of irritation at having produced a commonplace child, and he even went so far at times as to take a certain satisfaction in the thought that his wife had not lived to find her out. He was naturally slow in making this discovery himself, and it was not till Catherine had become a young lady grown that he regarded the matter as settled. He gave her the benefit of a great many doubts; he was in no haste to conclude. Mrs. Penniman frequently assured him that his daughter had a delightful nature; but he knew how to interpret this assurance. It meant, to his sense, that Catherine was not wise enough to discover that her aunt was a goose—a limitation of mind that could not fail to be agreeable to Mrs. Penniman. Both she and her brother, however, exaggerated the young girl's limitations; for Catherine, though she was very fond of her aunt, and conscious of the gratitude she owed her, regarded her without a particle of that gentle dread which gave its stamp to her admiration of her father. To her mind there was nothing of the infinite about Mrs. Penniman; Catherine saw her all at once, as it were, and was not dazzled by the apparition; whereas her father's great faculties seemed, as they stretched away, to lose themselves in a sort of luminous vagueness, which indicated, not that they stopped, but that Catherine's own mind ceased to follow them.

It must not be supposed that Dr. Sloper visited his disappointment upon the poor girl, or ever let her suspect that she had played him a trick. On the contrary, for fear of being unjust to her, he did his duty with exemplary zeal, and recognised that she was a faithful and affectionate child. Besides, he was a philosopher; he smoked a good many cigars over his disappointment, and in the fulness of time he got used to it. He satisfied himself that he had expected nothing, though, indeed, with a certain oddity of reasoning. "I expect nothing," he said to himself, "so that if she gives me a surprise, it will be all clear again. If she doesn't, it will be no loss." This was about the time Catherine had reached her eighteenth year, so that it will be seen her father had not been precipitate. At this time she seemed not only incapable of giving surprises; it was almost a question whether she could have received one—she was so quiet and irresponsive. People who expressed themselves roughly called her stolid. But she was irresponsive because she was shy, uncomfortably, painfully shy. This was not always understood, and she sometimes produced an impression of insensibility. In reality she was the softest creature in the world.

III

As a child she had promised to be tall, but when she was sixteen she ceased to grow, and her stature, like most other points in her composition, was not unusual. She was strong, however, and properly made, and, fortunately, her health was excellent. It has been noted that the Doctor was a philosopher, but I would not have answered for his philosophy if the poor girl had proved a sickly and suffering person. Her appearance of health constituted her principal claim to beauty, and her clear, fresh complexion, in which white and red were very equally distributed, was, indeed, an excellent thing to see. Her eye was small and quiet, her features were rather thick, her tresses brown and smooth. A dull, plain girl she was called by rigorous critics—a quiet, ladylike girl by those of the more imaginative sort; but by neither class was she very elaborately discussed. When it had been duly impressed upon her that she was a young lady—it was a good while before she could believe it—she suddenly developed a lively taste for dress: a lively taste is quite the expression to use. I feel as if I ought to write it very small, her judgement in this matter was by no means infallible; it was liable to confusions and embarrassments. Her great indulgence of it was really the desire of a rather inarticulate nature to manifest itself; she sought to be eloquent in her garments, and to make up for her diffidence of speech by a fine frankness of costume. But if she expressed herself in her clothes it is certain that people were not to blame for not thinking her a witty person. It must be added that though she had the expectation of a fortune—Dr. Sloper for a long time had been making twenty thousand dollars a year by his profession, and laying aside the half of it—the amount of money at her disposal was not greater than the allowance made to many poorer girls. In those days in New York there were still a few altar-fires flickering in the temple of Republican simplicity, and Dr. Sloper would have been glad to see his daughter present herself, with a classic grace, as a priestess of this mild faith. It made him fairly grimace, in private, to think that a child of his should be both ugly and overdressed. For himself, he was fond of the good things of life, and he made a considerable use of them;

but he had a dread of vulgarity, and even a theory that it was increasing in the society that surrounded him. Moreover, the standard of luxury in the United States thirty years ago was carried by no means so high as at present, and Catherine's clever father took the old-fashioned view of the education of young persons. He had no particular theory on the subject; it had scarcely as yet become a necessity of self-defence to have a collection of theories. It simply appeared to him proper and reasonable that a well-bred young woman should not carry half her fortune on her back. Catherine's back was a broad one, and would have carried a good deal; but to the weight of the paternal displeasure she never ventured to expose it, and our heroine was twenty years old before she treated herself, for evening wear, to a red satin gown trimmed with gold fringe; though this was an article which, for many years, she had coveted in secret. It made her look, when she sported it, like a woman of thirty; but oddly enough, in spite of her taste for fine clothes, she had not a grain of coquetry, and her anxiety when she put them on was as to whether they, and not she, would look well. It is a point on which history has not been explicit, but the assumption is warrantable; it was in the royal raiment just mentioned that she presented herself at a little entertainment given by her aunt, Mrs. Almond. The girl was at this time in her twenty-first year, and Mrs. Almond's party was the beginning of something very important.

Some three or four years before this Dr. Sloper had moved his household gods up town, as they say in New York. He had been living ever since his marriage in an edifice of red brick, with granite copings and an enormous fanlight over the door, standing in a street within five minutes' walk of the City Hall, which saw its best days (from the social point of view) about 1820. After this, the tide of fashion began to set steadily northward, as, indeed, in New York, thanks to the narrow channel in which it flows, it is obliged to do, and the great hum of traffic rolled farther to the right and left of Broadway. By the time the Doctor changed his residence the murmur of trade had become a mighty uproar, which was music in the ears of all good citizens interested in the commercial development, as they delighted to call it, of their fortunate isle. Dr. Sloper's interest in this phenomenon was only indirect—though, seeing that, as the years went on, half his patients came to be overworked men of business, it might have been more immediate—

and when most of his neighbours' dwellings (also ornamented with granite copings and large fanlights) had been converted into offices, warehouses, and shipping agencies, and otherwise applied to the base uses of commerce, he determined to look out for a quieter home. The ideal of quiet and of genteel retirement, in 1835, was found in Washington Square, where the Doctor built himself a handsome, modern, wide-fronted house, with a big balcony before the drawing-room windows, and a flight of marble steps ascending to a portal which was also faced with white marble. This structure, and many of its neighbours, which it exactly resembled, were supposed, forty years ago, to embody the last results of architectural science, and they remain to this day very solid and honourable dwellings. In front of them was the Square, containing a considerable quantity of inexpensive vegetation, enclosed by a wooden paling, which increased its rural and accessible appearance; and round the corner was the more august precinct of the Fifth Avenue, taking its origin at this point with a spacious and confident air which already marked it for high destinies. I know not whether it is owing to the tenderness of early associations, but this portion of New York appears to many persons the most delectable. It has a kind of established repose which is not of frequent occurrence in other quarters of the long, shrill city; it has a riper, richer, more honourable look than any of the upper ramifications of the great longitudinal thoroughfare—the look of having had something of a social history. It was here, as you might have been informed on good authority, that you had come into a world which appeared to offer a variety of sources of interest; it was here that your grandmother lived, in venerable solitude, and dispensed a hospitality which commended itself alike to the infant imagination and the infant palate; it was here that you took your first walks abroad, following the nursery-maid with unequal step and sniffing up the strange odour of the ailantus-trees which at that time formed the principal umbrage of the Square, and diffused an aroma that you were not yet critical enough to dislike as it deserved; it was here, finally, that your first school, kept by a broad-bosomed, broad-based old lady with a ferule, who was always having tea in a blue cup, with a saucer that didn't match, enlarged the circle both of your observations and your sensations. It was here, at any rate, that my heroine spent many years of her life; which is my excuse for this topographical parenthesis.

171

Mrs. Almond lived much farther up town, in an embryonic street with a high number—a region where the extension of the city began to assume a theoretic air, where poplars grew beside the pavement (when there was one), and mingled their shade with the steep roofs of desultory Dutch houses, and where pigs and chickens disported themselves in the gutter. These elements of rural picturesqueness have now wholly departed from New York street scenery; but they were to be found within the memory of middle-aged persons, in quarters which now would blush to be reminded of them. Catherine had a great many cousins, and with her Aunt Almond's children, who ended by being nine in number, she lived on terms of considerable intimacy. When she was younger they had been rather afraid of her; she was believed, as the phrase is, to be highly educated, and a person who lived in the intimacy of their Aunt Penniman had something of reflected grandeur. Mrs. Penniman, among the little Almonds, was an object of more admiration than sympathy. Her manners were strange and formidable, and her mourning robes—she dressed in black for twenty years after her husband's death, and then suddenly appeared one morning with pink roses in her cap—were complicated in odd, unexpected places with buckles, bugles, and pins, which discouraged familiarity. She took children too hard, both for good and for evil, and had an oppressive air of expecting subtle things of them, so that going to see her was a good deal like being taken to church and made to sit in a front pew. It was discovered after a while, however, that Aunt Penniman was but an accident in Catherine's existence, and not a part of its essence, and that when the girl came to spend a Saturday with her cousins, she was available for "follow-my-master," and even for leapfrog. On this basis an understanding was easily arrived at, and for several years Catherine fraternised with her young kinsmen. I say young kinsmen, because seven of the little Almonds were boys, and Catherine had a preference for those games which are most conveniently played in trousers. By degrees, however, the little Almonds' trousers began to lengthen, and the wearers to disperse and settle themselves in life. The elder children were older than Catherine, and the boys were sent to college or placed in counting-rooms. Of the girls, one married very punctually, and the other as punctually became engaged. It was to celebrate this latter event that Mrs. Almond gave the little party I have mentioned. Her daughter was to marry a stout young stockbroker, a boy of twenty; it was thought a very good thing.

IV

MRS. PENNIMAN, with more buckles and bangles than ever, came, of course, to the entertainment, accompanied by her niece; the Doctor, too, had promised to look in later in the evening. There was to be a good deal of dancing, and before it had gone very far, Marian Almond came up to Catherine, in company with a tall young man. She introduced the young man as a person who had a great desire to make our heroine's acquaintance, and as a cousin of Arthur Townsend, her own intended.

Marian Almond was a pretty little person of seventeen, with a very small figure and a very big sash, to the elegance of whose manners matrimony had nothing to add. She already had all the airs of a hostess, receiving the company, shaking her fan, saying that with so many people to attend to she should have no time to dance. She made a long speech about Mr. Townsend's cousin, to whom she administered a tap with her fan before turning away to other cares. Catherine had not understood all that she said; her attention was given to enjoying Marian's ease of manner and flow of ideas, and to looking at the young man, who was remarkably handsome. She had succeeded, however, as she often failed to do when people were presented to her, in catching his name, which appeared to be the same as that of Marian's little stockbroker. Catherine was always agitated by an introduction; it seemed a difficult moment, and she wondered that some people—her new acquaintance at this moment, for instance—should mind it so little. She wondered what she ought to say, and what would be the consequences of her saying nothing. The consequences at present were very agreeable. Mr. Townsend, leaving her no time for embarrassment, began to talk with an easy smile, as if he had known her for a year.

"What a delightful party! What a charming house! What an interesting family! What a pretty girl your cousin is!"

These observations, in themselves of no great profundity, Mr. Townsend seemed to offer for what they were worth, and as a contribution to an acquaintance. He looked straight into Catherine's eyes. She answered nothing; she only listened, and looked at him; and he, as if he expected no particular reply, went on to say many other things in the same comfortable and natural manner. Catherine, though she felt tongue-tied, was conscious of no embarrassment; it seemed proper that he should talk, and that she should simply look at him. What made it natural was that he was so handsome, or rather, as she phrased it to herself, so beautiful. The music had been silent for a while, but it suddenly began again; and then he asked her, with a deeper, intenser smile, if she would do him the honour of dancing with him. Even to this inquiry she gave no audible assent; she simply let him put his arm round her waist—as she did so it occurred to her more vividly than it had ever done before, that this was a singular place for a gentleman's arm to be—and in a moment he was guiding her round the room in the harmonious rotation of the polka. When they paused she felt that she was red; and then, for some moments, she stopped looking at him. She fanned herself, and looked at the flowers that were painted on her fan. He asked her if she would begin again, and she hesitated to answer, still looking at the flowers.

"Does it make you dizzy?" he asked, in a tone of great kindness.

Then Catherine looked up at him; he was certainly beautiful, and not at all red. "Yes," she said; she hardly knew why, for dancing had never made her dizzy.

"Ah, well, in that case," said Mr. Townsend, "we will sit still and talk. I will find a good place to sit."

He found a good place—a charming place; a little sofa that seemed meant only for two persons. The rooms by this time were very full; the dancers increased in number, and people stood close in front of them, turning their backs, so that Catherine and her companion seemed secluded and unobserved. "*We* will talk," the young man had said; but he still did all the talking. Catherine leaned back in her place, with her eyes fixed upon him, smiling and thinking him very clever. He had features like young men in pictures; Catherine had never seen such features—so delicate, so chiselled and finished—among the young New Yorkers whom she passed in the streets and met at parties. He was tall and slim, but he looked extremely strong. Catherine thought he looked like a statue. But a statue would not talk like that, and, above all, would not have eyes of so rare a colour. He had never been at Mrs. Almond's before; he felt very much like a stranger; and it was very kind of Catherine to take pity on him. He was Arthur Townsend's cousin—not very near; several times removed—and Arthur had brought him to present him to the family. In fact, he was a great stranger in New York. It was his native place; but he had not been there for many years. He had been knocking about the world, and living in far-away lands; he had only come back a month or two before. New York was very pleasant, only he felt lonely.

"You see, people forget you," he said, smiling at Catherine with his delightful gaze, while he leaned forward obliquely, turning towards her, with his elbows on his knees.

It seemed to Catherine that no one who had once seen him would ever forget him; but though she made this reflexion she kept it to herself, almost as you would keep something precious.

They sat there for some time. He was very amusing. He asked her about the people that were near them; he tried to guess who some of them were, and he made the most laughable mistakes. He criticised them very freely, in a positive, off-hand way. Catherine had never heard any one—especially any young man—talk just like that. It was the way a young man might talk in a novel; or better still, in a play, on the stage, close before the footlights, looking at the audience, and with every one looking at him, so that you wondered at his presence of mind. And yet Mr. Townsend was not like an actor; he seemed so sincere, so natural. This was very interesting; but in the midst of it Marian Almond came pushing through the crowd, with a little ironical cry, when she found these young people still together, which made every one turn round, and cost Catherine a conscious blush. Marian broke up their talk, and told Mr. Townsend—whom she treated as if she were already married, and he had become her cousin—to run away to her mother, who had been wishing for the last half-hour to introduce him to Mr. Almond.

"We shall meet again!" he said to Catherine as he left her, and Catherine thought it a very original speech.

Her cousin took her by the arm, and made her walk about. "I needn't ask you what you think of Morris!" the young girl exclaimed.

"Is that his name?"

"I don't ask you what you think of his name, but what you think of himself," said Marian.

"Oh, nothing particular!" Catherine answered, dissembling for the first time in her life.

"I have half a mind to tell him that!" cried Marian. "It will do him good. He's so terribly conceited."

"Conceited?" said Catherine, staring.

"So Arthur says, and Arthur knows about him."

"Oh, don't tell him!" Catherine murmured imploringly.

"Don't tell him he's conceited? I have told him so a dozen times."

At this profession of audacity Catherine looked down at her little companion in amazement. She supposed it was because Marian was going to be married that she took so much on herself; but she wondered too, whether, when she herself should become engaged, such exploits would be expected of her.

Half an hour later she saw her Aunt Penniman sitting in the embrasure of a window, with her head a little on one side, and her gold eye-glass raised to her eyes, which were wandering about the room. In front of her was a gentleman, bending forward a little, with his back turned to Catherine. She knew his back immediately, though she had never seen it; for when he had left her, at Marian's instigation, he had retreated in the best order, without turning round. Morris Townsend—the name had already become very familiar to her, as if some one had been repeating it in her ear for the last half-hour—Morris Townsend was giving his impressions of the company to her aunt, as he had done to herself; he was saying clever things, and Mrs. Penniman was smiling, as if she approved of them. As soon as Catherine had perceived this she moved away; she would not have liked him to turn round and see her. But it gave her pleasure—the whole thing. That he should talk with Mrs. Penniman, with whom she lived and whom she saw and talked with every day—that seemed to keep him near her, and to make him even easier to contemplate than if she herself had been the object of his civilities; and that Aunt Lavinia should like him, should not be shocked or startled by what he said, this also appeared to the girl a personal gain; for Aunt Lavinia's standard was extremely high, planted as it was over the grave of her late husband, in which, as she had convinced every one, the very genius of conversation was buried. One of the Almond boys, as Catherine called him, invited our heroine to dance a quadrille, and for a quarter of an hour her feet at least were occupied. This time she was not dizzy; her head was very clear. Just when the dance was over, she found herself in the crowd face to face with her father. Dr. Sloper had usually a little smile, never a very big one, and with his little smile playing in his clear eyes and on his neatly-shaved lips, he looked at his daughter's crimson gown.

"Is it possible that this magnificent person is my child?" he said.

You would have surprised him if you had told him so; but it is a literal fact that he almost never addressed his daughter save in the ironical form. Whenever he addressed her he gave her pleasure; but she had to cut her pleasure out of the piece, as it were. There were portions left over, light remnants and snippets of irony, which she never knew what to do with, which seemed too delicate for her own use; and yet Catherine, lamenting the limitations of her understanding, felt that they were too valuable to waste and had a belief that if they passed over her head they yet contributed to the general sum of human wisdom.

"I am not magnificent," she said mildly, wishing that she had put on another dress.

"You are sumptuous, opulent, expensive," her father rejoined. "You look as if you had eighty thousand a year."

"Well, so long as I haven't—" said Catherine illogically. Her conception of her prospective wealth was as yet very indefinite.

"So long as you haven't you shouldn't look as if you had. Have you enjoyed your party?"

Catherine hesitated a moment; and then, looking away, "I am rather tired," she murmured. I have said that this entertainment was the beginning of something important for Catherine. For the second time in her life she made an indirect answer; and the beginning of a period of dissimulation is certainly a significant date. Catherine was not so easily tired as that.

Nevertheless, in the carriage, as they drove home, she was as quiet as if fatigue had been her portion. Dr. Sloper's manner of addressing his sister Lavinia had a good deal of resemblance to the tone he had adopted towards Catherine.

"Who was the young man that was making love to you?" he presently asked.

"Oh, my good brother!" murmured Mrs. Penniman, in deprecation.

"He seemed uncommonly tender. Whenever I looked at you, for half an hour, he had the most devoted air."

"The devotion was not to me," said Mrs. Penniman. "It was to Catherine; he talked to me of her."

Catherine had been listening with all her ears. "Oh, Aunt Penniman!" she exclaimed faintly.

"He is very handsome; he is very clever; he expressed himself with a great deal—a great deal of felicity," her aunt went on.

"He is in love with this regal creature, then?" the Doctor inquired humorously.

"Oh, father," cried the girl, still more faintly, devoutly thankful the carriage was dark.

"I don't know that; but he admired her dress."

Catherine did not say to herself in the dark, "My dress only?" Mrs. Penniman's announcement struck her by its richness, not by its meagreness.

"You see," said her father, "he thinks you have eighty thousand a year."

"I don't believe he thinks of that," said Mrs. Penniman; "he is too refined."

"He must be tremendously refined not to think of that!"

"Well, he is!" Catherine exclaimed, before she knew it.

"I thought you had gone to sleep," her father answered. "The hour has come!" he added to himself. "Lavinia is going to get up a romance for Catherine. It's a shame to play such tricks on the girl. What is the gentleman's name?" he went on, aloud.

"I didn't catch it, and I didn't like to ask him. He asked to be introduced to me," said Mrs. Penniman, with a certain grandeur; "but you know how indistinctly Jefferson speaks." Jefferson was Mr. Almond. "Catherine, dear, what was the gentleman's name?"

For a minute, if it had not been for the rumbling of the carriage, you might have heard a pin drop.

"I don't know, Aunt Lavinia," said Catherine, very softly. And, with all his irony, her father believed her.

V

He learned what he had asked some three or four days later, after Morris Townsend, with his cousin, had called in Washington Square. Mrs. Penniman did not tell her brother, on the drive home, that she had intimated to this agreeable young man, whose name she did not know, that, with her niece, she should be very glad to see him; but she was greatly pleased, and even a little flattered, when, late on a Sunday afternoon, the two gentlemen made their appearance. His coming with Arthur Townsend made it more natural and easy; the latter young man was on the point of becoming connected with the family, and Mrs. Penniman had remarked to Catherine that, as he was going to marry Marian, it would be polite in him to call. These events came to pass late in the autumn, and Catherine and her aunt had been sitting together in the closing dusk, by the firelight, in the high back parlour.

Arthur Townsend fell to Catherine's portion, while his companion placed himself on the sofa, beside Mrs. Penniman. Catherine had hitherto not been a harsh critic; she was easy to please—she liked to talk with young men. But Marian's betrothed, this evening, made her feel vaguely fastidious; he sat looking at the fire and rubbing his knees with his hands. As for Catherine, she scarcely even pretended to keep up the conversation; her attention had fixed itself on the other side of the room; she was listening to what went on between the other Mr. Townsend and her aunt. Every now and then he looked over at Catherine herself and smiled, as if to show that what he said was for her benefit too. Catherine would have liked to change her place, to go and sit near them, where she might see and hear him better. But she was afraid of seeming bold—of looking eager; and, besides, it would not have been polite to Marian's little suitor. She wondered why the other gentleman had picked out her aunt—how he came to have so much to say to Mrs. Penniman, to whom, usually, young men were not especially devoted. She was not at all jealous of Aunt Lavinia, but she was a little envious, and above all she wondered; for Morris Townsend was an object on which she found that her imagination could exercise itself indefinitely. His cousin had been describing a house that he had taken in view of his union with Marian, and the domestic conveniences he meant to introduce into it; how Marian wanted a larger one, and Mrs. Almond recommended a smaller one, and how he himself was convinced that he had got the neatest house in New York.

"It doesn't matter," he said; "it's only for three or four years. At the end of three or four years we'll move. That's the way to live in New York—to move every three or four years. Then you always get the last thing. It's because the city's growing so quick—you've got to keep up with it. It's going straight up town—that's where New York's going. If I wasn't afraid Marian would be lonely, I'd go up there—right up to the top—and wait for it. Only have to wait ten years—they'd all come up after you. But Marian says she wants some neighbours—she doesn't want to be a pioneer. She says that if she's got to be the first settler she had better go out to Minnesota. I guess we'll move up little by little; when we get tired of one street we'll go higher. So you see we'll always have a new house; it's a great advantage to have a new house; you get all the latest improvements. They invent everything all over again about every five years, and it's a great thing to keep up with the new things. I always try and keep up with the new things of every kind. Don't you think that's a good motto for a young couple—to keep 'going higher'? That's the name of that piece of poetry—what do they call it?—*Excelsior!*"

Catherine bestowed on her junior visitor only just enough attention to feel that this was not the way Mr. Morris Townsend had talked the other night, or that he was talking now to her fortunate aunt. But suddenly his aspiring kinsman became more interesting. He seemed to have become conscious that she was affected by his companion's presence, and he thought it proper to explain it.

"My cousin asked me to bring him, or I shouldn't have taken the liberty. He seemed to want very much to come; you know he's awfully sociable. I told him I wanted to ask you first, but he said Mrs. Penniman had invited him. He isn't particular what he says when he wants to come somewhere! But Mrs. Penniman seems to think it's all right."

"We are very glad to see him," said Catherine. And she wished to talk more about him; but she hardly knew what to say. "I never saw him before," she went on presently.

Arthur Townsend stared.

"Why, he told me he talked with you for over half an hour the other night."

"I mean before the other night. That was the first time."

"Oh, he has been away from New York—he has been all round the world. He doesn't know many people here, but he's very sociable, and he wants to know every one."

"Every one?" said Catherine.

"Well, I mean all the good ones. All the pretty young ladies—like Mrs. Penniman!" and Arthur Townsend gave a private laugh.

"My aunt likes him very much," said Catherine.

"Most people like him—he's so brilliant."

"He's more like a foreigner," Catherine suggested.

"Well, I never knew a foreigner!" said young Townsend, in a tone which seemed to indicate that his ignorance had been optional.

"Neither have I," Catherine confessed, with more humility. "They say they are generally brilliant," she added vaguely.

"Well, the people of this city are clever enough for me. I know some of them that think they are too clever for me; but they ain't!"

"I suppose you can't be too clever," said Catherine, still with humility.

"I don't know. I know some people that call my cousin too clever."

Catherine listened to this statement with extreme interest, and a feeling that if Morris Townsend had a fault it would naturally be that one. But she did not commit herself, and in a moment she asked: "Now that he has come back, will he stay here always?"

"Ah," said Arthur, "if he can get something to do."

"Something to do?"

"Some place or other; some business."

"Hasn't he got any?" said Catherine, who had never heard of a young man—of the upper class—in this situation.

"No; he's looking round. But he can't find anything."

"I am very sorry," Catherine permitted herself to observe.

"Oh, he doesn't mind," said young Townsend. "He takes it easy—he isn't in a hurry. He is very particular."

Catherine thought he naturally would be, and gave herself up for some moments to the contemplation of this idea, in several of its bearings.

"Won't his father take him into his business—his office?" she at last inquired.

"He hasn't got any father—he has only got a sister. Your sister can't help you much."

It seemed to Catherine that if she were his sister she would disprove this axiom. "Is she—is she pleasant?" she asked in a moment.

"I don't know—I believe she's very respectable," said young Townsend. And then he looked across to his cousin and began to laugh. "Look here, we are talking about you," he added.

Morris Townsend paused in his conversation with Mrs. Penniman, and stared, with a little smile. Then he got up, as if he were going.

"As far as you are concerned, I can't return the compliment," he said to Catherine's companion. "But as regards Miss Sloper, it's another affair."

Catherine thought this little speech wonderfully well turned; but she was embarrassed by it, and she also got up. Morris Townsend stood looking at her and smiling; he put out his hand for farewell. He was going, without having said anything to her; but even on these terms she was glad to have seen him.

"I will tell her what you have said—when you go!" said Mrs. Penniman, with an insinuating laugh.

Catherine blushed, for she felt almost as if they were making sport of her. What in the world could this beautiful young man have said? He looked at her still, in spite of her blush; but very kindly and respectfully.

"I have had no talk with you," he said, "and that was what I came for. But it will be a good reason for coming another time; a little pretext—if I am obliged to give one. I am not afraid of what your aunt will say when I go."

With this the two young men took their departure; after which Catherine, with her blush still lingering, directed a serious and interrogative eye to Mrs. Penniman. She was incapable of elaborate artifice, and she resorted to no jocular device—to no affectation of the belief that she had been maligned—to learn what she desired.

"What did you say you would tell me?" she asked.

Mrs. Penniman came up to her, smiling and nodding a little, looked at her all over, and gave a twist to the knot of ribbon in her neck. "It's a great secret, my dear child; but he is coming a-courting!"

Catherine was serious still. "Is that what he told you!"

"He didn't say so exactly. But he left me to guess it. I'm a good guesser."

"Do you mean a-courting me?"

"Not me, certainly, miss; though I must say he is a hundred times more polite to a person who has no longer extreme youth to recommend her than most of the young men. He is thinking of some one else." And Mrs. Penniman gave her niece a delicate little kiss. "You must be very gracious to him."

Catherine stared—she was bewildered. "I don't understand you," she said; "he doesn't know me."

"Oh yes, he does; more than you think. I have told him all about you."

"Oh, Aunt Penniman!" murmured Catherine, as if this had been a breach of trust. "He is a perfect stranger—we don't know him." There was infinite, modesty in the poor girl's "we."

Aunt Penniman, however, took no account of it; she spoke even with a touch of acrimony. "My dear Catherine, you know very well that you admire him!"

"Oh, Aunt Penniman!" Catherine could only murmur again. It might very well be that she admired him—though this did not seem to her a thing to talk about. But that this brilliant stranger—this sudden apparition, who had barely heard the sound of her voice—took that sort of interest in her that was expressed by the romantic phrase of which Mrs. Penniman had just made use: this could only be a figment of the restless brain of Aunt Lavinia, whom every one knew to be a woman of powerful imagination.

VI

Mrs. Penniman even took for granted at times that other people had as much imagination as herself; so that when, half an hour later, her brother came in, she addressed him quite on this principle.

"He has just been here, Austin; it's such a pity you missed him."

"Whom in the world have I missed?" asked the Doctor.

"Mr. Morris Townsend; he has made us such a delightful visit."

"And who in the world is Mr. Morris Townsend?"

"Aunt Penniman means the gentleman—the gentleman whose name I couldn't remember," said Catherine.

"The gentleman at Elizabeth's party who was so struck with Catherine," Mrs. Penniman added.

"Oh, his name is Morris Townsend, is it? And did he come here to propose to you?"

"Oh, father," murmured the girl for all answer, turning away to the window, where the dusk had deepened to darkness.

"I hope he won't do that without your permission," said Mrs. Penniman, very graciously.

"After all, my dear, he seems to have yours," her brother answered.

Lavinia simpered, as if this might not be quite enough, and Catherine, with her forehead touching the window-panes, listened to this exchange of epigrams as reservedly as if they had not each been a pin-prick in her own destiny.

"The next time he comes," the Doctor added, "you had better call me. He might like to see me."

Morris Townsend came again, some five days afterwards; but Dr. Sloper was not called, as he was absent from home at the time. Catherine was with her aunt when the young man's name was brought in, and Mrs. Penniman, effacing herself and protesting, made a great point of her niece's going into the drawing-room alone.

"This time it's for you—for you only," she said. "Before, when he talked to me, it was only preliminary—it was to gain my confidence. Literally, my dear, I should not have the *courage* to show myself to-day."

And this was perfectly true. Mrs. Penniman was not a brave woman, and Morris Townsend had struck her as a young man of great force of character, and of remarkable powers of satire; a keen, resolute, brilliant nature, with which one must exercise a great deal of tact. She said to herself that he was "imperious," and she liked the word and the idea. She was not the least jealous of her niece, and she had been perfectly happy with Mr. Penniman, but in the bottom of her heart she permitted herself the observation: "That's the sort of husband I should have had!" He was certainly much more imperious—she ended by calling it imperial—than Mr. Penniman.

So Catherine saw Mr. Townsend alone, and her aunt did not come in even at the end of the visit. The visit was a long one; he sat there—in the front parlour, in the biggest armchair—for more than an hour. He seemed more at home this time—more familiar; lounging a little in the chair, slapping a cushion that was near him with his stick, and looking round the room a good deal, and at the objects it contained, as well as at Catherine; whom, however, he also contemplated freely. There was a smile of respectful devotion in his handsome eyes which seemed to Catherine almost solemnly beautiful; it made her think of a young knight in a poem. His talk, however, was not particularly knightly; it was light and easy and friendly; it took a practical turn, and he asked a number of questions about herself—what were her tastes—if she liked this and that—what were her habits. He said to her, with his charming smile, "Tell me about yourself; give me a little sketch." Catherine had very little to tell, and she had no talent for sketching; but before he went she had confided to him that she had a secret passion for the theatre, which had been but scantily gratified, and a taste for operatic music—that of Bellini and Donizetti, in especial (it must be remembered in extenuation of this primitive young woman that she held these opinions in an age of general darkness)—which she rarely had an occasion to hear, except on the hand-organ. She confessed that she was not particularly fond of literature. Morris Townsend agreed with her that books were tiresome things; only, as he said, you had to read a good many before you found it out. He had been to places that people had written books about, and they were not a bit like the descriptions. To see for yourself—that was the great thing; he always tried to see for himself. He had seen all the principal actors—he had been to all the best theatres in London and Paris. But the actors were always like the authors—they always exaggerated. He liked everything to be natural. Suddenly he stopped, looking at Catherine with his smile.

"That's what I like you for; you are so natural! Excuse me," he added; "you see I am natural myself!"

And before she had time to think whether she excused him or not—which afterwards, at leisure, she became conscious that she did—he began to talk about music, and to say that it was his greatest pleasure in life. He had heard all the great singers in Paris and London—Pasta and Rubini and Lablache—and when you had done that, you could say that you knew what singing was.

"I sing a little myself," he said; "some day I will show you. Not to-day, but some other time."

And then he got up to go; he had omitted, by accident, to say that he would sing to her if she would play to him. He thought of this after he got into the street; but he might have spared his compunction, for Catherine had not noticed the lapse. She was thinking only that "some other time" had a delightful sound; it seemed to spread itself over the future.

This was all the more reason, however, though she was ashamed and uncomfortable, why she should tell her father that Mr. Morris Townsend had called again. She announced the fact abruptly, almost violently, as soon as the Doctor came into the house; and having done so—it was her duty—she took measures to leave the room. But she could not leave it fast enough; her father stopped her just as she reached the door.

"Well, my dear, did he propose to you to-day?" the Doctor asked.

This was just what she had been afraid he would say; and yet she had no answer ready. Of course she would have liked to take it as a joke—as her father must have meant it; and yet she would have liked, also, in denying it, to be a little positive, a little sharp; so that he would perhaps not ask the question again. She didn't like it—it made her unhappy. But Catherine could never be sharp; and for a moment she only stood, with her hand on the door-knob, looking at her satiric parent, and giving a little laugh.

"Decidedly," said the Doctor to himself, "my daughter is not brilliant."

But he had no sooner made this reflexion than Catherine found something; she had decided, on the whole, to take the thing as a joke.

"Perhaps he will do it the next time!" she exclaimed, with a repetition of her laugh. And she quickly got out of the room.

The Doctor stood staring; he wondered whether his daughter were serious. Catherine went straight to her own room, and by the time she reached it she bethought herself that there was something else—something better—she might have said. She almost wished, now, that her father would ask his question again, so that she might reply: "Oh yes, Mr. Morris Townsend proposed to me, and I refused him!"

The Doctor, however, began to put his questions elsewhere; it naturally having occurred to him that he ought to inform himself properly about this handsome young man who had formed the habit of running in and out of his house. He addressed himself to the younger of his sisters, Mrs. Almond—not going to her for the purpose; there was no such hurry as that—but having made a note of the matter for the first opportunity. The Doctor was never eager, never impatient nor nervous; but he made notes of everything, and he regularly consulted his notes. Among them the information he obtained from Mrs. Almond about Morris Townsend took its place.

"Lavinia has already been to ask me," she said. "Lavinia is most excited; I don't understand it. It's not, after all, Lavinia that the young man is supposed to have designs upon. She is very peculiar."

"Ah, my dear," the Doctor replied, "she has not lived with me these twelve years without my finding it out!"

"She has got such an artificial mind," said Mrs. Almond, who always enjoyed an opportunity to discuss Lavinia's peculiarities with her brother. "She didn't want me to tell you that she had asked me about Mr. Townsend; but I told her I would. She always wants to conceal everything."

"And yet at moments no one blurts things out with such crudity. She is like a revolving lighthouse; pitch darkness alternating with a dazzling brilliancy! But what did you tell her?" the Doctor asked.

"What I tell you; that I know very little of him."

"Lavinia must have been disappointed at that," said the Doctor; "she would prefer him to have been guilty of some romantic crime. However, we must make the best of people. They tell me our gentleman is the cousin of the little boy to whom you are about to entrust the future of your little girl."

"Arthur is not a little boy; he is a very old man; you and I will never be so old. He is a distant relation of Lavinia's *protégé*. The name is the same, but I am given to understand that there are Townsends and Townsends. So Arthur's mother tells me; she talked about 'branches'—younger branches, elder branches, inferior branches—as if it were a royal house. Arthur, it appears, is of the reigning line, but poor Lavinia's young man is not. Beyond this, Arthur's mother knows very little about him; she has only a vague story that he has been 'wild.' But I know his sister a little, and she is a very nice woman. Her name is Mrs. Montgomery; she is a widow, with a little property and five children. She lives in the Second Avenue."

"What does Mrs. Montgomery say about him?"

"That he has talents by which he might distinguish himself."

"Only he is lazy, eh?"

"She doesn't say so."

"That's family pride," said the Doctor. "What is his profession?"

"He hasn't got any; he is looking for something. I believe he was once in the Navy."

"Once? What is his age?"

"I suppose he is upwards of thirty. He must have gone into the Navy very young. I think Arthur told me that he inherited a small property—which was perhaps the cause of his leaving the Navy—and that he spent it all in a few years. He travelled all over the world, lived abroad, amused himself. I believe it was a kind of system, a theory he had. He has lately come back to America, with the intention, as he tells Arthur, of beginning life in earnest."

"Is he in earnest about Catherine, then?"

"I don't see why you should be incredulous," said Mrs. Almond. "It seems to me that you have never done Catherine justice. You must remember that she has the prospect of thirty thousand a year."

The Doctor looked at his sister a moment, and then, with the slightest touch of bitterness: "You at least appreciate her," he said.

Mrs. Almond blushed.

"I don't mean that is her only merit; I simply mean that it is a great one. A great many young men think so; and you appear to me never to have been properly aware of that. You have always had a little way of alluding to her as an unmarriageable girl."

"My allusions are as kind as yours, Elizabeth," said the Doctor frankly. "How many suitors has Catherine had, with all her expectations—how much attention has she ever received? Catherine is not unmarriageable, but she is absolutely unattractive. What other reason is there for Lavinia being so charmed with the idea that there is a lover in the house? There has never been one before, and Lavinia, with her sensitive, sympathetic nature, is not used to the idea. It affects her imagination. I must do the young men of New York the justice to say that they strike me as very disinterested. They prefer pretty girls—lively girls—girls like your own. Catherine is neither pretty nor lively."

"Catherine does very well; she has a style of her own—which is more than my poor Marian has, who has no style at all," said Mrs. Almond. "The reason Catherine has received so little attention is that she seems to all the young men to be older than themselves. She is so large, and she dresses—so richly. They are rather afraid of her, I think; she looks as if she had been married already, and you know they don't like married women. And if our young men appear disinterested," the Doctor's wiser sister went on, "it is because they marry, as a general thing, so young; before twenty-five, at the age of innocence and sincerity, before the age of calculation. If they only waited a little, Catherine would fare better."

"As a calculation? Thank you very much," said the Doctor.

"Wait till some intelligent man of forty comes along, and he will be delighted with Catherine," Mrs. Almond continued.

"Mr. Townsend is not old enough, then; his motives may be pure."

"It is very possible that his motives are pure; I should be very sorry to take the contrary for granted. Lavinia is sure of it, and, as he is a very prepossessing youth, you might give him the benefit of the doubt."

Dr. Sloper reflected a moment.

"What are his present means of subsistence?"

"I have no idea. He lives, as I say, with his sister."

"A widow, with five children? Do you mean he lives *upon* her?"

Mrs. Almond got up, and with a certain impatience: "Had you not better ask Mrs. Montgomery herself?" she inquired.

"Perhaps I may come to that," said the Doctor. "Did you say the Second Avenue?" He made a note of the Second Avenue.

VII

HE was, however, by no means so much in earnest as this might seem to indicate; and, indeed, he was more than anything else amused with the whole situation. He was not in the least in a state of tension or of vigilance with regard to Catherine's prospects; he was even on his guard against the ridicule that might attach itself to the spectacle of a house thrown into agitation by its daughter and heiress receiving attentions unprecedented in its annals. More than this, he went so far as to promise himself some entertainment from the little drama—if drama it was—of which Mrs. Penniman desired to represent the ingenious Mr. Townsend as the hero. He had no intention, as yet, of regulating the *dénouement*. He was perfectly willing, as Elizabeth had suggested, to give the young man the benefit of every doubt. There was no great danger in it; for Catherine, at the age of twenty-two, was, after all, a rather mature blossom, such as could be plucked from the stem only by a vigorous jerk. The fact that Morris Townsend was poor—was not of necessity against him; the Doctor had never made up his mind that his daughter should marry a rich man. The fortune she would inherit struck him as a very sufficient provision for two reasonable persons, and if a penniless swain who could give a good account of himself should enter the lists, he should be judged quite upon his personal merits. There were other things besides. The Doctor thought it very vulgar to be precipitate in accusing people of mercenary motives, inasmuch as his door had as yet not been in the least besieged by fortune-hunters; and, lastly, he was very curious to see whether Catherine might really be loved for her moral worth. He smiled as he reflected that poor Mr. Townsend had been only twice to the house, and he said to Mrs. Penniman that the next time he should come she must ask him to dinner.

He came very soon again, and Mrs. Penniman had of course great pleasure in executing this mission. Morris Townsend accepted her invitation with equal good grace, and the dinner took place a few days later. The Doctor had said to himself, justly enough, that they must not have the young man alone; this would partake too much of the nature of encouragement. So two or three other persons were invited; but Morris Townsend, though he was by no means the ostensible, was the real, occasion of the feast. There is every reason to suppose that he desired to make a good impression; and if he fell short of this result, it was not for want of a good deal of intelligent effort. The Doctor talked to him very little during dinner; but he observed him attentively, and after the ladies had gone out he pushed him the wine and asked him several questions. Morris was not a young man who needed to be pressed, and he found quite enough encouragement in the superior quality of the claret. The Doctor's wine was admirable, and it may be communicated to the reader that while he sipped it Morris reflected that a cellar-full of good liquor—there was evidently a cellar-full here—would be a most attractive idiosyncrasy in a father-in-law. The Doctor was struck with his appreciative guest; he saw that he was not a commonplace young man. "He has ability," said Catherine's father, "decided ability; he has a very good head if he chooses to use it. And he is uncommonly well turned out; quite the sort of figure that pleases the ladies. But I don't think I like him." The Doctor, however, kept his reflexions to himself, and talked to his visitors about foreign lands, concerning which Morris offered him more information than he was ready, as he mentally phrased it, to swallow. Dr. Sloper had travelled but little, and he took the liberty of not believing everything this anecdotical idler narrated. He prided himself on being something of a physiognomist, and while the young man, chatting with easy assurance, puffed his cigar and filled his glass again, the Doctor sat with his eyes quietly fixed on his bright, expressive face. "He has the assurance of the devil himself," said Morris's host; "I don't think I ever saw such assurance. And his powers of invention are most remarkable. He is very knowing; they were not so knowing as that in my time. And a good head, did I say? I should think so—after a bottle of Madeira and a bottle and a half of claret!"

After dinner Morris Townsend went and stood before Catherine, who was standing before the fire in her red satin gown.

"He doesn't like me—he doesn't like me at all!" said the young man.

"Who doesn't like you?" asked Catherine.

"Your father; extraordinary man!"

"I don't see how you know," said Catherine, blushing.

"I feel; I am very quick to feel."

"Perhaps you are mistaken."

"Ah, well; you ask him and you will see."

"I would rather not ask him, if there is any danger of his saying what you think."

Morris looked at her with an air of mock melancholy.

"It wouldn't give you any pleasure to contradict him?"

"I never contradict him," said Catherine.

"Will you hear me abused without opening your lips in my defence?"

"My father won't abuse you. He doesn't know you enough."

Morris Townsend gave a loud laugh, and Catherine began to blush again.

"I shall never mention you," she said, to take refuge from her confusion.

"That is very well; but it is not quite what I should have liked you to say. I should have liked you to say: 'If my father doesn't think well of you, what does it matter?'"

"Ah, but it would matter; I couldn't say that!" the girl exclaimed.

He looked at her for a moment, smiling a little; and the Doctor, if he had been watching him just then, would have seen a gleam of fine impatience in the sociable softness of his eye. But there was no impatience in his rejoinder—none, at least, save what was expressed in a little appealing sigh. "Ah, well, then, I must not give up the hope of bringing him round!"

He expressed it more frankly to Mrs. Penniman later in the evening. But before that he sang two or three songs at Catherine's timid request; not that he flattered himself that this would help to bring her father round. He had a sweet, light tenor voice, and when he had finished every one made some exclamation—every one, that is, save Catherine, who remained intensely silent. Mrs. Penniman declared that his manner of singing was "most artistic," and Dr. Sloper said it was "very taking—very taking indeed"; speaking loudly and distinctly, but with a certain dryness.

"He doesn't like me—he doesn't like me at all," said Morris Townsend, addressing the aunt in the same manner as he had done the niece. "He thinks I'm all wrong."

Unlike her niece, Mrs. Penniman asked for no explanation. She only smiled very sweetly, as if she understood everything; and, unlike Catherine too, she made no attempt to contradict him. "Pray, what does it matter?" she murmured softly.

"Ah, you say the right thing!" said Morris, greatly to the gratification of Mrs. Penniman, who prided herself on always saying the right thing.

The Doctor, the next time he saw his sister Elizabeth, let her know that he had made the acquaintance of Lavinia's *protégé*.

"Physically," he said, "he's uncommonly well set up. As an anatomist, it is really a pleasure to me to see such a beautiful structure; although, if people were all like him, I suppose there would be very little need for doctors."

"Don't you see anything in people but their bones?" Mrs. Almond rejoined. "What do you think of him as a father?"

"As a father? Thank Heaven I am not his father!"

"No; but you are Catherine's. Lavinia tells me she is in love."

"She must get over it. He is not a gentleman."

"Ah, take care! Remember that he is a branch of the Townsends."

"He is not what I call a gentleman. He has not the soul of one. He is extremely insinuating; but it's a vulgar nature. I saw through it in a minute. He is altogether too familiar—I hate familiarity. He is a plausible coxcomb."

"Ah, well," said Mrs. Almond; "if you make up your mind so easily, it's a great advantage."

"I don't make up my mind easily. What I tell you is the result of thirty years of observation; and in order to be able to form that judgement in a single evening, I have had to spend a lifetime in study."

"Very possibly you are right. But the thing is for Catherine to see it."

"I will present her with a pair of spectacles!" said the Doctor.

VIII

IF it were true that she was in love, she was certainly very quiet about it; but the Doctor was of course prepared to admit that her quietness might mean volumes. She had told Morris Townsend that she would not mention him to her father, and she saw no reason to retract this vow of discretion. It was no more than decently civil, of course, that after having dined in Washington Square, Morris should call there again; and it was no more than natural that, having been kindly received on this occasion, he should continue to present himself. He had had plenty of leisure on his hands; and thirty years ago, in New York, a young man of leisure had reason to be thankful for aids to self-oblivion. Catherine said nothing to her father about these visits, though they had rapidly become the most important, the most absorbing thing in her life. The girl was very happy. She knew not as yet what would come of it; but the present had suddenly grown rich and solemn. If she had been told she was in love, she would have been a good deal surprised; for she had an idea that love was an eager and exacting passion, and her own heart was filled in these days with the impulse of self-effacement and sacrifice. Whenever Morris Townsend had left the house, her imagination projected itself, with all its strength, into the idea of his soon coming back; but if she had been told at such a moment that he would not return for a year, or even that he would never return, she would not have complained nor rebelled, but would have humbly accepted the decree, and sought for consolation in thinking over the times she had already seen him, the words he had spoken, the sound of his voice, of his tread, the expression of his face. Love demands certain things as a right; but Catherine had no sense of her rights; she had only a consciousness of immense and unexpected favours. Her very gratitude for these things had hushed itself; for it seemed to her that there would be something of impudence in making a festival of her secret. Her father suspected Morris Townsend's visits, and noted her reserve. She seemed to beg pardon for it; she looked at him constantly in silence, as if she meant to say that she said nothing because she was afraid of irritating him. But the poor girl's dumb eloquence irritated him more than anything else would have done, and he caught himself murmuring more than once that it was a grievous pity his only child was a simpleton. His murmurs, however, were inaudible; and for a while he said nothing to any one. He would have liked to know exactly how often young Townsend came; but he had determined to ask no questions of the girl herself—to say nothing more to her that would show that he watched her. The Doctor had a great idea of being largely just: he wished to leave his daughter her liberty, and interfere only when the danger should be proved. It was not in his manner to obtain information by indirect methods, and it never even occurred to him to question the servants. As for Lavinia, he hated to talk to her about the matter; she annoyed him with her mock romanticism. But he had to come to this. Mrs. Penniman's convictions as regards the relations of her niece and the clever young visitor who saved appearances by coming ostensibly for both the ladies—Mrs. Penniman's convictions had passed into a riper and richer phase. There was to be no crudity in Mrs. Penniman's treatment of the situation; she had become as uncommunicative as Catherine herself. She was tasting of the sweets of concealment; she had taken up the line of mystery. "She would be enchanted to be able to prove to herself that she is persecuted," said the Doctor; and when at last he questioned her, he was sure she would contrive to extract from his words a pretext for this belief.

"Be so good as to let me know what is going on in the house," he said to her, in a tone which, under the circumstances, he himself deemed genial.

"Going on, Austin?" Mrs. Penniman exclaimed. "Why, I am sure I don't know! I believe that last night the old grey cat had kittens!"

"At her age?" said the Doctor. "The idea is startling—almost shocking. Be so good as to see that they are all drowned. But what else has happened?"

"Ah, the dear little kittens!" cried Mrs. Penniman. "I wouldn't have them drowned for the world!"

Her brother puffed his cigar a few moments in silence. "Your sympathy with kittens, Lavinia," he presently resumed, "arises from a feline element in your own character."

"Cats are very graceful, and very clean," said Mrs. Penniman, smiling.

"And very stealthy. You are the embodiment both of grace and of neatness; but you are wanting in frankness."

"You certainly are not, dear brother."

"I don't pretend to be graceful, though I try to be neat. Why haven't you let me know that Mr. Morris Townsend is coming to the house four times a week?"

Mrs. Penniman lifted her eyebrows. "Four times a week?"

"Five times, if you prefer it. I am away all day, and I see nothing. But when such things happen, you should let me know."

Mrs. Penniman, with her eyebrows still raised, reflected intently. "Dear Austin," she said at last, "I am incapable of betraying a confidence. I would rather suffer anything."

"Never fear; you shall not suffer. To whose confidence is it you allude? Has Catherine made you take a vow of eternal secrecy?"

"By no means. Catherine has not told me as much as she might. She has not been very trustful."

"It is the young man, then, who has made you his confidante? Allow me to say that it is extremely indiscreet of you to form secret alliances with young men. You don't know where they may lead you."

"I don't know what you mean by an alliance," said Mrs. Penniman. "I take a great interest in Mr. Townsend; I won't conceal that. But that's all."

"Under the circumstances, that is quite enough. What is the source of your interest in Mr. Townsend?"

"Why," said Mrs. Penniman, musing, and then breaking into her smile, "that he is so interesting!"

The Doctor felt that he had need of his patience. "And what makes him interesting?—his good looks?"

"His misfortunes, Austin."

"Ah, he has had misfortunes? That, of course, is always interesting. Are you at liberty to mention a few of Mr. Townsend's?"

"I don't know that he would like it," said Mrs. Penniman. "He has told me a great deal about himself—he has told me, in fact, his whole history. But I don't think I ought to repeat those things. He would tell them to you, I am sure, if he thought you would listen to him kindly. With kindness you may do anything with him."

The Doctor gave a laugh. "I shall request him very kindly, then, to leave Catherine alone."

"Ah!" said Mrs. Penniman, shaking her forefinger at her brother, with her little finger turned out, "Catherine had probably said something to him kinder than that."

"Said that she loved him? Do you mean that?"

Mrs. Penniman fixed her eyes on the floor. "As I tell you, Austin, she doesn't confide in me."

"You have an opinion, I suppose, all the same. It is that I ask you for; though I don't conceal from you that I shall not regard it as conclusive."

Mrs. Penniman's gaze continued to rest on the carpet; but at last she lifted it, and then her brother thought it very expressive. "I think Catherine is very happy; that is all I can say."

"Townsend is trying to marry her—is that what you mean?"

"He is greatly interested in her."

"He finds her such an attractive girl?"

"Catherine has a lovely nature, Austin," said Mrs. Penniman, "and Mr. Townsend has had the intelligence to discover that."

"With a little help from you, I suppose. My dear Lavinia," cried the Doctor, "you are an admirable aunt!"

"So Mr. Townsend says," observed Lavinia, smiling.

"Do you think he is sincere?" asked her brother.

"In saying that?"

"No; that's of course. But in his admiration for Catherine?"

"Deeply sincere. He has said to me the most appreciative, the most charming things about her. He would say them to you, if he were sure you would listen to him—gently."

"I doubt whether I can undertake it. He appears to require a great deal of gentleness."

"He is a sympathetic, sensitive nature," said Mrs. Penniman.

Her brother puffed his cigar again in silence. "These delicate qualities have survived his vicissitudes, eh? All this while you haven't told me about his misfortunes."

"It is a long story," said Mrs. Penniman, "and I regard it as a sacred trust. But I suppose there is no objection to my saying that he has been wild—he frankly confesses that. But he has paid for it."

"That's what has impoverished him, eh?"

"I don't mean simply in money. He is very much alone in the world."

"Do you mean that he has behaved so badly that his friends have given him up?"

"He has had false friends, who have deceived and betrayed him."

"He seems to have some good ones too. He has a devoted sister, and half-a-dozen nephews and nieces."

Mrs. Penniman was silent a minute. "The nephews and nieces are children, and the sister is not a very attractive person."

"I hope he doesn't abuse her to you," said the Doctor; "for I am told he lives upon her."

"Lives upon her?"

"Lives with her, and does nothing for himself; it is about the same thing."

"He is looking for a position—most earnestly," said Mrs. Penniman. "He hopes every day to find one."

"Precisely. He is looking for it here—over there in the front parlour. The position of husband of a weak-minded woman with a large fortune would suit him to perfection!"

Mrs. Penniman was truly amiable, but she now gave signs of temper. She rose with much animation, and stood for a moment looking at her brother. "My dear Austin," she remarked, "if you regard Catherine as a weak-minded woman, you are particularly mistaken!" And with this she moved majestically away.

IX

It was a regular custom with the family in Washington Square to go and spend Sunday evening at Mrs. Almond's. On the Sunday after the conversation I have just narrated, this custom was not intermitted and on this occasion, towards the middle of the evening, Dr. Sloper found reason to withdraw to the library, with his brother-in-law, to talk over a matter of business. He was absent some twenty minutes, and when he came back into the circle, which was enlivened by the presence of several friends of the family, he saw that Morris Townsend had come in and had lost as little time as possible in seating himself on a small sofa, beside Catherine. In the large room, where several different groups had been formed, and the hum of voices and of laughter was loud, these two young persons might confabulate, as the Doctor phrased it to himself, without attracting attention. He saw in a moment, however, that his daughter was painfully conscious of his own observation. She sat motionless, with her eyes bent down, staring at her open fan, deeply flushed, shrinking together as if to minimise the indiscretion of which she confessed herself guilty.

The Doctor almost pitied her. Poor Catherine was not defiant; she had no genius for bravado; and as she felt that her father viewed her companion's attentions with an unsympathising eye, there was nothing but discomfort for her in the accident of seeming to challenge him. The Doctor felt, indeed, so sorry for her that he turned away, to spare her the sense of being watched; and he was so intelligent a man that, in his thoughts, he rendered a sort of poetic justice to her situation.

"It must be deucedly pleasant for a plain inanimate girl like that to have a beautiful young fellow come and sit down beside her and whisper to her that he is her slave—if that is what this one whispers. No wonder she likes it, and that she thinks me a cruel tyrant; which of course she does, though she is afraid—she hasn't the animation necessary—to admit it to herself. Poor old Catherine!" mused the Doctor; "I verily believe she is capable of defending me when Townsend abuses me!"

And the force of this reflexion, for the moment, was such in making him feel the natural opposition between his point of view and that of an infatuated child, that he said to himself that he was perhaps, after all, taking things too hard and crying out before he was hurt. He must not condemn Morris Townsend unheard. He had a great aversion to taking things too hard; he thought that half the discomfort and many of the disappointments of life come from it; and for an instant he asked himself whether, possibly, he did not appear ridiculous to this intelligent young man, whose private perception of incongruities he suspected of being keen. At the end of a quarter of an hour Catherine had got rid of him, and Townsend was now standing before the fireplace in conversation with Mrs. Almond.

"We will try him again," said the Doctor. And he crossed the room and joined his sister and her companion, making her a sign that she should leave the young man to him. She presently did so, while Morris looked at him, smiling, without a sign of evasiveness in his affable eye.

"He's amazingly conceited!" thought the Doctor; and then he said aloud: "I am told you are looking out for a position."

"Oh, a position is more than I should presume to call it," Morris Townsend answered. "That sounds so fine. I should like some quiet work—something to turn an honest penny."

"What sort of thing should you prefer?"

"Do you mean what am I fit for? Very little, I am afraid. I have nothing but my good right arm, as they say in the melodramas."

"You are too modest," said the Doctor. "In addition to your good right arm, you have your subtle brain. I know nothing of you but what I see; but I see by your physiognomy that you are extremely intelligent."

"Ah," Townsend murmured, "I don't know what to answer when you say that! You advise me, then, not to despair?"

And he looked at his interlocutor as if the question might have a double meaning. The Doctor caught the look and weighed it a moment before he replied. "I should be very sorry to admit that a robust and well-disposed young man need ever despair. If he doesn't succeed in one thing, he can try another. Only, I should add, he should choose his line with discretion."

"Ah, yes, with discretion," Morris Townsend repeated sympathetically. "Well, I have been indiscreet, formerly; but I think I have got over it. I am very steady now." And he stood a moment, looking down at his remarkably neat shoes. Then at last, "Were you kindly intending to propose something for my advantage?" he inquired, looking up and smiling.

"Damn his impudence!" the Doctor exclaimed privately. But in a moment he reflected that he himself had, after all, touched first upon this delicate point, and that his words might have been construed as an offer of assistance. "I have no particular proposal to make," he presently said; "but it occurred to me to let you know that I have you in my mind. Sometimes one hears of opportunities. For instance—should you object to leaving New York—to going to a distance?"

"I am afraid I shouldn't be able to manage that. I must seek my fortune here or nowhere. You see," added Morris Townsend, "I have ties—I have responsibilities here. I have a sister, a widow, from whom I have been separated for a long time, and to whom I am almost everything. I shouldn't like to say to her that I must leave her. She rather depends upon me, you see."

"Ah, that's very proper; family feeling is very proper," said Dr. Sloper. "I often think there is not enough of it in our city. I think I have heard of your sister."

"It is possible, but I rather doubt it; she lives so very quietly."

"As quietly, you mean," the Doctor went on, with a short laugh, "as a lady may do who has several young children."

"Ah, my little nephews and nieces—that's the very point! I am helping to bring them up," said Morris Townsend. "I am a kind of amateur tutor; I give them lessons."

"That's very proper, as I say; but it is hardly a career."

"It won't make my fortune!" the young man confessed.

"You must not be too much bent on a fortune," said the Doctor. "But I assure you I will keep you in mind; I won't lose sight of you!"

"If my situation becomes desperate I shall perhaps take the liberty of reminding you!" Morris rejoined, raising his voice a little, with a brighter smile, as his interlocutor turned away.

Before he left the house the Doctor had a few words with Mrs. Almond.

"I should like to see his sister," he said. "What do you call her? Mrs. Montgomery. I should like to have a little talk with her."

"I will try and manage it," Mrs. Almond responded. "I will take the first opportunity of inviting her, and you shall come and meet her. Unless, indeed," Mrs. Almond added, "she first takes it into her head to be sick and to send for you."

"Ah no, not that; she must have trouble enough without that. But it would have its advantages, for then I should see the children. I should like very much to see the children."

"You are very thorough. Do you want to catechise them about their uncle!"

"Precisely. Their uncle tells me he has charge of their education, that he saves their mother the expense of school-bills. I should like to ask them a few questions in the commoner branches."

"He certainly has not the cut of a schoolmaster!" Mrs. Almond said to herself a short time afterwards, as she saw Morris Townsend in a corner bending over her niece, who was seated.

And there was, indeed, nothing in the young man's discourse at this moment that savoured of the pedagogue.

"Will you meet me somewhere to-morrow or next day?" he said, in a low tone, to Catherine.

"Meet you?" she asked, lifting her frightened eyes.

"I have something particular to say to you—very particular."

"Can't you come to the house? Can't you say it there?"

Townsend shook his head gloomily. "I can't enter your doors again!"

"Oh, Mr. Townsend!" murmured Catherine. She trembled as she wondered what had happened, whether her father had forbidden it.

"I can't in self-respect," said the young man. "Your father has insulted me."

"Insulted you!"

"He has taunted me with my poverty."

"Oh, you are mistaken—you misunderstood him!" Catherine spoke with energy, getting up from her chair.

"Perhaps I am too proud—too sensitive. But would you have me otherwise?" he asked tenderly.

"Where my father is concerned, you must not be sure. He is full of goodness," said Catherine.

"He laughed at me for having no position! I took it quietly; but only because he belongs to you."

"I don't know," said Catherine; "I don't know what he thinks. I am sure he means to be kind. You must not be too proud."

"I will be proud only of you," Morris answered. "Will you meet me in the Square in the afternoon?"

A great blush on Catherine's part had been the answer to the declaration I have just quoted. She turned away, heedless of his question.

"Will you meet me?" he repeated. "It is very quiet there; no one need see us—toward dusk?"

"It is you who are unkind, it is you who laugh, when you say such things as that."

"My dear girl!" the young man murmured.

"You know how little there is in me to be proud of. I am ugly and stupid."

Morris greeted this remark with an ardent murmur, in which she recognised nothing articulate but an assurance that she was his own dearest.

But she went on. "I am not even—I am not even—" And she paused a moment.

"You are not what?"

"I am not even brave."

"Ah, then, if you are afraid, what shall we do?"

She hesitated a while; then at last—"You must come to the house," she said; "I am not afraid of that."

"I would rather it were in the Square," the young man urged. "You know how empty it is, often. No one will see us."

"I don't care who sees us! But leave me now."

He left her resignedly; he had got what he wanted. Fortunately he was ignorant that half an hour later, going home with her father and feeling him near, the poor girl, in spite of her sudden declaration of courage, began to tremble again. Her father said nothing; but she had an idea his eyes were fixed upon her in the darkness. Mrs. Penniman also was silent; Morris Townsend had told her that her niece preferred, unromantically, an interview in a chintz-covered parlour to a sentimental tryst beside a fountain sheeted with dead leaves, and she was lost in wonderment at the oddity—almost the perversity—of the choice.

X

CATHERINE received the young man the next day on the ground she had chosen—amid the chaste upholstery of a New York drawing-room furnished in the fashion of fifty years ago. Morris had swallowed his pride and made the effort necessary to cross the threshold of her too derisive parent—an act of magnanimity which could not fail to render him doubly interesting.

"We must settle something—we must take a line," he declared, passing his hand through his hair and giving a glance at the long narrow mirror which adorned the space between the two windows, and which had at its base a little gilded bracket covered by a thin slab of white marble, supporting in its turn a backgammon board folded together in the shape of two volumes, two shining folios inscribed in letters of greenish gilt, *History of England*. If Morris had been pleased to describe the master of the house as a heartless scoffer, it is because he thought him too much on his guard, and this was the easiest way to express his own dissatisfaction—a dissatisfaction which he had made a point of concealing from the Doctor. It will probably seem to the reader, however, that the Doctor's vigilance was by no means excessive, and that these two young people had an open field. Their intimacy was now considerable, and it may appear that for a shrinking and retiring person our heroine had been liberal of her favours. The young man, within a few days, had made her listen to things for which she had not supposed that she was prepared; having a lively foreboding of difficulties, he proceeded to gain as much ground as possible in the present. He remembered that fortune favours the brave, and even if he had forgotten it, Mrs. Penniman would have remembered it for him. Mrs. Penniman delighted of all things in a drama, and she flattered herself that a drama would now be enacted. Combining as she did the zeal of the prompter with the impatience of the spectator, she had long since done her utmost to pull up the curtain. She too expected to figure in the performance—to be the confidante, the Chorus, to speak the epilogue. It may even be said that there were times when she lost sight altogether of the modest heroine of the play, in the contemplation of certain great passages which would naturally occur between the hero and herself.

What Morris had told Catherine at last was simply that he loved her, or rather adored her. Virtually, he had made known as much already—his visits had been a series of eloquent intimations of it. But now he had affirmed it in lover's vows, and, as a memorable sign of it, he had passed his arm round the girl's waist and taken a kiss. This happy certitude had come sooner than Catherine expected, and she had regarded it, very naturally, as a priceless treasure. It may even be doubted whether she had ever definitely expected to possess it; she had not been waiting for it, and she had never said to herself that at a given moment it must come. As I have tried to explain, she was not eager and exacting; she took what was given her from day to day; and if the delightful custom of her lover's visits, which yielded her a happiness in which confidence and timidity were strangely blended, had suddenly come to an end, she would not only not have spoken of herself as one of the forsaken, but she would not have thought of herself as one of the disappointed. After Morris had kissed her, the last time he was with her, as a ripe assurance of his devotion, she begged him to go away, to leave her alone, to let her think. Morris went away, taking another kiss first. But Catherine's meditations had lacked a certain coherence. She felt his kisses on her lips and on her cheeks for a long time afterwards; the sensation was rather an obstacle than an aid to reflexion. She would have liked to see her situation all clearly before her, to make up her mind what she should do if, as she feared, her father should tell her that he disapproved of Morris Townsend. But all that she could see with any vividness was that it was terribly strange that anyone should disapprove of him; that there must in that case be some mistake, some mystery, which in a little while would be set at rest. She put off deciding and choosing; before the vision of a conflict with her father she dropped her eyes and sat motionless, holding her breath and waiting. It made her heart beat, it was intensely painful. When Morris kissed her and said these things—that also made her heart beat; but this was worse, and it frightened her. Nevertheless, to-day, when the young man spoke of settling something, taking a line, she felt that it was the truth, and she answered very simply and without hesitating.

"We must do our duty," she said; "we must speak to my father. I will do it to-night; you must do it to-morrow."

"It is very good of you to do it first," Morris answered. "The young man—the happy lover—generally does that. But just as you please!"

It pleased Catherine to think that she should be brave for his sake, and in her satisfaction she even gave a little smile. "Women have more tact," she said "they ought to do it first. They are more conciliating; they can persuade better."

"You will need all your powers of persuasion. But, after all," Morris added, "you are irresistible."

"Please don't speak that way—and promise me this. To-morrow, when you talk with father, you will be very gentle and respectful."

"As much so as possible," Morris promised. "It won't be much use, but I shall try. I certainly would rather have you easily than have to fight for you."

"Don't talk about fighting; we shall not fight."

"Ah, we must be prepared," Morris rejoined; "you especially, because for you it must come hardest. Do you know the first thing your father will say to you?"

"No, Morris; please tell me."

"He will tell you I am mercenary."

"Mercenary?"

"It's a big word; but it means a low thing. It means that I am after your money."

"Oh!" murmured Catherine softly.

The exclamation was so deprecating and touching that Morris indulged in another little demonstration of affection. "But he will be sure to say it," he added.

"It will be easy to be prepared for that," Catherine said. "I shall simply say that he is mistaken—that other men may be that way, but that you are not."

"You must make a great point of that, for it will be his own great point."

Catherine looked at her lover a minute, and then she said, "I shall persuade him. But I am glad we shall be rich," she added.

Morris turned away, looking into the crown of his hat. "No, it's a misfortune," he said at last. "It is from that our difficulty will come."

"Well, if it is the worst misfortune, we are not so unhappy. Many people would not think it so bad. I will persuade him, and after that we shall be very glad we have money."

Morris Townsend listened to this robust logic in silence. "I will leave my defence to you; it's a charge that a man has to stoop to defend himself from."

Catherine on her side was silent for a while; she was looking at him while he looked, with a good deal of fixedness, out of the window. "Morris," she said abruptly, "are you very sure you love me?"

He turned round, and in a moment he was bending over her. "My own dearest, can you doubt it?"

"I have only known it five days," she said; "but now it seems to me as if I could never do without it."

"You will never be called upon to try!" And he gave a little tender, reassuring laugh. Then, in a moment, he added, "There is something you must tell me, too." She had closed her eyes after the last word she uttered, and kept them closed; and at this she nodded her head, without opening them. "You must tell me," he went on, "that if your father is dead against me, if he absolutely forbids our marriage, you will still be faithful."

Catherine opened her eyes, gazing at him, and she could give no better promise than what he read there.

"You will cleave to me?" said Morris. "You know you are your own mistress—you are of age."

"Ah, Morris!" she murmured, for all answer. Or rather not for all; for she put her hand into his own. He kept it a while, and presently he kissed her again. This is all that need be recorded of their conversation; but Mrs. Penniman, if she had been present, would probably have admitted that it was as well it had not taken place beside the fountain in Washington Square.

XI

CATHERINE listened for her father when he came in that evening, and she heard him go to his study. She sat quiet, though her heart was beating fast, for nearly half an hour; then she went and knocked at his door—a ceremony without which she never crossed the threshold of this apartment. On entering it now she found him in his chair beside the fire, entertaining himself with a cigar and the evening paper.

"I have something to say to you," she began very gently; and she sat down in the first place that offered.

"I shall be very happy to hear it, my dear," said her father. He waited—waited, looking at her, while she stared, in a long silence, at the fire. He was curious and impatient, for he was sure she was going to speak of Morris Townsend; but he let her take her own time, for he was determined to be very mild.

"I am engaged to be married!" Catherine announced at last, still staring at the fire.

The Doctor was startled; the accomplished fact was more than he had expected. But he betrayed no surprise. "You do right to tell me," he simply said. "And who is the happy mortal whom you have honoured with your choice?"

"Mr. Morris Townsend." And as she pronounced her lover's name, Catherine looked at him. What she saw was her father's still grey eye and his clear-cut, definite smile. She contemplated these objects for a moment, and then she looked back at the fire; it was much warmer.

"When was this arrangement made?" the Doctor asked.

"This afternoon—two hours ago."

"Was Mr. Townsend here?"

"Yes, father; in the front parlour." She was very glad that she was not obliged to tell him that the ceremony of their betrothal had taken place out there under the bare ailantus-trees.

"Is it serious?" said the Doctor.

"Very serious, father."

Her father was silent a moment. "Mr. Townsend ought to have told me."

"He means to tell you to-morrow."

"After I know all about it from you? He ought to have told me before. Does he think I didn't care—because I left you so much liberty?"

"Oh no," said Catherine; "he knew you would care. And we have been so much obliged to you for—for the liberty."

The Doctor gave a short laugh. "You might have made a better use of it, Catherine."

"Please don't say that, father," the girl urged softly, fixing her dull and gentle eyes upon him.

He puffed his cigar awhile, meditatively. "You have gone very fast," he said at last.

"Yes," Catherine answered simply; "I think we have."

Her father glanced at her an instant, removing his eyes from the fire. "I don't wonder Mr. Townsend likes you. You are so simple and so good."

"I don't know why it is—but he *does* like me. I am sure of that."

"And are you very fond of Mr. Townsend?"

"I like him very much, of course—or I shouldn't consent to marry him."

"But you have known him a very short time, my dear."

"Oh," said Catherine, with some eagerness, "it doesn't take long to like a person—when once you begin."

"You must have begun very quickly. Was it the first time you saw him—that night at your aunt's party?"

"I don't know, father," the girl answered. "I can't tell you about that."

"Of course; that's your own affair. You will have observed that I have acted on that principle. I have not interfered, I have left you your liberty, I have remembered that you are no longer a little girl—that you have arrived at years of discretion."

"I feel very old—and very wise," said Catherine, smiling faintly.

"I am afraid that before long you will feel older and wiser yet. I don't like your engagement."

"Ah!" Catherine exclaimed softly, getting up from her chair.

"No, my dear. I am sorry to give you pain; but I don't like it. You should have consulted me before you settled it. I have been too easy with you, and I feel as if you had taken advantage of my indulgence. Most decidedly, you should have spoken to me first."

Catherine hesitated a moment, and then—"It was because I was afraid you wouldn't like it!" she confessed.

"Ah, there it is! You had a bad conscience."

"No, I have not a bad conscience, father!" the girl cried out, with considerable energy. "Please don't accuse me of anything so dreadful." These words, in fact, represented to her imagination something very terrible indeed, something base and cruel, which she associated with malefactors and prisoners. "It was because I was afraid—afraid—" she went on.

"If you were afraid, it was because you had been foolish!"

"I was afraid you didn't like Mr. Townsend."

"You were quite right. I don't like him."

"Dear father, you don't know him," said Catherine, in a voice so timidly argumentative that it might have touched him.

"Very true; I don't know him intimately. But I know him enough. I have my impression of him. You don't know him either."

She stood before the fire, with her hands lightly clasped in front of her; and her father, leaning back in his chair and looking up at her, made this remark with a placidity that might have been irritating.

I doubt, however, whether Catherine was irritated, though she broke into a vehement protest. "I don't know him?" she cried. "Why, I know him—better than I have ever known any one!"

"You know a part of him—what he has chosen to show you. But you don't know the rest."

"The rest? What is the rest?"

"Whatever it may be. There is sure to be plenty of it."

"I know what you mean," said Catherine, remembering how Morris had forewarned her. "You mean that he is mercenary."

Her father looked up at her still, with his cold, quiet reasonable eye. "If I meant it, my dear, I should say it! But there is an error I wish particularly to avoid—that of rendering Mr. Townsend more interesting to you by saying hard things about him."

"I won't think them hard if they are true," said Catherine.

"If you don't, you will be a remarkably sensible young woman!"

"They will be your reasons, at any rate, and you will want me to hear your reasons."

The Doctor smiled a little. "Very true. You have a perfect right to ask for them." And he puffed his cigar a few moments. "Very well, then, without accusing Mr. Townsend of being in love only with your fortune—and with the fortune that you justly expect—I will say that there is every reason to suppose that these good things have entered into his calculation more largely than a tender solicitude for your happiness strictly requires. There is, of course, nothing impossible in an intelligent young man entertaining a disinterested affection for you. You are an honest, amiable girl, and an intelligent young man might easily find it out. But the principal thing that we know about this young man—who is, indeed, very intelligent—leads us to suppose that, however much he may value your personal merits, he values your money more. The principal thing we know about him is that he has led a life of dissipation, and has spent a fortune of his own in doing so. That is enough for me, my dear. I wish you to marry a young man with other antecedents—a young man who could give positive guarantees. If Morris Townsend has spent his own fortune in amusing himself, there is every reason to believe that he would spend yours."

The Doctor delivered himself of these remarks slowly, deliberately, with occasional pauses and prolongations of accent, which made no great allowance for poor Catherine's suspense as to his conclusion. She sat down at last, with her head bent and her eyes still fixed upon him; and strangely enough—I hardly know how to tell it—even while she felt that what he said went so terribly against her, she admired his neatness and nobleness of expression. There was something hopeless and oppressive in having to argue with her father; but she too, on her side, must try to be clear. He was so quiet; he was not at all angry; and she too must be quiet. But her very effort to be quiet made her tremble.

"That is not the principal thing we know about him," she said; and there was a touch of her tremor in her voice. "There are other things—many other things. He has very high abilities—he wants so much to do something. He is kind, and generous, and true," said poor Catherine, who had not suspected hitherto the resources of her eloquence. "And his fortune—his fortune that he spent—was very small!"

"All the more reason he shouldn't have spent it," cried the Doctor, getting up, with a laugh. Then as Catherine, who had also risen to her feet again, stood there in her rather angular earnestness, wishing so much and expressing so little, he drew her towards him and kissed her. "You won't think me cruel?" he said, holding her a moment.

This question was not reassuring; it seemed to Catherine, on the contrary, to suggest possibilities which made her feel sick. But she answered coherently enough—"No, dear father; because if you knew how I feel—and you must know, you know everything—you would be so kind, so gentle."

"Yes, I think I know how you feel," the Doctor said. "I will be very kind—be sure of that. And I will see Mr. Townsend to-morrow. Meanwhile, and for the present, be so good as to mention to no one that you are engaged."

XII

On the morrow, in the afternoon, he stayed at home, awaiting Mr. Townsend's call—a proceeding by which it appeared to him (justly perhaps, for he was a very busy man) that he paid Catherine's suitor great honour, and gave both these young people so much the less to complain of. Morris presented himself with a countenance sufficiently serene—he appeared to have forgotten the "insult" for which he had solicited Catherine's sympathy two evenings before, and Dr. Sloper lost no time in letting him know that he had been prepared for his visit.

"Catherine told me yesterday what has been going on between you," he said. "You must allow me to say that it would have been becoming of you to give me notice of your intentions before they had gone so far."

"I should have done so," Morris answered, "if you had not had so much the appearance of leaving your daughter at liberty. She seems to me quite her own mistress."

"Literally, she is. But she has not emancipated herself morally quite so far, I trust, as to choose a husband without consulting me. I have left her at liberty, but I have not been in the least indifferent. The truth is that your little affair has come to a head with a rapidity that surprises me. It was only the other day that Catherine made your acquaintance."

"It was not long ago, certainly," said Morris, with great gravity. "I admit that we have not been slow to—to arrive at an understanding. But that was very natural, from the moment we were sure of ourselves—and of each other. My interest in Miss Sloper began the first time I saw her."

"Did it not by chance precede your first meeting?" the Doctor asked.

Morris looked at him an instant. "I certainly had already heard that she was a charming girl."

"A charming girl—that's what you think her?"

"Assuredly. Otherwise I should not be sitting here."

The Doctor meditated a moment. "My dear young man," he said at last, "you must be very susceptible. As Catherine's father, I have, I trust, a just and tender appreciation of her many good qualities; but I don't mind telling you that I have never thought of her as a charming girl, and never expected any one else to do so."

Morris Townsend received this statement with a smile that was not wholly devoid of deference. "I don't know what I might think of her if I were her father. I can't put myself in that place. I speak from my own point of view."

"You speak very well," said the Doctor; "but that is not all that is necessary. I told Catherine yesterday that I disapproved of her engagement."

"She let me know as much, and I was very sorry to hear it. I am greatly disappointed." And Morris sat in silence awhile, looking at the floor.

"Did you really expect I would say I was delighted, and throw my daughter into your arms?"

"Oh no; I had an idea you didn't like me."

"What gave you the idea?"

"The fact that I am poor."

"That has a harsh sound," said the Doctor, "but it is about the truth—speaking of you strictly as a son-in-law. Your absence of means, of a profession, of visible resources or prospects, places you in a category from which it would be imprudent for me to select a husband for my daughter, who is a weak young woman with a large fortune. In any other capacity I am perfectly prepared to like you. As a son-in-law, I abominate you!"

Morris Townsend listened respectfully. "I don't think Miss Sloper is a weak woman," he presently said.

"Of course you must defend her—it's the least you can do. But I have known my child twenty years, and you have known her six weeks. Even if she were not weak, however, you would still be a penniless man."

"Ah, yes; that is *my* weakness! And therefore, you mean, I am mercenary—I only want your daughter's money."

"I don't say that. I am not obliged to say it; and to say it, save under stress of compulsion, would be very bad taste. I say simply that you belong to the wrong category."

"But your daughter doesn't marry a category," Townsend urged, with his handsome smile. "She marries an individual—an individual whom she is so good as to say she loves."

"An individual who offers so little in return!"

"Is it possible to offer more than the most tender affection and a lifelong devotion?" the young man demanded.

"It depends how we take it. It is possible to offer a few other things besides; and not only is it possible, but it's usual. A lifelong devotion is measured after the fact; and meanwhile it is customary in these cases to give a few material securities. What are yours? A very handsome face and figure, and a very good manner. They are excellent as far as they go, but they don't go far enough."

"There is one thing you should add to them," said Morris; "the word of a gentleman!"

"The word of a gentleman that you will always love Catherine? You must be a very fine gentleman to be sure of that."

"The word of a gentleman that I am not mercenary; that my affection for Miss Sloper is as pure and disinterested a sentiment as was ever lodged in a human breast! I care no more for her fortune than for the ashes in that grate."

"I take note—I take note," said the Doctor. "But having done so, I turn to our category again. Even with that solemn vow on your lips, you take your place in it. There is nothing against you but an accident, if you will; but with my thirty years' medical practice, I have seen that accidents may have far-reaching consequences."

Morris smoothed his hat—it was already remarkably glossy—and continued to display a self-control which, as the Doctor was obliged to admit, was extremely creditable to him. But his disappointment was evidently keen.

"Is there nothing I can do to make you believe in me?"

"If there were I should be sorry to suggest it, for—don't you see?—I don't want to believe in you!" said the Doctor, smiling.

"I would go and dig in the fields."

"That would be foolish."

"I will take the first work that offers, to-morrow."

"Do so by all means—but for your own sake, not for mine."

"I see; you think I am an idler!" Morris exclaimed, a little too much in the tone of a man who has made a discovery. But he saw his error immediately, and blushed.

"It doesn't matter what I think, when once I have told you I don't think of you as a son-in-law."

But Morris persisted. "You think I would squander her money."

The Doctor smiled. "It doesn't matter, as I say; but I plead guilty to that."

"That's because I spent my own, I suppose," said Morris. "I frankly confess that. I have been wild. I have been foolish. I will tell you every crazy thing I ever did, if you like. There were some great follies among the number—I have never concealed that. But I have sown my wild oats. Isn't there some proverb about a reformed rake? I was not a rake, but I assure you I have reformed. It is better to have amused oneself for a while and have done with it. Your daughter would never care for a milksop; and I will take the liberty of saying that you would like one quite as little. Besides, between my money and hers there is a great difference. I spent my own; it was because it was my own that I spent it. And I made no debts; when it was gone I stopped. I don't owe a penny in the world."

"Allow me to inquire what you are living on now—though I admit," the Doctor added, "that the question, on my part, is inconsistent."

"I am living on the remnants of my property," said Morris Townsend.

"Thank you!" the Doctor gravely replied.

Yes, certainly, Morris's self-control was laudable. "Even admitting I attach an undue importance to Miss Sloper's fortune," he went on, "would not that be in itself an assurance that I should take much care of it?"

"That you should take too much care would be quite as bad as that you should take too little. Catherine might suffer as much by your economy as by your extravagance."

"I think you are very unjust!" The young man made this declaration decently, civilly, without violence.

"It is your privilege to think so, and I surrender my reputation to you! I certainly don't flatter myself I gratify you."

"Don't you care a little to gratify your daughter? Do you enjoy the idea of making her miserable?"

"I am perfectly resigned to her thinking me a tyrant for a twelvemonth."

"For a twelvemonth!" exclaimed Morris, with a laugh.

"For a lifetime, then! She may as well be miserable in that way as in the other."

Here at last Morris lost his temper. "Ah, you are not polite, sir!" he cried.

"You push me to it—you argue too much."

"I have a great deal at stake."

"Well, whatever it is," said the Doctor, "you have lost it!"

"Are you sure of that?" asked Morris; "are you sure your daughter will give me up?"

"I mean, of course, you have lost it as far as I am concerned. As for Catherine's giving you up—no, I am not sure of it. But as I shall strongly recommend it, as I have a great fund of respect and affection in my daughter's mind to draw upon, and as she has the sentiment of duty developed in a very high degree, I think it extremely possible."

Morris Townsend began to smooth his hat again. "I too have a fund of affection to draw upon!" he observed at last.

The Doctor at this point showed his own first symptoms of irritation. "Do you mean to defy me?"

"Call it what you please, sir! I mean not to give your daughter up."

The Doctor shook his head. "I haven't the least fear of your pining away your life. You are made to enjoy it."

Morris gave a laugh. "Your opposition to my marriage is all the more cruel, then! Do you intend to forbid your daughter to see me again?"

"She is past the age at which people are forbidden, and I am not a father in an old-fashioned novel. But I shall strongly urge her to break with you."

"I don't think she will," said Morris Townsend.

"Perhaps not. But I shall have done what I could."

"She has gone too far," Morris went on.

"To retreat? Then let her stop where she is."

"Too far to stop, I mean."

The Doctor looked at him a moment; Morris had his hand on the door. "There is a great deal of impertinence in your saying it."

"I will say no more, sir!" Morris answered; and, making his bow, he left the room.

XIII

It may be thought the Doctor was too positive, and Mrs. Almond intimated as much. But, as he said, he had his impression; it seemed to him sufficient, and he had no wish to modify it. He had passed his life in estimating people (it was part of the medical trade), and in nineteen cases out of twenty he was right.

"Perhaps Mr. Townsend is the twentieth case," Mrs. Almond suggested.

"Perhaps he is, though he doesn't look to me at all like a twentieth case. But I will give him the benefit of the doubt, and, to make sure, I will go and talk with Mrs. Montgomery. She will almost certainly tell me I have done right; but it is just possible that she will prove to me that I have made the greatest mistake of my life. If she does, I will beg Mr. Townsend's pardon. You needn't invite her to meet me, as you kindly proposed; I will write her a frank letter, telling her how matters stand, and asking leave to come and see her."

"I am afraid the frankness will be chiefly on your side. The poor little woman will stand up for her brother, whatever he may be."

"Whatever he may be? I doubt that. People are not always so fond of their brothers."

"Ah," said Mrs. Almond, "when it's a question of thirty thousand a year coming into a family—"

"If she stands up for him on account of the money, she will be a humbug. If she is a humbug I shall see it. If I see it, I won't waste time with her."

"She is not a humbug—she is an exemplary woman. She will not wish to play her brother a trick simply because he is selfish."

"If she is worth talking to, she will sooner play him a trick than that he should play Catherine one. Has she seen Catherine, by the way—does she know her?"

"Not to my knowledge. Mr. Townsend can have had no particular interest in bringing them together."

"If she is an exemplary woman, no. But we shall see to what extent she answers your description."

"I shall be curious to hear her description of you!" said Mrs. Almond, with a laugh. "And, meanwhile, how is Catherine taking it?"

"As she takes everything—as a matter of course."

"Doesn't she make a noise? Hasn't she made a scene?"

"She is not scenic."

"I thought a love-lorn maiden was always scenic."

"A fantastic widow is more so. Lavinia has made me a speech; she thinks me very arbitrary."

"She has a talent for being in the wrong," said Mrs. Almond. "But I am very sorry for Catherine, all the same."

"So am I. But she will get over it."

"You believe she will give him up?"

"I count upon it. She has such an admiration for her father."

"Oh, we know all about that! But it only makes me pity her the more. It makes her dilemma the more painful, and the effort of choosing between you and her lover almost impossible."

"If she can't choose, all the better."

"Yes, but he will stand there entreating her to choose, and Lavinia will pull on that side."

"I am glad she is not on my side; she is capable of ruining an excellent cause. The day Lavinia gets into your boat it capsizes. But she had better be careful," said the Doctor. "I will have no treason in my house!"

"I suspect she will be careful; for she is at bottom very much afraid of you."

"They are both afraid of me—harmless as I am!" the Doctor answered. "And it is on that that I build—on the salutary terror I inspire!"

XIV

HE wrote his frank letter to Mrs. Montgomery, who punctually answered it, mentioning an hour at which he might present himself in the Second Avenue. She lived in a neat little house of red brick, which had been freshly painted, with the edges of the bricks very sharply marked out in white. It has now disappeared, with its companions, to make room for a row of structures more majestic. There were green shutters upon the windows, without slats, but pierced with little holes, arranged in groups; and before the house was a diminutive yard, ornamented with a bush of mysterious character, and surrounded by a low wooden paling, painted in the same green as the shutters. The place looked like a magnified baby-house, and might have been taken down from a shelf in a toy-shop. Dr. Sloper, when he went to call, said to himself, as he glanced at the objects I have enumerated, that Mrs. Montgomery was evidently a thrifty and self-respecting little person— the modest proportions of her dwelling seemed to indicate that she was of small stature—who took a virtuous satisfaction in keeping herself tidy, and had resolved that, since she might not be splendid, she would at least be immaculate. She received him in a little parlour, which was precisely the parlour he had expected: a small unspeckled bower, ornamented with a desultory foliage of tissue-paper, and with clusters of glass drops, amid which—to carry out the analogy—the temperature of the leafy season was maintained by means of a cast-iron stove, emitting a dry blue flame, and smelling strongly of varnish. The walls were embellished with engravings swathed in pink gauze, and the tables ornamented with volumes of extracts from the poets, usually bound in black cloth stamped with florid designs in jaundiced gilt. The Doctor had time to take cognisance of these details, for Mrs. Montgomery, whose conduct he pronounced under the circumstances inexcusable, kept him waiting some ten minutes before she appeared. At last, however, she rustled in, smoothing down a stiff poplin dress, with a little frightened flush in a gracefully-rounded cheek.

She was a small, plump, fair woman, with a bright, clear eye, and an extraordinary air of neatness and briskness. But these qualities were evidently combined with an unaffected humility, and the Doctor gave her his esteem as soon as he had looked at her. A brave little person, with lively perceptions, and yet a disbelief in her own talent for social, as distinguished from practical, affairs—this was his rapid mental *résumé* of Mrs. Montgomery, who, as he saw, was flattered by what she regarded as the honour of his visit. Mrs. Montgomery, in her little red house in the Second Avenue, was a person for whom Dr. Sloper was one of the great men, one of the fine gentlemen of New York; and while she fixed her agitated eyes upon him, while she clasped her mittened hands together in her glossy poplin lap, she had the appearance of saying to herself that he quite answered her idea of what a distinguished guest would naturally be. She apologised for being late; but he interrupted her.

"It doesn't matter," he said; "for while I sat here I had time to think over what I wish to say to you, and to make up my mind how to begin."

"Oh, do begin!" murmured Mrs. Montgomery.

"It is not so easy," said the Doctor, smiling. "You will have gathered from my letter that I wish to ask you a few questions, and you may not find it very comfortable to answer them."

"Yes; I have thought what I should say. It is not very easy."

"But you must understand my situation—my state of mind. Your brother wishes to marry my daughter, and I wish to find out what sort of a young man he is. A good way to do so seemed to be to come and ask you; which I have proceeded to do."

Mrs. Montgomery evidently took the situation very seriously; she was in a state of extreme moral concentration. She kept her pretty eyes, which were illumined by a sort of brilliant modesty, attached to his own countenance, and evidently paid the most earnest attention to each of his words. Her expression indicated that she thought his idea of coming to see her a very superior conception, but that she was really afraid to have opinions on strange subjects.

231

"I am extremely glad to see you," she said, in a tone which seemed to admit, at the same time, that this had nothing to do with the question.

The Doctor took advantage of this admission. "I didn't come to see you for your pleasure; I came to make you say disagreeable things—and you can't like that. What sort of a gentleman is your brother?"

Mrs. Montgomery's illuminated gaze grew vague, and began to wander. She smiled a little, and for some time made no answer, so that the Doctor at last became impatient. And her answer, when it came, was not satisfactory. "It is difficult to talk about one's brother."

"Not when one is fond of him, and when one has plenty of good to say."

"Yes, even then, when a good deal depends on it," said Mrs. Montgomery.

"Nothing depends on it, for you."

"I mean for—for—" and she hesitated.

"For your brother himself. I see!"

"I mean for Miss Sloper," said Mrs. Montgomery. The Doctor liked this; it had the accent of sincerity. "Exactly; that's the point. If my poor girl should marry your brother, everything—as regards her happiness—would depend on his being a good fellow. She is the best creature in the world, and she could never do him a grain of injury. He, on the other hand, if he should not be all that we desire, might make her very miserable. That is why I want you to throw some light upon his character, you know. Of course you are not bound to do it. My daughter, whom you have never seen, is nothing to you; and I, possibly, am only an indiscreet and impertinent old man. It is perfectly open to you to tell me that my visit is in very bad taste and that I had better go about my business. But I don't think you will do this; because I think we shall interest you, my poor girl and I. I am sure that if you were to see Catherine, she would interest you very much. I don't mean because she is interesting in the usual sense of the word, but because you would feel sorry for her. She is so soft, so simple-minded, she would be such an easy victim! A bad husband would have remarkable facilities for making her miserable; for she would have neither the intelligence nor the resolution to get the better of him, and yet she would have an exaggerated power of suffering. I see," added the Doctor, with his most insinuating, his most professional laugh, "you are already interested!"

"I have been interested from the moment he told me he was engaged," said Mrs. Montgomery.

"Ah! he says that—he calls it an engagement?"

"Oh, he has told me you didn't like it."

"Did he tell you that I don't like *him?*"

"Yes, he told me that too. I said I couldn't help it!" added Mrs. Montgomery.

"Of course you can't. But what you can do is to tell me I am right—to give me an attestation, as it were." And the Doctor accompanied this remark with another professional smile.

Mrs. Montgomery, however, smiled not at all; it was obvious that she could not take the humorous view of his appeal. "That is a good deal to ask," she said at last.

"There can be no doubt of that; and I must, in conscience, remind you of the advantages a young man marrying my daughter would enjoy. She has an income of ten thousand dollars in her own right, left her by her mother; if she marries a husband I approve, she will come into almost twice as much more at my death."

Mrs. Montgomery listened in great earnestness to this splendid financial statement; she had never heard thousands of dollars so familiarly talked about. She flushed a little with excitement. "Your daughter will be immensely rich," she said softly.

"Precisely—that's the bother of it."

"And if Morris should marry her, he—he—" And she hesitated timidly.

"He would be master of all that money? By no means. He would be master of the ten thousand a year that she has from her mother; but I should leave every penny of my own fortune, earned in the laborious exercise of my profession, to public institutions."

Mrs. Montgomery dropped her eyes at this, and sat for some time gazing at the straw matting which covered her floor.

"I suppose it seems to you," said the Doctor, laughing, "that in so doing I should play your brother a very shabby trick."

"Not at all. That is too much money to get possession of so easily, by marrying. I don't think it would be right."

"It's right to get all one can. But in this case your brother wouldn't be able. If Catherine marries without my consent, she doesn't get a penny from my own pocket."

"Is that certain?" asked Mrs. Montgomery, looking up.

"As certain as that I sit here!"

"Even if she should pine away?"

"Even if she should pine to a shadow, which isn't probable."

"Does Morris know this?"

"I shall be most happy to inform him!" the Doctor exclaimed.

Mrs. Montgomery resumed her meditations, and her visitor, who was prepared to give time to the affair, asked himself whether, in spite of her little conscientious air, she was not playing into her brother's hands. At the same time he was half ashamed of the ordeal to which he had subjected her, and was touched by the gentleness with which she bore it. "If she were a humbug," he said, "she would get angry; unless she be very deep indeed. It is not probable that she is as deep as that."

"What makes you dislike Morris so much?" she presently asked, emerging from her reflexions.

"I don't dislike him in the least as a friend, as a companion. He seems to me a charming fellow, and I should think he would be excellent company. I dislike him, exclusively, as a son-in-law. If the only office of a son-in-law were to dine at the paternal table, I should set a high value upon your brother. He dines capitally. But that is a small part of his function, which, in general, is to be a protector and caretaker of my child, who is singularly ill-adapted to take care of herself. It is there that he doesn't satisfy me. I confess I have nothing but my impression to go by; but I am in the habit of trusting my impression. Of course you are at liberty to contradict it flat. He strikes me as selfish and shallow."

Mrs. Montgomery's eyes expanded a little, and the Doctor fancied he saw the light of admiration in them. "I wonder you have discovered he is selfish!" she exclaimed.

"Do you think he hides it so well?"

"Very well indeed," said Mrs. Montgomery. "And I think we are all rather selfish," she added quickly.

"I think so too; but I have seen people hide it better than he. You see I am helped by a habit I have of dividing people into classes, into types. I may easily be mistaken about your brother as an individual, but his type is written on his whole person."

"He is very good-looking," said Mrs. Montgomery.

The Doctor eyed her a moment. "You women are all the same! But the type to which your brother belongs was made to be the ruin of you, and you were made to be its handmaids and victims. The sign of the type in question is the determination—sometimes terrible in its quiet intensity—to accept nothing of life but its pleasures, and to secure these pleasures chiefly by the aid of your complaisant sex. Young men of this class never do anything for themselves that they can get other people to do for them, and it is the infatuation, the devotion, the superstition of others that keeps them going. These others in ninety-nine cases out of a hundred are women. What our young friends chiefly insist upon is that some one else shall suffer for them; and women do that sort of thing, as you must know, wonderfully well." The

Doctor paused a moment, and then he added abruptly, "You have suffered immensely for your brother!"

This exclamation was abrupt, as I say, but it was also perfectly calculated. The Doctor had been rather disappointed at not finding his compact and comfortable little hostess surrounded in a more visible degree by the ravages of Morris Townsend's immorality; but he had said to himself that this was not because the young man had spared her, but because she had contrived to plaster up her wounds. They were aching there, behind the varnished stove, the festooned engravings, beneath her own neat little poplin bosom; and if he could only touch the tender spot, she would make a movement that would betray her. The words I have just quoted were an attempt to put his finger suddenly upon the place; and they had some of the success that he looked for. The tears sprang for a moment to Mrs. Montgomery's eyes, and she indulged in a proud little jerk of the head.

"I don't know how you have found that out!" she exclaimed.

"By a philosophic trick—by what they call induction. You know you have always your option of contradicting me. But kindly answer me a question. Don't you give your brother money? I think you ought to answer that."

"Yes, I have given him money," said Mrs. Montgomery.

"And you have not had much to give him?"

She was silent a moment. "If you ask me for a confession of poverty, that is easily made. I am very poor."

"One would never suppose it from your—your charming house," said the Doctor. "I learned from my sister that your income was moderate, and your family numerous."

"I have five children," Mrs. Montgomery observed; "but I am happy to say I can bring them up decently."

"Of course you can—accomplished and devoted as you are! But your brother has counted them over, I suppose?"

"Counted them over?"

"He knows there are five, I mean. He tells me it is he that brings them up."

Mrs. Montgomery stared a moment, and then quickly—"Oh yes; he teaches them Spanish."

The Doctor laughed out. "That must take a great deal off your hands! Your brother also knows, of course, that you have very little money."

"I have often told him so!" Mrs. Montgomery exclaimed, more unreservedly than she had yet spoken. She was apparently taking some comfort in the Doctor's clairvoyancy.

"Which means that you have often occasion to, and that he often sponges on you. Excuse the crudity of my language; I simply express a fact. I don't ask you how much of your money he has had, it is none of my business. I have ascertained what I suspected—what I wished." And the Doctor got up, gently smoothing his hat. "Your brother lives on you," he said as he stood there.

Mrs. Montgomery quickly rose from her chair, following her visitor's movements with a look of fascination. But then, with a certain inconsequence—"I have never complained of him!" she said.

"You needn't protest—you have not betrayed him. But I advise you not to give him any more money."

"Don't you see it is in my interest that he should marry a rich person?" she asked. "If, as you say, he lives on me, I can only wish to get rid of him, and to put obstacles in the way of his marrying is to increase my own difficulties."

"I wish very much you would come to me with your difficulties," said the Doctor. "Certainly, if I throw him back on your hands, the least I can do is to help you to bear the burden. If you will allow me to say so, then, I shall take the liberty of placing in your hands, for the present, a certain fund for your brother's support."

Mrs. Montgomery stared; she evidently thought he was jesting; but she presently saw that he was not, and the complication of her feelings became painful. "It seems to me that I ought to be very much offended with you," she murmured.

"Because I have offered you money? That's a superstition," said the Doctor. "You must let me come and see you again, and we will talk about these things. I suppose that some of your children are girls."

"I have two little girls," said Mrs. Montgomery.

"Well, when they grow up, and begin to think of taking husbands, you will see how anxious you will be about the moral character of these gentlemen. Then you will understand this visit of mine!"

"Ah, you are not to believe that Morris's moral character is bad!"

The Doctor looked at her a little, with folded arms. "There is something I should greatly like—as a moral satisfaction. I should like to hear you say— 'He is abominably selfish!'"

The words came out with the grave distinctness of his voice, and they seemed for an instant to create, to poor Mrs. Montgomery's troubled vision, a material image. She gazed at it an instant, and then she turned away. "You distress me, sir!" she exclaimed. "He is, after all, my brother, and his talents, his talents—" On these last words her voice quavered, and before he knew it she had burst into tears.

"His talents are first-rate!" said the Doctor. "We must find a proper field for them!" And he assured her most respectfully of his regret at having so greatly discomposed her. "It's all for my poor Catherine," he went on. "You must know her, and you will see."

Mrs. Montgomery brushed away her tears, and blushed at having shed them. "I should like to know your daughter," she answered; and then, in an instant—"Don't let her marry him!"

Dr. Sloper went away with the words gently humming in his ears— "Don't let her marry him!" They gave him the moral satisfaction of which he had just spoken, and their value was the greater that they had evidently cost a pang to poor little Mrs. Montgomery's family pride.

XV

HE had been puzzled by the way that Catherine carried herself; her attitude at this sentimental crisis seemed to him unnaturally passive. She had not spoken to him again after that scene in the library, the day before his interview with Morris; and a week had elapsed without making any change in her manner. There was nothing in it that appealed for pity, and he was even a little disappointed at her not giving him an opportunity to make up for his harshness by some manifestation of liberality which should operate as a compensation. He thought a little of offering to take her for a tour in Europe; but he was determined to do this only in case she should seem mutely to reproach him. He had an idea that she would display a talent for mute reproaches, and he was surprised at not finding himself exposed to these silent batteries. She said nothing, either tacitly or explicitly, and as she was never very talkative, there was now no especial eloquence in her reserve. And poor Catherine was not sulky—a style of behaviour for which she had too little histrionic talent; she was simply very patient. Of course she was thinking over her situation, and she was apparently doing so in a deliberate and unimpassioned manner, with a view of making the best of it.

"She will do as I have bidden her," said the Doctor, and he made the further reflexion that his daughter was not a woman of a great spirit. I know not whether he had hoped for a little more resistance for the sake of a little more entertainment; but he said to himself, as he had said before, that though it might have its momentary alarms, paternity was, after all, not an exciting vocation.

Catherine, meanwhile, had made a discovery of a very different sort; it had become vivid to her that there was a great excitement in trying to be a good daughter. She had an entirely new feeling, which may be described as a state of expectant suspense about her own actions. She watched herself as she would have watched another person, and wondered what she would do. It was as if this other person, who was both herself and not herself, had suddenly sprung into being, inspiring her with a natural curiosity as to the performance of untested functions.

"I am glad I have such a good daughter," said her father, kissing her, after the lapse of several days.

"I am trying to be good," she answered, turning away, with a conscience not altogether clear.

"If there is anything you would like to say to me, you know you must not hesitate. You needn't feel obliged to be so quiet. I shouldn't care that Mr. Townsend should be a frequent topic of conversation, but whenever you have anything particular to say about him I shall be very glad to hear it."

"Thank you," said Catherine; "I have nothing particular at present."

He never asked her whether she had seen Morris again, because he was sure that if this had been the case she would tell him. She had, in fact, not seen him, she had only written him a long letter. The letter at least was long for her; and, it may be added, that it was long for Morris; it consisted of five pages, in a remarkably neat and handsome hand. Catherine's handwriting was beautiful, and she was even a little proud of it; she was extremely fond of copying, and possessed volumes of extracts which testified to this accomplishment; volumes which she had exhibited one day to her lover, when the bliss of feeling that she was important in his eyes was exceptionally keen. She told Morris in writing that her father had expressed the wish that she should not see him again, and that she begged he would not come to the house until she should have "made up her mind." Morris replied with a passionate epistle, in which he asked to what, in Heaven's name, she wished to make up her mind. Had not her mind been made up two weeks before, and could it be possible that she entertained the idea of throwing him off? Did she mean to break down at the very beginning of their ordeal, after all the promises of fidelity she had both given and extracted? And he gave an account of his own interview with her father—an account not identical at all points with that offered in these pages. "He was terribly violent," Morris wrote; "but you know my self-control. I have need of it all when I remember that I have it in my power to break in upon your cruel captivity." Catherine sent him, in answer to this, a note of three lines. "I am in great trouble; do not doubt of my affection, but let me wait a little and think." The idea of a struggle with her father, of setting up her will against his own, was heavy on her soul, and it kept her formally submissive, as a great physical weight keeps us motionless. It never entered into her mind to throw her lover off; but from the first she tried to assure herself that there would be a peaceful way out of their difficulty. The assurance was vague, for it contained no element of positive conviction that her father would change his mind. She only had an idea that if she should be very good, the situation would in some mysterious manner improve. To be good, she must be patient, respectful, abstain from judging her father too harshly, and from committing any act of open defiance. He was perhaps right, after all, to think as he did; by which Catherine meant not in the least that his judgement of Morris's motives in seeking to marry her was perhaps a just one, but that it was probably natural and proper that conscientious parents should be suspicious and even unjust. There were probably people in the world as bad as her father supposed Morris to be, and if there were the slightest chance of Morris being one of these sinister persons, the Doctor was right in taking it into account. Of course he could not know what she knew, how the purest love and truth were seated in the young man's eyes; but Heaven, in its time, might appoint a way of bringing him to such knowledge. Catherine expected a good deal of Heaven, and referred to the skies the initiative, as the French say, in dealing with her dilemma. She could not imagine herself imparting any kind of knowledge to her father, there was something superior even in his injustice and absolute in his mistakes. But she could at least be good, and if she were only good enough, Heaven would invent some way of reconciling all things—the dignity of her father's errors and the sweetness of her own confidence, the strict performance of her filial duties and the enjoyment of Morris Townsend's affection. Poor Catherine would have been glad to regard Mrs. Penniman as an illuminating agent, a part which this lady herself indeed was but imperfectly prepared to play. Mrs. Penniman took too much satisfaction in the sentimental shadows of this little drama to have, for the moment, any great interest in dissipating them. She wished the plot to thicken, and the advice that she gave her niece tended, in her own imagination, to produce this result. It was rather incoherent counsel, and from one day to another it contradicted itself; but it was pervaded by an earnest desire that Catherine should do something striking. "You must *act*, my dear; in your situation the great thing is to act," said Mrs. Penniman, who found her niece altogether beneath her opportunities. Mrs. Penniman's real hope was that the girl would make a secret marriage, at which she should officiate as brideswoman or duenna. She had a vision of this ceremony being performed in some subterranean chapel—subterranean chapels in New York were not frequent, but Mrs. Penniman's imagination was not chilled by trifles—and of the guilty couple—she liked to think of poor Catherine and her suitor as the guilty couple—being shuffled away in a fast-whirling vehicle to some obscure lodging in the suburbs, where she would pay them (in a thick veil) clandestine visits, where they would endure a period of romantic privation, and where ultimately, after she should have been their earthly providence, their intercessor, their advocate, and their medium of communication with the world, they should be reconciled to her brother in an artistic tableau, in which she herself should be somehow the central figure. She hesitated as yet to recommend this course to Catherine, but she attempted to draw an attractive picture of it to Morris Townsend. She was in daily communication with the young man, whom she kept informed by letters of the state of affairs in Washington Square. As he had been banished, as she said, from the house, she no longer saw him; but she ended by writing to him that she longed for an interview. This interview could take place only on neutral ground, and she bethought herself greatly before selecting a place of meeting. She had an inclination for Greenwood Cemetery, but she gave it up as too distant; she could not absent herself for so long, as she said, without exciting suspicion. Then she thought of the Battery, but that was rather cold and windy, besides one's being exposed to intrusion from the Irish emigrants who at this point alight, with large appetites, in the New World and at last she fixed upon an oyster saloon in the Seventh Avenue, kept by a negro—an establishment of which she knew nothing save that she had noticed it in passing. She made an appointment with Morris Townsend to meet him there, and she went to the tryst at dusk, enveloped in an impenetrable veil. He kept her waiting for half an hour—he had almost the whole width of the city to traverse—but she liked to wait, it seemed to intensify the situation.

She ordered a cup of tea, which proved excessively bad, and this gave her a sense that she was suffering in a romantic cause. When Morris at last arrived, they sat together for half an hour in the duskiest corner of a back shop; and it is hardly too much to say that this was the happiest half-hour that Mrs. Penniman had known for years. The situation was really thrilling, and it scarcely seemed to her a false note when her companion asked for an oyster stew, and proceeded to consume it before her eyes. Morris, indeed, needed all the satisfaction that stewed oysters could give him, for it may be intimated to the reader that he regarded Mrs. Penniman in the light of a fifth wheel to his coach. He was in a state of irritation natural to a gentleman of fine parts who had been snubbed in a benevolent attempt to confer a distinction upon a young woman of inferior characteristics, and the insinuating sympathy of this somewhat desiccated matron appeared to offer him no practical relief. He thought her a humbug, and he judged of humbugs with a good deal of confidence. He had listened and made himself agreeable to her at first, in order to get a footing in Washington Square; and at present he needed all his self-command to be decently civil. It would have gratified him to tell her that she was a fantastic old woman, and that he should like to put her into an omnibus and send her home. We know, however, that Morris possessed the virtue of self-control, and he had, moreover, the constant habit of seeking to be agreeable; so that, although Mrs. Penniman's demeanour only exasperated his already unquiet nerves, he listened to her with a sombre deference in which she found much to admire.

<u>XVI</u>

THEY had of course immediately spoken of Catherine. "Did she send me a message, or—or anything?" Morris asked. He appeared to think that she might have sent him a trinket or a lock of her hair.

Mrs. Penniman was slightly embarrassed, for she had not told her niece of her intended expedition. "Not exactly a message," she said; "I didn't ask her for one, because I was afraid to—to excite her."

"I am afraid she is not very excitable!" And Morris gave a smile of some bitterness.

"She is better than that. She is steadfast—she is true!"

"Do you think she will hold fast, then?"

"To the death!"

"Oh, I hope it won't come to that," said Morris.

"We must be prepared for the worst, and that is what I wish to speak to you about."

"What do you call the worst?"

"Well," said Mrs. Penniman, "my brother's hard, intellectual nature."

"Oh, the devil!"

"He is impervious to pity," Mrs. Penniman added, by way of explanation.

"Do you mean that he won't come round?"

"He will never be vanquished by argument. I have studied him. He will be vanquished only by the accomplished fact."

"The accomplished fact?"

"He will come round afterwards," said Mrs. Penniman, with extreme significance. "He cares for nothing but facts; he must be met by facts!"

"Well," rejoined Morris, "it is a fact that I wish to marry his daughter. I met him with that the other day, but he was not at all vanquished."

Mrs. Penniman was silent a little, and her smile beneath the shadow of her capacious bonnet, on the edge of which her black veil was arranged curtain-wise, fixed itself upon Morris's face with a still more tender brilliancy. "Marry Catherine first and meet him afterwards!" she exclaimed.

"Do you recommend that?" asked the young man, frowning heavily.

She was a little frightened, but she went on with considerable boldness. "That is the way I see it: a private marriage—a private marriage." She repeated the phrase because she liked it.

"Do you mean that I should carry Catherine off? What do they call it—elope with her?"

"It is not a crime when you are driven to it," said Mrs. Penniman. "My husband, as I have told you, was a distinguished clergyman; one of the most eloquent men of his day. He once married a young couple that had fled from the house of the young lady's father. He was so interested in their story. He had no hesitation, and everything came out beautifully. The father was afterwards reconciled, and thought everything of the young man. Mr. Penniman married them in the evening, about seven o'clock. The church was so dark, you could scarcely see; and Mr. Penniman was intensely agitated; he was so sympathetic. I don't believe he could have done it again."

"Unfortunately Catherine and I have not Mr. Penniman to marry us," said Morris.

"No, but you have me!" rejoined Mrs. Penniman expressively. "I can't perform the ceremony, but I can help you. I can watch."

"The woman's an idiot," thought Morris; but he was obliged to say something different. It was not, however, materially more civil. "Was it in order to tell me this that you requested I would meet you here?"

Mrs. Penniman had been conscious of a certain vagueness in her errand, and of not being able to offer him any very tangible reward for his long walk.

"I thought perhaps you would like to see one who is so near to Catherine," she observed, with considerable majesty. "And also," she added, "that you would value an opportunity of sending her something."

Morris extended his empty hands with a melancholy smile. "I am greatly obliged to you, but I have nothing to send."

"Haven't you a *word*?" asked his companion, with her suggestive smile coming back.

Morris frowned again. "Tell her to hold fast," he said rather curtly.

"That is a good word—a noble word. It will make her happy for many days. She is very touching, very brave," Mrs. Penniman went on, arranging her mantle and preparing to depart. While she was so engaged she had an inspiration. She found the phrase that she could boldly offer as a vindication of the step she had taken. "If you marry Catherine at all risks," she said, "you will give my brother a proof of your being what he pretends to doubt."

"What he pretends to doubt?"

"Don't you know what that is?" Mrs. Penniman asked almost playfully.

"It does not concern me to know," said Morris grandly.

"Of course it makes you angry."

"I despise it," Morris declared.

"Ah, you know what it is, then?" said Mrs. Penniman, shaking her finger at him. "He pretends that you like—you like the money."

Morris hesitated a moment; and then, as if he spoke advisedly— "I *do* like the money!"

"Ah, but not—but not as he means it. You don't like it more than Catherine?"

He leaned his elbows on the table and buried his head in his hands. "You torture me!" he murmured. And, indeed, this was almost the effect of the poor lady's too importunate interest in his situation.

But she insisted on making her point. "If you marry her in spite of him, he will take for granted that you expect nothing of him, and are prepared to do without it. And so he will see that you are disinterested."

Morris raised his head a little, following this argument, "And what shall I gain by that?"

"Why, that he will see that he has been wrong in thinking that you wished to get his money."

"And seeing that I wish he would go to the deuce with it, he will leave it to a hospital. Is that what you mean?" asked Morris.

"No, I don't mean that; though that would be very grand!" Mrs. Penniman quickly added. "I mean that having done you such an injustice, he will think it his duty, at the end, to make some amends."

Morris shook his head, though it must be confessed he was a little struck with this idea. "Do you think he is so sentimental?"

"He is not sentimental," said Mrs. Penniman; "but, to be perfectly fair to him, I think he has, in his own narrow way, a certain sense of duty."

There passed through Morris Townsend's mind a rapid wonder as to what he might, even under a remote contingency, be indebted to from the action of this principle in Dr. Sloper's breast, and the inquiry exhausted itself in his sense of the ludicrous. "Your brother has no duties to me," he said presently, "and I none to him."

"Ah, but he has duties to Catherine."

"Yes, but you see that on that principle Catherine has duties to him as well."

Mrs. Penniman got up, with a melancholy sigh, as if she thought him very unimaginative. "She has always performed them faithfully; and now, do you think she has no duties to *you*?" Mrs. Penniman always, even in conversation, italicised her personal pronouns.

"It would sound harsh to say so! I am so grateful for her love," Morris added.

"I will tell her you said that! And now, remember that if you need me, I am there." And Mrs. Penniman, who could think of nothing more to say, nodded vaguely in the direction of Washington Square.

Morris looked some moments at the sanded floor of the shop; he seemed to be disposed to linger a moment. At last, looking up with a certain abruptness, "It is your belief that if she marries me he will cut her off?" he asked.

Mrs. Penniman stared a little, and smiled. "Why, I have explained to you what I think would happen—that in the end it would be the best thing to do."

"You mean that, whatever she does, in the long run she will get the money?"

"It doesn't depend upon her, but upon you. Venture to appear as disinterested as you are!" said Mrs. Penniman ingeniously. Morris dropped his eyes on the sanded floor again, pondering this; and she pursued. "Mr. Penniman and I had nothing, and we were very happy. Catherine, moreover, has her mother's fortune, which, at the time my sister-in-law married, was considered a very handsome one."

"Oh, don't speak of that!" said Morris; and, indeed, it was quite superfluous, for he had contemplated the fact in all its lights.

"Austin married a wife with money—why shouldn't you?"

"Ah! but your brother was a doctor," Morris objected.

"Well, all young men can't be doctors!"

"I should think it an extremely loathsome profession," said Morris, with an air of intellectual independence. Then in a moment, he went on rather inconsequently, "Do you suppose there is a will already made in Catherine's favour?"

"I suppose so—even doctors must die; and perhaps a little in mine," Mrs. Penniman frankly added.

"And you believe he would certainly change it—as regards Catherine?"

"Yes; and then change it back again."

"Ah, but one can't depend on that!" said Morris.

"Do you want to *depend* on it?" Mrs. Penniman asked.

Morris blushed a little. "Well, I am certainly afraid of being the cause of an injury to Catherine."

"Ah! you must not be afraid. Be afraid of nothing, and everything will go well!"

And then Mrs. Penniman paid for her cup of tea, and Morris paid for his oyster stew, and they went out together into the dimly-lighted wilderness of the Seventh Avenue. The dusk had closed in completely and the street lamps were separated by wide intervals of a pavement in which cavities and fissures played a disproportionate part. An omnibus, emblazoned with strange pictures, went tumbling over the dislocated cobble-stones.

"How will you go home?" Morris asked, following this vehicle with an interested eye. Mrs. Penniman had taken his arm.

She hesitated a moment. "I think this manner would be pleasant," she said; and she continued to let him feel the value of his support.

So he walked with her through the devious ways of the west side of the town, and through the bustle of gathering nightfall in populous streets, to the quiet precinct of Washington Square. They lingered a moment at the foot of Dr. Sloper's white marble steps, above which a spotless white door, adorned with a glittering silver plate, seemed to figure, for Morris, the closed portal of happiness; and then Mrs. Penniman's companion rested a melancholy eye upon a lighted window in the upper part of the house.

"That is my room—my dear little room!" Mrs. Penniman remarked.

Morris started. "Then I needn't come walking round the Square to gaze at it."

"That's as you please. But Catherine's is behind; two noble windows on the second floor. I think you can see them from the other street."

"I don't want to see them, ma'am!" And Morris turned his back to the house.

"I will tell her you have been *here*, at any rate," said Mrs. Penniman, pointing to the spot where they stood; "and I will give her your message—that she is to hold fast!"

"Oh, yes! of course. You know I write her all that."

"It seems to say more when it is spoken! And remember, if you need me, that I am *there*"; and Mrs. Penniman glanced at the third floor.

On this they separated, and Morris, left to himself, stood looking at the house a moment; after which he turned away, and took a gloomy walk round the Square, on the opposite side, close to the wooden fence. Then he came back, and paused for a minute in front of Dr. Sloper's dwelling. His eyes travelled over it; they even rested on the ruddy windows of Mrs. Penniman's apartment. He thought it a devilish comfortable house.

XVII

Mrs. Penniman told Catherine that evening—the two ladies were sitting in the back parlour—that she had had an interview with Morris Townsend; and on receiving this news the girl started with a sense of pain. She felt angry for the moment; it was almost the first time she had ever felt angry. It seemed to her that her aunt was meddlesome; and from this came a vague apprehension that she would spoil something.

"I don't see why you should have seen him. I don't think it was right," Catherine said.

"I was so sorry for him—it seemed to me some one ought to see him."

"No one but I," said Catherine, who felt as if she were making the most presumptuous speech of her life, and yet at the same time had an instinct that she was right in doing so.

"But you wouldn't, my dear," Aunt Lavinia rejoined; "and I didn't know what might have become of him."

"I have not seen him, because my father has forbidden it," Catherine said very simply.

There was a simplicity in this, indeed, which fairly vexed Mrs. Penniman. "If your father forbade you to go to sleep, I suppose you would keep awake!" she commented.

Catherine looked at her. "I don't understand you. You seem to be very strange."

"Well, my dear, you will understand me some day!" And Mrs. Penniman, who was reading the evening paper, which she perused daily from the first line to the last, resumed her occupation. She wrapped herself in silence; she was determined Catherine should ask her for an account of her interview with Morris. But Catherine was silent for so long, that she almost lost patience; and she was on the point of remarking to her that she was very heartless, when the girl at last spoke.

"What did he say?" she asked.

"He said he is ready to marry you any day, in spite of everything."

Catherine made no answer to this, and Mrs. Penniman almost lost patience again; owing to which she at last volunteered the information that Morris looked very handsome, but terribly haggard.

"Did he seem sad?" asked her niece.

"He was dark under the eyes," said Mrs. Penniman. "So different from when I first saw him; though I am not sure that if I had seen him in this condition the first time, I should not have been even more struck with him. There is something brilliant in his very misery."

This was, to Catherine's sense, a vivid picture, and though she disapproved, she felt herself gazing at it. "Where did you see him?" she asked presently.

"In—in the Bowery; at a confectioner's," said Mrs. Penniman, who had a general idea that she ought to dissemble a little.

"Whereabouts is the place?" Catherine inquired, after another pause.

"Do you wish to go there, my dear?" said her aunt.

"Oh no!" And Catherine got up from her seat and went to the fire, where she stood looking a while at the glowing coals.

"Why are you so dry, Catherine?" Mrs. Penniman said at last.

"So dry?"

"So cold—so irresponsive."

The girl turned very quickly. "Did *he* say that?"

Mrs. Penniman hesitated a moment. "I will tell you what he said. He said he feared only one thing—that you would be afraid."

"Afraid of what?"

"Afraid of your father."

Catherine turned back to the fire again, and then, after a pause, she said—"I *am* afraid of my father."

Mrs. Penniman got quickly up from her chair and approached her niece. "Do you mean to give him up, then?"

Catherine for some time never moved; she kept her eyes on the coals. At last she raised her head and looked at her aunt. "Why do you push me so?" she asked.

"I don't push you. When have I spoken to you before?"

"It seems to me that you have spoken to me several times."

"I am afraid it is necessary, then, Catherine," said Mrs. Penniman, with a good deal of solemnity. "I am afraid you don't feel the importance—" She paused a little; Catherine was looking at her. "The importance of not disappointing that gallant young heart!" And Mrs. Penniman went back to her chair, by the lamp, and, with a little jerk, picked up the evening paper again.

Catherine stood there before the fire, with her hands behind her, looking at her aunt, to whom it seemed that the girl had never had just this dark fixedness in her gaze. "I don't think you understand—or that you know me," she said.

"If I don't, it is not wonderful; you trust me so little."

Catherine made no attempt to deny this charge, and for some time more nothing was said. But Mrs. Penniman's imagination was restless, and the evening paper failed on this occasion to enchain it.

"If you succumb to the dread of your father's wrath," she said, "I don't know what will become of us."

"Did *he* tell you to say these things to me?"

"He told me to use my influence."

"You must be mistaken," said Catherine. "He trusts me."

"I hope he may never repent of it!" And Mrs. Penniman gave a little sharp slap to her newspaper. She knew not what to make of her niece, who had suddenly become stern and contradictious.

This tendency on Catherine's part was presently even more apparent. "You had much better not make any more appointments with Mr. Townsend," she said. "I don't think it is right."

Mrs. Penniman rose with considerable majesty. "My poor child, are you jealous of me?" she inquired.

"Oh, Aunt Lavinia!" murmured Catherine, blushing.

"I don't think it is your place to teach me what is right."

On this point Catherine made no concession. "It can't be right to deceive."

"I certainly have not deceived *you!*"

"Yes; but I promised my father—"

"I have no doubt you promised your father. But I have promised him nothing!"

Catherine had to admit this, and she did so in silence. "I don't believe Mr. Townsend himself likes it," she said at last.

"Doesn't like meeting me?"

"Not in secret."

"It was not in secret; the place was full of people."

"But it was a secret place—away off in the Bowery."

Mrs. Penniman flinched a little. "Gentlemen enjoy such things," she remarked presently. "I know what gentlemen like."

"My father wouldn't like it, if he knew."

"Pray, do you propose to inform him?" Mrs. Penniman inquired.

"No, Aunt Lavinia. But please don't do it again."

"If I do it again, you will inform him: is that what you mean? I do not share your dread of my brother; I have always known how to defend my own position. But I shall certainly never again take any step on your behalf; you are much too thankless. I knew you were not a spontaneous nature, but I believed you were firm, and I told your father that he would find you so. I am disappointed—but your father will not be!" And with this, Mrs. Penniman offered her niece a brief good-night, and withdrew to her own apartment.

XVIII

CATHERINE sat alone by the parlour fire—sat there for more than an hour, lost in her meditations. Her aunt seemed to her aggressive and foolish, and to see it so clearly—to judge Mrs. Penniman so positively—made her feel old and grave. She did not resent the imputation of weakness; it made no impression on her, for she had not the sense of weakness, and she was not hurt at not being appreciated. She had an immense respect for her father, and she felt that to displease him would be a misdemeanour analogous to an act of profanity in a great temple; but her purpose had slowly ripened, and she believed that her prayers had purified it of its violence. The evening advanced, and the lamp burned dim without her noticing it; her eyes were fixed upon her terrible plan. She knew her father was in his study—that he had been there all the evening; from time to time she expected to hear him move. She thought he would perhaps come, as he sometimes came, into the parlour. At last the clock struck eleven, and the house was wrapped in silence; the servants had gone to bed. Catherine got up and went slowly to the door of the library, where she waited a moment, motionless. Then she knocked, and then she waited again. Her father had answered her, but she had not the courage to turn the latch. What she had said to her aunt was true enough— she was afraid of him; and in saying that she had no sense of weakness she meant that she was not afraid of herself. She heard him move within, and he came and opened the door for her.

"What is the matter?" asked the Doctor. "You are standing there like a ghost."

She went into the room, but it was some time before she contrived to say what she had come to say. Her father, who was in his dressing-gown and slippers, had been busy at his writing-table, and after looking at her for some moments, and waiting for her to speak, he went and seated himself at his papers again. His back was turned to her—she began to hear the scratching of his pen. She remained near the door, with her heart thumping beneath her bodice; and she was very glad that his back was turned, for it seemed to her that she could more easily address herself to this portion of his person than to his face. At last she began, watching it while she spoke.

"You told me that if I should have anything more to say about Mr. Townsend you would be glad to listen to it."

"Exactly, my dear," said the Doctor, not turning round, but stopping his pen.

Catherine wished it would go on, but she herself continued. "I thought I would tell you that I have not seen him again, but that I should like to do so."

"To bid him good-bye?" asked the Doctor.

The girl hesitated a moment. "He is not going away."

The Doctor wheeled slowly round in his chair, with a smile that seemed to accuse her of an epigram; but extremes meet, and Catherine had not intended one. "It is not to bid him good-bye, then?" her father said.

"No, father, not that; at least, not for ever. I have not seen him again, but I should like to see him," Catherine repeated.

The Doctor slowly rubbed his under lip with the feather of his quill.

"Have you written to him?"

"Yes, four times."

"You have not dismissed him, then. Once would have done that."

"No," said Catherine; "I have asked him—asked him to wait."

Her father sat looking at her, and she was afraid he was going to break out into wrath; his eyes were so fine and cold.

"You are a dear, faithful child," he said at last. "Come here to your father." And he got up, holding out his hands toward her.

The words were a surprise, and they gave her an exquisite joy. She went to him, and he put his arm round her tenderly, soothingly; and then he kissed her. After this he said:

"Do you wish to make me very happy?"

"I should like to—but I am afraid I can't," Catherine answered.

"You can if you will. It all depends on your will."

"Is it to give him up?" said Catherine.

"Yes, it is to give him up."

And he held her still, with the same tenderness, looking into her face and resting his eyes on her averted eyes. There was a long silence; she wished he would release her.

"You are happier than I, father," she said, at last.

"I have no doubt you are unhappy just now. But it is better to be unhappy for three months and get over it, than for many years and never get over it."

"Yes, if that were so," said Catherine.

"It would be so; I am sure of that." She answered nothing, and he went on. "Have you no faith in my wisdom, in my tenderness, in my solicitude for your future?"

"Oh, father!" murmured the girl.

"Don't you suppose that I know something of men: their vices, their follies, their falsities?"

She detached herself, and turned upon him. "He is not vicious—he is not false!"

Her father kept looking at her with his sharp, pure eye. "You make nothing of my judgement, then?"

"I can't believe that!"

"I don't ask you to believe it, but to take it on trust."

Catherine was far from saying to herself that this was an ingenious sophism; but she met the appeal none the less squarely. "What has he done—what do you know?"

"He has never done anything—he is a selfish idler."

"Oh, father, don't abuse him!" she exclaimed pleadingly.

"I don't mean to abuse him; it would be a great mistake. You may do as you choose," he added, turning away.

"I may see him again?"

"Just as you choose."

"Will you forgive me?"

"By no means."

"It will only be for once."

"I don't know what you mean by once. You must either give him up or continue the acquaintance."

"I wish to explain—to tell him to wait."

"To wait for what?"

"Till you know him better—till you consent."

"Don't tell him any such nonsense as that. I know him well enough, and I shall never consent."

"But we can wait a long time," said poor Catherine, in a tone which was meant to express the humblest conciliation, but which had upon her father's nerves the effect of an iteration not characterised by tact.

The Doctor answered, however, quietly enough: "Of course you can wait till I die, if you like." Catherine gave a cry of natural horror.

"Your engagement will have one delightful effect upon you; it will make you extremely impatient for that event."

Catherine stood staring, and the Doctor enjoyed the point he had made. It came to Catherine with the force—or rather with the vague impressiveness—of a logical axiom which it was not in her province to controvert; and yet, though it was a scientific truth, she felt wholly unable to accept it.

"I would rather not marry, if that were true," she said.

"Give me a proof of it, then; for it is beyond a question that by engaging yourself to Morris Townsend you simply wait for my death."

She turned away, feeling sick and faint; and the Doctor went on. "And if you wait for it with impatience, judge, if you please, what *his* eagerness will be!"

Catherine turned it over—her father's words had such an authority for her that her very thoughts were capable of obeying him. There was a dreadful ugliness in it, which seemed to glare at her through the interposing medium of her own feebler reason. Suddenly, however, she had an inspiration—she almost knew it to be an inspiration.

"If I don't marry before your death, I will not after," she said.

To her father, it must be admitted, this seemed only another epigram; and as obstinacy, in unaccomplished minds, does not usually select such a mode of expression, he was the more surprised at this wanton play of a fixed idea.

"Do you mean that for an impertinence?" he inquired; an inquiry of which, as he made it, he quite perceived the grossness.

"An impertinence? Oh, father, what terrible things you say!"

"If you don't wait for my death, you might as well marry immediately; there is nothing else to wait for."

For some time Catherine made no answer; but finally she said:

"I think Morris—little by little—might persuade you."

"I shall never let him speak to me again. I dislike him too much."

Catherine gave a long, low sigh; she tried to stifle it, for she had made up her mind that it was wrong to make a parade of her trouble, and to endeavour to act upon her father by the meretricious aid of emotion. Indeed, she even thought it wrong—in the sense of being inconsiderate—to attempt to act upon his feelings at all; her part was to effect some gentle, gradual change in his intellectual perception of poor Morris's character. But the means of effecting such a change were at present shrouded in mystery, and she felt miserably helpless and hopeless. She had exhausted all arguments, all replies. Her father might have pitied her, and in fact he did so; but he was sure he was right.

"There is one thing you can tell Mr. Townsend when you see him again," he said: "that if you marry without my consent, I don't leave you a farthing of money. That will interest him more than anything else you can tell him."

"That would be very right," Catherine answered. "I ought not in that case to have a farthing of your money."

"My dear child," the Doctor observed, laughing, "your simplicity is touching. Make that remark, in that tone, and with that expression of countenance, to Mr. Townsend, and take a note of his answer. It won't be polite—it will, express irritation; and I shall be glad of that, as it will put me in the right; unless, indeed—which is perfectly possible—you should like him the better for being rude to you."

"He will never be rude to me," said Catherine gently.

"Tell him what I say, all the same."

She looked at her father, and her quiet eyes filled with tears.

"I think I will see him, then," she murmured, in her timid voice.

"Exactly as you choose!" And he went to the door and opened it for her to go out. The movement gave her a terrible sense of his turning her off.

"It will be only once, for the present," she added, lingering a moment.

261

"Exactly as you choose," he repeated, standing there with his hand on the door. "I have told you what I think. If you see him, you will be an ungrateful, cruel child; you will have given your old father the greatest pain of his life."

This was more than the poor girl could bear; her tears overflowed, and she moved towards her grimly consistent parent with a pitiful cry. Her hands were raised in supplication, but he sternly evaded this appeal. Instead of letting her sob out her misery on his shoulder, he simply took her by the arm and directed her course across the threshold, closing the door gently but firmly behind her. After he had done so, he remained listening. For a long time there was no sound; he knew that she was standing outside. He was sorry for her, as I have said; but he was so sure he was right. At last he heard her move away, and then her footstep creaked faintly upon the stairs.

The Doctor took several turns round his study, with his hands in his pockets, and a thin sparkle, possibly of irritation, but partly also of something like humour, in his eye. "By Jove," he said to himself, "I believe she will stick—I believe she will stick!" And this idea of Catherine "sticking" appeared to have a comical side, and to offer a prospect of entertainment. He determined, as he said to himself, to see it out.

XIX

IT was for reasons connected with this determination that on the morrow he sought a few words of private conversation with Mrs. Penniman. He sent for her to the library, and he there informed her that he hoped very much that, as regarded this affair of Catherine's, she would mind her *p*'s and *q*'s.

"I don't know what you mean by such an expression," said his sister. "You speak as if I were learning the alphabet."

"The alphabet of common sense is something you will never learn," the Doctor permitted himself to respond.

"Have you called me here to insult me?" Mrs. Penniman inquired.

"Not at all. Simply to advise you. You have taken up young Townsend; that's your own affair. I have nothing to do with your sentiments, your fancies, your affections, your delusions; but what I request of you is that you will keep these things to yourself. I have explained my views to Catherine; she understands them perfectly, and anything that she does further in the way of encouraging Mr. Townsend's attentions will be in deliberate opposition to my wishes. Anything that you should do in the way of giving her aid and comfort will be—permit me the expression—distinctly treasonable. You know high treason is a capital offence; take care how you incur the penalty."

Mrs. Penniman threw back her head, with a certain expansion of the eye which she occasionally practised. "It seems to me that you talk like a great autocrat."

"I talk like my daughter's father."

"Not like your sister's brother!" cried Lavinia. "My dear Lavinia," said the Doctor, "I sometimes wonder whether I am your brother. We are so extremely different. In spite of differences, however, we can, at a pinch, understand each other; and that is the essential thing just now. Walk straight with regard to Mr. Townsend; that's all I ask. It is highly probable you have been corresponding with him for the last three weeks—perhaps even seeing him. I don't ask you—you needn't tell me." He had a moral conviction that she would contrive to tell a fib about the matter, which it would disgust him to listen to. "Whatever you have done, stop doing it. That's all I wish."

"Don't you wish also by chance to murder our child?" Mrs. Penniman inquired.

"On the contrary, I wish to make her live and be happy."

"You will kill her; she passed a dreadful night."

"She won't die of one dreadful night, nor of a dozen. Remember that I am a distinguished physician."

Mrs. Penniman hesitated a moment. Then she risked her retort. "Your being a distinguished physician has not prevented you from already losing *two members* of your family!"

She had risked it, but her brother gave her such a terribly incisive look—a look so like a surgeon's lancet—that she was frightened at her courage. And he answered her in words that corresponded to the look: "It may not prevent me, either, from losing the society of still another."

Mrs. Penniman took herself off, with whatever air of depreciated merit was at her command, and repaired to Catherine's room, where the poor girl was closeted. She knew all about her dreadful night, for the two had met again, the evening before, after Catherine left her father. Mrs. Penniman was on the landing of the second floor when her niece came upstairs. It was not remarkable that a person of so much subtlety should have discovered that Catherine had been shut up with the Doctor. It was still less remarkable that she should have felt an extreme curiosity to learn the result of this interview, and that this sentiment, combined with her great amiability and generosity, should have prompted her to regret the sharp words lately exchanged between her niece and herself. As the unhappy girl came into sight, in the dusky corridor, she made a lively demonstration of sympathy. Catherine's bursting heart was equally oblivious. She only knew that her aunt was taking her into her arms. Mrs. Penniman drew her into Catherine's own room, and the two women sat there together, far into the small hours; the younger one with her head on the other's lap, sobbing and sobbing at first in a soundless, stifled manner, and then at last perfectly still. It gratified Mrs. Penniman to be able to feel conscientiously that this scene virtually removed the interdict which Catherine had placed upon her further communion with Morris Townsend. She was not gratified, however, when, in coming back to her niece's room before breakfast, she found that Catherine had risen and was preparing herself for this meal.

"You should not go to breakfast," she said; "you are not well enough, after your fearful night."

"Yes, I am very well, and I am only afraid of being late."

"I can't understand you!" Mrs. Penniman cried. "You should stay in bed for three days."

"Oh, I could never do that!" said Catherine, to whom this idea presented no attractions.

Mrs. Penniman was in despair, and she noted, with extreme annoyance, that the trace of the night's tears had completely vanished from Catherine's eyes. She had a most impracticable *physique*. "What effect do you expect to have upon your father," her aunt demanded, "if you come plumping down, without a vestige of any sort of feeling, as if nothing in the world had happened?"

"He would not like me to lie in bed," said Catherine simply.

"All the more reason for your doing it. How else do you expect to move him?"

Catherine thought a little. "I don't know how; but not in that way. I wish to be just as usual." And she finished dressing, and, according to her aunt's expression, went plumping down into the paternal presence. She was really too modest for consistent pathos.

And yet it was perfectly true that she had had a dreadful night. Even after Mrs. Penniman left her she had had no sleep. She lay staring at the uncomforting gloom, with her eyes and ears filled with the movement with which her father had turned her out of his room, and of the words in which he had told her that she was a heartless daughter. Her heart was breaking. She had heart enough for that. At moments it seemed to her that she believed him, and that to do what she was doing, a girl must indeed be bad. She *was* bad; but she couldn't help it. She would try to appear good, even if her heart were perverted; and from time to time she had a fancy that she might accomplish something by ingenious concessions to form, though she should persist in caring for Morris. Catherine's ingenuities were indefinite, and we are not called upon to expose their hollowness. The best of them perhaps showed itself in that freshness of aspect which was so discouraging to Mrs. Penniman, who was amazed at the absence of haggardness in a young woman who for a whole night had lain quivering beneath a father's curse. Poor Catherine was conscious of her freshness; it gave her a feeling about the future which rather added to the weight upon her mind. It seemed a proof that she was strong and solid and dense, and would live to a great age— longer than might be generally convenient; and this idea was depressing, for it appeared to saddle her with a pretension the more, just when the cultivation of any pretension was inconsistent with her doing right. She wrote that day to Morris Townsend, requesting him to come and see her on the morrow; using very few words, and explaining nothing. She would explain everything face to face.

XX

ON the morrow, in the afternoon, she heard his voice at the door, and his step in the hall. She received him in the big, bright front parlour, and she instructed the servant that if any one should call she was particularly engaged. She was not afraid of her father's coming in, for at that hour he was always driving about town. When Morris stood there before her, the first thing that she was conscious of was that he was even more beautiful to look at than fond recollection had painted him; the next was that he had pressed her in his arms. When she was free again it appeared to her that she had now indeed thrown herself into the gulf of defiance, and even, for an instant, that she had been married to him.

He told her that she had been very cruel, and had made him very unhappy; and Catherine felt acutely the difficulty of her destiny, which forced her to give pain in such opposite quarters. But she wished that, instead of reproaches, however tender, he would give her help; he was certainly wise enough, and clever enough, to invent some issue from their troubles. She expressed this belief, and Morris received the assurance as if he thought it natural; but he interrogated, at first—as was natural too—rather than committed himself to marking out a course.

"You should not have made me wait so long," he said. "I don't know how I have been living; every hour seemed like years. You should have decided sooner."

"Decided?" Catherine asked.

"Decided whether you would keep me or give me up."

"Oh, Morris," she cried, with a long tender murmur, "I never thought of giving you up!"

"What, then, were you waiting for?" The young man was ardently logical.

"I thought my father might—might—" and she hesitated.

"Might see how unhappy you were?"

"Oh no! But that he might look at it differently."

"And now you have sent for me to tell me that at last he does so. Is that it?"

This hypothetical optimism gave the poor girl a pang. "No, Morris," she said solemnly, "he looks at it still in the same way."

"Then why have you sent for me?"

"Because I wanted to see you!" cried Catherine piteously.

"That's an excellent reason, surely. But did you want to look at me only? Have you nothing to tell me?"

His beautiful persuasive eyes were fixed upon her face, and she wondered what answer would be noble enough to make to such a gaze as that. For a moment her own eyes took it in, and then—"I *did* want to look at you!" she said gently. But after this speech, most inconsistently, she hid her face.

Morris watched her for a moment, attentively. "Will you marry me to-morrow?" he asked suddenly.

"To-morrow?"

"Next week, then. Any time within a month."

"Isn't it better to wait?" said Catherine.

"To wait for what?"

She hardly knew for what; but this tremendous leap alarmed her. "Till we have thought about it a little more."

He shook his head, sadly and reproachfully. "I thought you had been thinking about it these three weeks. Do you want to turn it over in your mind for five years? You have given me more than time enough. My poor girl," he added in a moment, "you are not sincere!"

Catherine coloured from brow to chin, and her eyes filled with tears. "Oh, how can you say that?" she murmured.

"Why, you must take me or leave me," said Morris, very reasonably. "You can't please your father and me both; you must choose between us."

"I have chosen you!" she said passionately.

"Then marry me next week."

She stood gazing at him. "Isn't there any other way?"

"None that I know of for arriving at the same result. If there is, I should be happy to hear of it."

Catherine could think of nothing of the kind, and Morris's luminosity seemed almost pitiless. The only thing she could think of was that her father might, after all, come round, and she articulated, with an awkward sense of her helplessness in doing so, a wish that this miracle might happen.

"Do you think it is in the least degree likely?" Morris asked.

"It would be, if he could only know you!"

"He can know me if he will. What is to prevent it?"

"His ideas, his reasons," said Catherine. "They are so—so terribly strong." She trembled with the recollection of them yet.

"Strong?" cried Morris. "I would rather you should think them weak."

"Oh, nothing about my father is weak!" said the girl.

Morris turned away, walking to the window, where he stood looking out. "You are terribly afraid of him!" he remarked at last.

She felt no impulse to deny it, because she had no shame in it; for if it was no honour to herself, at least it was an honour to him. "I suppose I must be," she said simply.

"Then you don't love me—not as I love me. If you fear your father more than you love me, then your love is not what I hoped it was."

"Ah, my friend!" she said, going to him.

"Do *I* fear anything?" he demanded, turning round on her. "For your sake what am I not ready to face?"

"You are noble—you are brave!" she answered, stopping short at a distance that was almost respectful.

"Small good it does me, if you are so timid."

"I don't think that I am—*really*," said Catherine.

"I don't know what you mean by 'really.' It is really enough to make us miserable."

"I should be strong enough to wait—to wait a long time."

"And suppose after a long time your father should hate me worse than ever?"

"He wouldn't—he couldn't!"

"He would be touched by my fidelity? Is that what you mean? If he is so easily touched, then why should you be afraid of him?"

This was much to the point, and Catherine was struck by it. "I will try not to be," she said. And she stood there submissively, the image, in advance, of a dutiful and responsible wife. This image could not fail to recommend itself to Morris Townsend, and he continued to give proof of the high estimation in which he held her. It could only have been at the prompting of such a sentiment that he presently mentioned to her that the course recommended by Mrs. Penniman was an immediate union, regardless of consequences.

"Yes, Aunt Penniman would like that," Catherine said simply—and yet with a certain shrewdness. It must, however, have been in pure simplicity, and from motives quite untouched by sarcasm, that, a few moments after, she went on to say to Morris that her father had given her a message for him. It was quite on her conscience to deliver this message, and had the mission been ten times more painful she would have as scrupulously performed it. "He told me to tell you—to tell you very distinctly, and directly from himself, that if I marry without his consent, I shall not inherit a penny of his fortune. He made a great point of this. He seemed to think—he seemed to think—"

Morris flushed, as any young man of spirit might have flushed at an imputation of baseness.

"What did he seem to think?"

"That it would make a difference."

"It *will* make a difference—in many things. We shall be by many thousands of dollars the poorer; and that is a great difference. But it will make none in my affection."

"We shall not want the money," said Catherine; "for you know I have a good deal myself."

"Yes, my dear girl, I know you have something. And he can't touch that!"

"He would never," said Catherine. "My mother left it to me."

Morris was silent a while. "He was very positive about this, was he?" he asked at last. "He thought such a message would annoy me terribly, and make me throw off the mask, eh?"

"I don't know what he thought," said Catherine wearily.

"Please tell him that I care for his message as much as for that!" And Morris snapped his fingers sonorously.

"I don't think I could tell him that."

"Do you know you sometimes disappoint me?" said Morris.

"I should think I might. I disappoint every one—father and Aunt Penniman."

"Well, it doesn't matter with me, because I am fonder of you than they are."

"Yes, Morris," said the girl, with her imagination—what there was of it—swimming in this happy truth, which seemed, after all, invidious to no one.

"Is it your belief that he will stick to it—stick to it for ever, to this idea of disinheriting you?—that your goodness and patience will never wear out his cruelty?"

"The trouble is that if I marry you, he will think I am not good. He will think that a proof."

"Ah, then, he will never forgive you!"

This idea, sharply expressed by Morris's handsome lips, renewed for a moment, to the poor girl's temporarily pacified conscience, all its dreadful vividness. "Oh, you must love me very much!" she cried.

"There is no doubt of that, my dear!" her lover rejoined. "You don't like that word 'disinherited,'" he added in a moment.

"It isn't the money; it is that he should—that he should feel so."

"I suppose it seems to you a kind of curse," said Morris. "It must be very dismal. But don't you think," he went on presently, "that if you were to try to be very clever, and to set rightly about it, you might in the end conjure it away? Don't you think," he continued further, in a tone of sympathetic speculation, "that a really clever woman, in your place, might bring him round at last? Don't you think?"

Here, suddenly, Morris was interrupted; these ingenious inquiries had not reached Catherine's ears. The terrible word "disinheritance," with all its impressive moral reprobation, was still ringing there; seemed indeed to gather force as it lingered. The mortal chill of her situation struck more deeply into her child-like heart, and she was overwhelmed by a feeling of loneliness and danger. But her refuge was there, close to her, and she put out her hands to grasp it. "Ah, Morris," she said, with a shudder, "I will marry you as soon as you please." And she surrendered herself, leaning her head on his shoulder.

"My dear good girl!" he exclaimed, looking down at his prize. And then he looked up again, rather vaguely, with parted lips and lifted eyebrows.

XXI

Dr. Sloper very soon imparted his conviction to Mrs. Almond, in the same terms in which he had announced it to himself. "She's going to stick, by Jove! she's going to stick."

"Do you mean that she is going to marry him?" Mrs. Almond inquired.

"I don't know that; but she is not going to break down. She is going to drag out the engagement, in the hope of making me relent."

"And shall you not relent?"

"Shall a geometrical proposition relent? I am not so superficial."

"Doesn't geometry treat of surfaces?" asked Mrs. Almond, who, as we know, was clever, smiling.

"Yes; but it treats of them profoundly. Catherine and her young man are my surfaces; I have taken their measure."

"You speak as if it surprised you."

"It is immense; there will be a great deal to observe."

"You are shockingly cold-blooded!" said Mrs. Almond.

"I need to be with all this hot blood about me. Young Townsend indeed is cool; I must allow him that merit."

"I can't judge him," Mrs. Almond answered; "but I am not at all surprised at Catherine."

"I confess I am a little; she must have been so deucedly divided and bothered."

"Say it amuses you outright! I don't see why it should be such a joke that your daughter adores you."

"It is the point where the adoration stops that I find it interesting to fix."

"It stops where the other sentiment begins."

"Not at all—that would be simple enough. The two things are extremely mixed up, and the mixture is extremely odd. It will produce some third element, and that's what I am waiting to see. I wait with suspense—with positive excitement; and that is a sort of emotion that I didn't suppose Catherine would ever provide for me. I am really very much obliged to her."

"She will cling," said Mrs. Almond; "she will certainly cling."

"Yes; as I say, she will stick."

"Cling is prettier. That's what those very simple natures always do, and nothing could be simpler than Catherine. She doesn't take many impressions; but when she takes one she keeps it. She is like a copper kettle that receives a dent; you may polish up the kettle, but you can't efface the mark."

"We must try and polish up Catherine," said the Doctor. "I will take her to Europe."

"She won't forget him in Europe."

"He will forget her, then."

Mrs. Almond looked grave. "Should you really like that?"

"Extremely!" said the Doctor.

Mrs. Penniman, meanwhile, lost little time in putting herself again in communication with Morris Townsend. She requested him to favour her with another interview, but she did not on this occasion select an oyster saloon as the scene of their meeting. She proposed that he should join her at the door of a certain church, after service on Sunday afternoon, and she was careful not to appoint the place of worship which she usually visited, and where, as she said, the congregation would have spied upon her. She picked out a less elegant resort, and on issuing from its portal at the hour she had fixed she saw the young man standing apart. She offered him no recognition till she had crossed the street and he had followed her to some distance. Here, with a smile—"Excuse my apparent want of cordiality," she said. "You know what to believe about that. Prudence before everything." And on his asking her in what direction they should walk, "Where we shall be least observed," she murmured.

Morris was not in high good-humour, and his response to this speech was not particularly gallant. "I don't flatter myself we shall be much observed anywhere." Then he turned recklessly toward the centre of the town. "I hope you have come to tell me that he has knocked under," he went on.

"I am afraid I am not altogether a harbinger of good; and yet, too, I am to a certain extent a messenger of peace. I have been thinking a great deal, Mr. Townsend," said Mrs. Penniman.

"You think too much."

"I suppose I do; but I can't help it, my mind is so terribly active. When I give myself, I give myself. I pay the penalty in my headaches, my famous headaches—a perfect circlet of pain! But I carry it as a queen carries her crown. Would you believe that I have one now? I wouldn't, however, have missed our rendezvous for anything. I have something very important to tell you."

"Well, let's have it," said Morris.

"I was perhaps a little headlong the other day in advising you to marry immediately. I have been thinking it over, and now I see it just a little differently."

"You seem to have a great many different ways of seeing the same object."

"Their number is infinite!" said Mrs. Penniman, in a tone which seemed to suggest that this convenient faculty was one of her brightest attributes.

"I recommend you to take one way and stick to it," Morris replied.

"Ah! but it isn't easy to choose. My imagination is never quiet, never satisfied. It makes me a bad adviser, perhaps; but it makes me a capital friend!"

"A capital friend who gives bad advice!" said Morris.

"Not intentionally—and who hurries off, at every risk, to make the most humble excuses!"

"Well, what do you advise me now?"

"To be very patient; to watch and wait."

"And is that bad advice or good?"

"That is not for me to say," Mrs. Penniman rejoined, with some dignity. "I only pretend it's sincere."

"And will you come to me next week and recommend something different and equally sincere?"

"I may come to you next week and tell you that I am in the streets!"

"In the streets?"

"I have had a terrible scene with my brother, and he threatens, if anything happens, to turn me out of the house. You know I am a poor woman."

Morris had a speculative idea that she had a little property; but he naturally did not press this.

"I should be very sorry to see you suffer martyrdom for me," he said. "But you make your brother out a regular Turk."

Mrs. Penniman hesitated a little.

"I certainly do not regard Austin as a satisfactory Christian."

"And am I to wait till he is converted?"

"Wait, at any rate, till he is less violent. Bide your time, Mr. Townsend; remember the prize is great!"

Morris walked along some time in silence, tapping the railings and gateposts very sharply with his stick.

"You certainly are devilish inconsistent!" he broke out at last. "I have already got Catherine to consent to a private marriage."

Mrs. Penniman was indeed inconsistent, for at this news she gave a little jump of gratification.

"Oh! when and where?" she cried. And then she stopped short.

Morris was a little vague about this.

"That isn't fixed; but she consents. It's deuced awkward, now, to back out."

Mrs. Penniman, as I say, had stopped short; and she stood there with her eyes fixed brilliantly on her companion.

"Mr. Townsend," she proceeded, "shall I tell you something? Catherine loves you so much that you may do anything."

This declaration was slightly ambiguous, and Morris opened his eyes.

"I am happy to hear it! But what do you mean by 'anything'?"

"You may postpone—you may change about; she won't think the worse of you."

Morris stood there still, with his raised eyebrows; then he said simply and rather dryly—"Ah!" After this he remarked to Mrs. Penniman that if she walked so slowly she would attract notice, and he succeeded, after a fashion, in hurrying her back to the domicile of which her tenure had become so insecure.

XXII

HE had slightly misrepresented the matter in saying that Catherine had consented to take the great step. We left her just now declaring that she would burn her ships behind her; but Morris, after having elicited this declaration, had become conscious of good reasons for not taking it up. He avoided, gracefully enough, fixing a day, though he left her under the impression that he had his eye on one. Catherine may have had her difficulties; but those of her circumspect suitor are also worthy of consideration. The prize was certainly great; but it was only to be won by striking the happy mean between precipitancy and caution. It would be all very well to take one's jump and trust to Providence; Providence was more especially on the side of clever people, and clever people were known by an indisposition to risk their bones. The ultimate reward of a union with a young woman who was both unattractive and impoverished ought to be connected with immediate disadvantages by some very palpable chain. Between the fear of losing Catherine and her possible fortune altogether, and the fear of taking her too soon and finding this possible fortune as void of actuality as a collection of emptied bottles, it was not comfortable for Morris Townsend to choose; a fact that should be remembered by readers disposed to judge harshly of a young man who may have struck them as making but an indifferently successful use of fine natural parts. He had not forgotten that in any event Catherine had her own ten thousand a year; he had devoted an abundance of meditation to this circumstance. But with his fine parts he rated himself high, and he had a perfectly definite appreciation of his value, which seemed to him inadequately represented by the sum I have mentioned. At the same time he reminded himself that this sum was considerable, that everything is relative, and that if a modest income is less desirable than a large one, the complete absence of revenue is nowhere accounted an advantage. These reflexions gave him plenty of occupation, and made it necessary that he should trim his sail. Dr. Sloper's opposition was the unknown quantity in the problem he had to work out. The natural way to work it out was by marrying Catherine;

but in mathematics there are many short cuts, and Morris was not without a hope that he should yet discover one. When Catherine took him at his word and consented to renounce the attempt to mollify her father, he drew back skilfully enough, as I have said, and kept the wedding-day still an open question. Her faith in his sincerity was so complete that she was incapable of suspecting that he was playing with her; her trouble just now was of another kind. The poor girl had an admirable sense of honour; and from the moment she had brought herself to the point of violating her father's wish, it seemed to her that she had no right to enjoy his protection. It was on her conscience that she ought to live under his roof only so long as she conformed to his wisdom. There was a great deal of glory in such a position, but poor Catherine felt that she had forfeited her claim to it. She had cast her lot with a young man against whom he had solemnly warned her, and broken the contract under which he provided her with a happy home. She could not give up the young man, so she must leave the home; and the sooner the object of her preference offered her another the sooner her situation would lose its awkward twist. This was close reasoning; but it was commingled with an infinite amount of merely instinctive penitence. Catherine's days at this time were dismal, and the weight of some of her hours was almost more than she could bear. Her father never looked at her, never spoke to her. He knew perfectly what he was about, and this was part of a plan. She looked at him as much as she dared (for she was afraid of seeming to offer herself to his observation), and she pitied him for the sorrow she had brought upon him. She held up her head and busied her hands, and went about her daily occupations; and when the state of things in Washington Square seemed intolerable, she closed her eyes and indulged herself with an intellectual vision of the man for whose sake she had broken a sacred law. Mrs. Penniman, of the three persons in Washington Square, had much the most of the manner that belongs to a great crisis. If Catherine was quiet, she was quietly quiet, as I may say, and her pathetic effects, which there was no one to notice, were entirely unstudied and unintended. If the Doctor was stiff and dry and absolutely indifferent to the presence of his companions, it was so lightly, neatly, easily done, that you would have had to know him well to discover that, on the whole, he rather enjoyed having to be so disagreeable. But Mrs. Penniman was elaborately reserved and significantly silent; there was a richer rustle in the very deliberate movements to which she confined herself, and when she occasionally spoke, in connexion with some very trivial event, she had the air of meaning something deeper than what she said. Between Catherine and her father nothing had passed since the evening she went to speak to him in his study. She had something to say to him—it seemed to her she ought to say it; but she kept it back, for fear of irritating him. He also had something to say to her; but he was determined not to speak first. He was interested, as we know, in seeing how, if she were left to herself, she would "stick." At last she told him she had seen Morris Townsend again, and that their relations remained quite the same.

"I think we shall marry—before very long. And probably, meanwhile, I shall see him rather often; about once a week, not more."

The Doctor looked at her coldly from head to foot, as if she had been a stranger. It was the first time his eyes had rested on her for a week, which was fortunate, if that was to be their expression. "Why not three times a day?" he asked. "What prevents your meeting as often as you choose?"

She turned away a moment; there were tears in her eyes. Then she said, "It is better once a week."

"I don't see how it is better. It is as bad as it can be. If you flatter yourself that I care for little modifications of that sort, you are very much mistaken. It is as wrong of you to see him once a week as it would be to see him all day long. Not that it matters to me, however."

Catherine tried to follow these words, but they seemed to lead towards a vague horror from which she recoiled. "I think we shall marry pretty soon," she repeated at last.

Her father gave her his dreadful look again, as if she were some one else. "Why do you tell me that? It's no concern of mine."

"Oh, father!" she broke out, "don't you care, even if you do feel so?"

"Not a button. Once you marry, it's quite the same to me when or where or why you do it; and if you think to compound for your folly by hoisting your flag in this way, you may spare yourself the trouble."

With this he turned away. But the next day he spoke to her of his own accord, and his manner was somewhat changed. "Shall you be married within the next four or five months?" he asked.

"I don't know, father," said Catherine. "It is not very easy for us to make up our minds."

"Put it off, then, for six months, and in the meantime I will take you to Europe. I should like you very much to go."

It gave her such delight, after his words of the day before, to hear that he should "like" her to do something, and that he still had in his heart any of the tenderness of preference, that she gave a little exclamation of joy. But then she became conscious that Morris was not included in this proposal, and that—as regards really going—she would greatly prefer to remain at home with him. But she blushed, none the less, more comfortably than she had done of late. "It would be delightful to go to Europe," she remarked, with a sense that the idea was not original, and that her tone was not all it might be.

"Very well, then, we will go. Pack up your clothes."

"I had better tell Mr. Townsend," said Catherine.

Her father fixed his cold eyes upon her. "If you mean that you had better ask his leave, all that remains to me is to hope he will give it."

The girl was sharply touched by the pathetic ring of the words; it was the most calculated, the most dramatic little speech the Doctor had ever uttered. She felt that it was a great thing for her, under the circumstances, to have this fine opportunity of showing him her respect; and yet there was something else that she felt as well, and that she presently expressed. "I sometimes think that if I do what you dislike so much, I ought not to stay with you."

"To stay with me?"

"If I live with you, I ought to obey you."

"If that's your theory, it's certainly mine," said the Doctor, with a dry laugh.

"But if I don't obey you, I ought not to live with you—to enjoy your kindness and protection."

This striking argument gave the Doctor a sudden sense of having underestimated his daughter; it seemed even more than worthy of a young woman who had revealed the quality of unaggressive obstinacy. But it displeased him—displeased him deeply, and he signified as much. "That idea is in very bad taste," he said. "Did you get it from Mr. Townsend?"

"Oh no; it's my own!" said Catherine eagerly.

"Keep it to yourself, then," her father answered, more than ever determined she should go to Europe.

XXIII

IF Morris Townsend was not to be included in this journey, no more was Mrs. Penniman, who would have been thankful for an invitation, but who (to do her justice) bore her disappointment in a perfectly ladylike manner. "I should enjoy seeing the works of Raphael and the ruins—the ruins of the Pantheon," she said to Mrs. Almond; "but, on the other hand, I shall not be sorry to be alone and at peace for the next few months in Washington Square. I want rest; I have been through so much in the last four months." Mrs. Almond thought it rather cruel that her brother should not take poor Lavinia abroad; but she easily understood that, if the purpose of his expedition was to make Catherine forget her lover, it was not in his interest to give his daughter this young man's best friend as a companion. "If Lavinia had not been so foolish, she might visit the ruins of the Pantheon," she said to herself; and she continued to regret her sister's folly, even though the latter assured her that she had often heard the relics in question most satisfactorily described by Mr. Penniman. Mrs. Penniman was perfectly aware that her brother's motive in undertaking a foreign tour was to lay a trap for Catherine's constancy; and she imparted this conviction very frankly to her niece.

"He thinks it will make you forget Morris," she said (she always called the young man "Morris" now); "out of sight, out of mind, you know. He thinks that all the things you will see over there will drive him out of your thoughts."

Catherine looked greatly alarmed. "If he thinks that, I ought to tell him beforehand."

Mrs. Penniman shook her head. "Tell him afterwards, my dear! After he has had all the trouble and the expense! That's the way to serve him." And she added, in a softer key, that it must be delightful to think of those who love us among the ruins of the Pantheon.

Her father's displeasure had cost the girl, as we know, a great deal of deep-welling sorrow—sorrow of the purest and most generous kind, without a touch of resentment or rancour; but for the first time, after he had dismissed with such contemptuous brevity her apology for being a charge upon him, there was a spark of anger in her grief. She had felt his contempt; it had scorched her; that speech about her bad taste made her ears burn for three days. During this period she was less considerate; she had an idea—a rather vague one, but it was agreeable to her sense of injury—that now she was absolved from penance, and might do what she chose. She chose to write to Morris Townsend to meet her in the Square and take her to walk about the town. If she were going to Europe out of respect to her father, she might at least give herself this satisfaction. She felt in every way at present more free and more resolute; there was a force that urged her. Now at last, completely and unreservedly, her passion possessed her.

Morris met her at last, and they took a long walk. She told him immediately what had happened—that her father wished to take her away. It would be for six months, to Europe; she would do absolutely what Morris should think best. She hoped inexpressibly that he would think it best she should stay at home. It was some time before he said what he thought: he asked, as they walked along, a great many questions. There was one that especially struck her; it seemed so incongruous.

"Should you like to see all those celebrated things over there?"

"Oh no, Morris!" said Catherine, quite deprecatingly.

"Gracious Heaven, what a dull woman!" Morris exclaimed to himself.

"He thinks I will forget you," said Catherine: "that all these things will drive you out of my mind."

"Well, my dear, perhaps they will!"

"Please don't say that," Catherine answered gently, as they walked along. "Poor father will be disappointed."

Morris gave a little laugh. "Yes, I verily believe that your poor father will be disappointed! But you will have seen Europe," he added humorously. "What a take-in!"

"I don't care for seeing Europe," Catherine said.

"You ought to care, my dear. And it may mollify your father."

Catherine, conscious of her obstinacy, expected little of this, and could not rid herself of the idea that in going abroad and yet remaining firm, she should play her father a trick. "Don't you think it would be a kind of deception?" she asked.

"Doesn't he want to deceive you?" cried Morris. "It will serve him right! I really think you had better go."

"And not be married for so long?"

"Be married when you come back. You can buy your wedding clothes in Paris." And then Morris, with great kindness of tone, explained his view of the matter. It would be a good thing that she should go; it would put them completely in the right. It would show they were reasonable and willing to wait. Once they were so sure of each other, they could afford to wait—what had they to fear? If there was a particle of chance that her father would be favourably affected by her going, that ought to settle it; for, after all, Morris was very unwilling to be the cause of her being disinherited. It was not for himself, it was for her and for her children. He was willing to wait for her; it would be hard, but he could do it. And over there, among beautiful scenes and noble monuments, perhaps the old gentleman would be softened; such things were supposed to exert a humanising influence. He might be touched by her gentleness, her patience, her willingness to make any sacrifice but *that* one; and if she should appeal to him some day, in some celebrated spot—in Italy, say, in the evening; in Venice, in a gondola, by moonlight—if she should be a little clever about it and touch the right chord, perhaps he would fold her in his arms and tell her that he forgave her. Catherine was immensely struck with this conception of the affair, which seemed eminently worthy of her lover's brilliant intellect; though she viewed it askance in so far as it depended upon her own powers of execution. The idea of being "clever" in a gondola by moonlight appeared to her to involve elements of which her grasp was not active. But it was settled between them that she should tell her father that she was ready to follow him obediently anywhere, making the mental reservation that she loved Morris Townsend more than ever.

She informed the Doctor she was ready to embark, and he made rapid arrangements for this event. Catherine had many farewells to make, but with only two of them are we actively concerned. Mrs. Penniman took a discriminating view of her niece's journey; it seemed to her very proper that Mr. Townsend's destined bride should wish to embellish her mind by a foreign tour.

"You leave him in good hands," she said, pressing her lips to Catherine's forehead. (She was very fond of kissing people's foreheads; it was an involuntary expression of sympathy with the intellectual part.) "I shall see him often; I shall feel like one of the vestals of old, tending the sacred flame."

"You behave beautifully about not going with us," Catherine answered, not presuming to examine this analogy.

"It is my pride that keeps me up," said Mrs. Penniman, tapping the body of her dress, which always gave forth a sort of metallic ring.

Catherine's parting with her lover was short, and few words were exchanged.

"Shall I find you just the same when I come back?" she asked; though the question was not the fruit of scepticism.

"The same—only more so!" said Morris, smiling.

It does not enter into our scheme to narrate in detail Dr. Sloper's proceedings in the eastern hemisphere. He made the grand tour of Europe, travelled in considerable splendour, and (as was to have been expected in a man of his high cultivation) found so much in art and antiquity to interest him, that he remained abroad, not for six months, but for twelve. Mrs. Penniman, in Washington Square, accommodated herself to his absence. She enjoyed her uncontested dominion in the empty house, and flattered herself that she made it more attractive to their friends than when her brother was at home. To Morris Townsend, at least, it would have appeared that she made it singularly attractive. He was altogether her most frequent visitor, and Mrs. Penniman was very fond of asking him to tea. He had his chair—a very easy one at the fireside in the back parlour (when the great mahogany sliding-doors, with silver knobs and hinges, which divided this apartment from its more formal neighbour, were closed), and he used to smoke cigars in the Doctor's study, where he often spent an hour in turning over the curious collections of its absent proprietor. He thought Mrs. Penniman a goose, as we know; but he was no goose himself, and, as a young man of luxurious tastes and scanty resources, he found the house a perfect castle of indolence. It became for him a club with a single member. Mrs. Penniman saw much less of her sister than while the Doctor was at home; for Mrs. Almond had felt moved to tell her that she disapproved of her relations with Mr. Townsend. She had no business to be so friendly to a young man of whom their brother thought so meanly, and Mrs. Almond was surprised at her levity in foisting a most deplorable engagement upon Catherine.

"Deplorable?" cried Lavinia. "He will make her a lovely husband!"

"I don't believe in lovely husbands," said Mrs. Almond; "I only believe in good ones. If he marries her, and she comes into Austin's money, they may get on. He will be an idle, amiable, selfish, and doubtless tolerably good-natured fellow. But if she doesn't get the money and he finds himself tied to her, Heaven have mercy on her! He will have none. He will hate her for his disappointment, and take his revenge; he will be pitiless and cruel. Woe betide poor Catherine! I recommend you to talk a little with his sister; it's a pity Catherine can't marry *her!*"

Mrs. Penniman had no appetite whatever for conversation with Mrs. Montgomery, whose acquaintance she made no trouble to cultivate; and the effect of this alarming forecast of her niece's destiny was to make her think it indeed a thousand pities that Mr. Townsend's generous nature should be embittered. Bright enjoyment was his natural element, and how could he be comfortable if there should prove to be nothing to enjoy? It became a fixed idea with Mrs. Penniman that he should yet enjoy her brother's fortune, on which she had acuteness enough to perceive that her own claim was small.

"If he doesn't leave it to Catherine, it certainly won't be to leave it to me," she said.

XXIV

THE Doctor, during the first six months he was abroad, never spoke to his daughter of their little difference; partly on system, and partly because he had a great many other things to think about. It was idle to attempt to ascertain the state of her affections without direct inquiry, because, if she had not had an expressive manner among the familiar influences of home, she failed to gather animation from the mountains of Switzerland or the monuments of Italy. She was always her father's docile and reasonable associate—going through their sight-seeing in deferential silence, never complaining of fatigue, always ready to start at the hour he had appointed over-night, making no foolish criticisms and indulging in no refinements of appreciation. "She is about as intelligent as the bundle of shawls," the Doctor said; her main superiority being that while the bundle of shawls sometimes got lost, or tumbled out of the carriage, Catherine was always at her post, and had a firm and ample seat. But her father had expected this, and he was not constrained to set down her intellectual limitations as a tourist to sentimental depression; she had completely divested herself of the characteristics of a victim, and during the whole time that they were abroad she never uttered an audible sigh. He supposed she was in correspondence with Morris Townsend; but he held his peace about it, for he never saw the young man's letters, and Catherine's own missives were always given to the courier to post. She heard from her lover with considerable regularity, but his letters came enclosed in Mrs. Penniman's; so that whenever the Doctor handed her a packet addressed in his sister's hand, he was an involuntary instrument of the passion he condemned. Catherine made this reflexion, and six months earlier she would have felt bound to give him warning; but now she deemed herself absolved. There was a sore spot in her heart that his own words had made when once she spoke to him as she thought honour prompted; she would try and please him as far as she could, but she would never speak that way again. She read her lover's letters in secret.

One day at the end of the summer, the two travellers found themselves in a lonely valley of the Alps. They were crossing one of the passes, and on the long ascent they had got out of the carriage and had wandered much in advance. After a while the Doctor descried a footpath which, leading through a transverse valley, would bring them out, as he justly supposed, at a much higher point of the ascent. They followed this devious way, and finally lost the path; the valley proved very wild and rough, and their walk became rather a scramble. They were good walkers, however, and they took their adventure easily; from time to time they stopped, that Catherine might rest; and then she sat upon a stone and looked about her at the hard-featured rocks and the glowing sky. It was late in the afternoon, in the last of August; night was coming on, and, as they had reached a great elevation, the air was cold and sharp. In the west there was a great suffusion of cold, red light, which made the sides of the little valley look only the more rugged and dusky. During one of their pauses, her father left her and wandered away to some high place, at a distance, to get a view. He was out of sight; she sat there alone, in the stillness, which was just touched by the vague murmur, somewhere, of a mountain brook. She thought of Morris Townsend, and the place was so desolate and lonely that he seemed very far away. Her father remained absent a long time; she began to wonder what had become of him. But at last he reappeared, coming towards her in the clear twilight, and she got up, to go on. He made no motion to proceed, however, but came close to her, as if he had something to say. He stopped in front of her and stood looking at her, with eyes that had kept the light of the flushing snow-summits on which they had just been fixed. Then, abruptly, in a low tone, he asked her an unexpected question:

"Have you given him up?"

The question was unexpected, but Catherine was only superficially unprepared.

"No, father!" she answered.

He looked at her again for some moments, without speaking.

"Does he write to you?" he asked.

"Yes—about twice a month."

The Doctor looked up and down the valley, swinging his stick; then he said to her, in the same low tone:

"I am very angry."

She wondered what he meant—whether he wished to frighten her. If he did, the place was well chosen; this hard, melancholy dell, abandoned by the summer light, made her feel her loneliness. She looked around her, and her heart grew cold; for a moment her fear was great. But she could think of nothing to say, save to murmur gently, "I am sorry."

"You try my patience," her father went on, "and you ought to know what I am, I am not a very good man. Though I am very smooth externally, at bottom I am very passionate; and I assure you I can be very hard."

She could not think why he told her these things. Had he brought her there on purpose, and was it part of a plan? What was the plan? Catherine asked herself. Was it to startle her suddenly into a retractation—to take an advantage of her by dread? Dread of what? The place was ugly and lonely, but the place could do her no harm. There was a kind of still intensity about her father, which made him dangerous, but Catherine hardly went so far as to say to herself that it might be part of his plan to fasten his hand—the neat, fine, supple hand of a distinguished physician—in her throat. Nevertheless, she receded a step. "I am sure you can be anything you please," she said. And it was her simple belief.

"I am very angry," he replied, more sharply.

"Why has it taken you so suddenly?"

"It has not taken me suddenly. I have been raging inwardly for the last six months. But just now this seemed a good place to flare out. It's so quiet, and we are alone."

"Yes, it's very quiet," said Catherine vaguely, looking about her. "Won't you come back to the carriage?"

"In a moment. Do you mean that in all this time you have not yielded an inch?"

"I would if I could, father; but I can't."

The Doctor looked round him too. "Should you like to be left in such a place as this, to starve?"

"What do you mean?" cried the girl.

"That will be your fate—that's how he will leave you."

He would not touch her, but he had touched Morris. The warmth came back to her heart. "That is not true, father," she broke out, "and you ought not to say it! It is not right, and it's not true!"

He shook his head slowly. "No, it's not right, because you won't believe it. But it *is* true. Come back to the carriage."

He turned away, and she followed him; he went faster, and was presently much in advance. But from time to time he stopped, without turning round, to let her keep up with him, and she made her way forward with difficulty, her heart beating with the excitement of having for the first time spoken to him in violence. By this time it had grown almost dark, and she ended by losing sight of him. But she kept her course, and after a little, the valley making a sudden turn, she gained the road, where the carriage stood waiting. In it sat her father, rigid and silent; in silence, too, she took her place beside him.

It seemed to her, later, in looking back upon all this, that for days afterwards not a word had been exchanged between them. The scene had been a strange one, but it had not permanently affected her feeling towards her father, for it was natural, after all, that he should occasionally make a scene of some kind, and he had let her alone for six months. The strangest part of it was that he had said he was not a good man; Catherine wondered a great deal what he had meant by that. The statement failed to appeal to her credence, and it was not grateful to any resentment that she entertained. Even in the utmost bitterness that she might feel, it would give her no satisfaction to think him less complete. Such a saying as that was a part of his great subtlety—men so clever as he might say anything and mean anything. And as to his being hard, that surely, in a man, was a virtue.

He let her alone for six months more—six months during which she accommodated herself without a protest to the extension of their tour. But he spoke again at the end of this time; it was at the very last, the night before they embarked for New York, in the hotel at Liverpool. They had been dining together in a great dim, musty sitting-room; and then the cloth had been removed, and the Doctor walked slowly up and down. Catherine at last took her candle to go to bed, but her father motioned her to stay.

"What do you mean to do when you get home?" he asked, while she stood there with her candle in her hand.

"Do you mean about Mr. Townsend?"

"About Mr. Townsend."

"We shall probably marry."

The Doctor took several turns again while she waited. "Do you hear from him as much as ever?"

"Yes; twice a month," said Catherine promptly.

"And does he always talk about marriage?"

"Oh yes! That is, he talks about other things too, but he always says something about that."

"I am glad to hear he varies his subjects; his letters might otherwise be monotonous."

"He writes beautifully," said Catherine, who was very glad of a chance to say it.

"They always write beautifully. However, in a given case that doesn't diminish the merit. So, as soon as you arrive, you are going off with him?"

This seemed a rather gross way of putting it, and something that there was of dignity in Catherine resented it. "I cannot tell you till we arrive," she said.

"That's reasonable enough," her father answered. "That's all I ask of you—that you *do* tell me, that you give me definite notice. When a poor man is to lose his only child, he likes to have an inkling of it beforehand."

"Oh, father, you will not lose me!" Catherine said, spilling her candle-wax.

"Three days before will do," he went on, "if you are in a position to be positive then. He ought to be very thankful to me, do you know. I have done a mighty good thing for him in taking you abroad; your value is twice as great, with all the knowledge and taste that you have acquired. A year ago, you were perhaps a little limited—a little rustic; but now you have seen everything, and appreciated everything, and you will be a most entertaining companion. We have fattened the sheep for him before he kills it!" Catherine turned away, and stood staring at the blank door. "Go to bed," said her father; "and, as we don't go aboard till noon, you may sleep late. We shall probably have a most uncomfortable voyage."

XXV

THE voyage was indeed uncomfortable, and Catherine, on arriving in New York, had not the compensation of "going off," in her father's phrase, with Morris Townsend. She saw him, however, the day after she landed; and, in the meantime, he formed a natural subject of conversation between our heroine and her Aunt Lavinia, with whom, the night she disembarked, the girl was closeted for a long time before either lady retired to rest.

"I have seen a great deal of him," said Mrs. Penniman. "He is not very easy to know. I suppose you think you know him; but you don't, my dear. You will some day; but it will only be after you have lived with him. I may almost say *I* have lived with him," Mrs. Penniman proceeded, while Catherine stared. "I think I know him now; I have had such remarkable opportunities. You will have the same—or rather, you will have better!" and Aunt Lavinia smiled. "Then you will see what I mean. It's a wonderful character, full of passion and energy, and just as true!"

Catherine listened with a mixture of interest and apprehension. Aunt Lavinia was intensely sympathetic, and Catherine, for the past year, while she wandered through foreign galleries and churches, and rolled over the smoothness of posting roads, nursing the thoughts that never passed her lips, had often longed for the company of some intelligent person of her own sex. To tell her story to some kind woman—at moments it seemed to her that this would give her comfort, and she had more than once been on the point of taking the landlady, or the nice young person from the dressmaker's, into her confidence. If a woman had been near her she would on certain occasions have treated such a companion to a fit of weeping; and she had an apprehension that, on her return, this would form her response to Aunt Lavinia's first embrace. In fact, however, the two ladies had met, in Washington Square, without tears, and when they found themselves alone together a certain dryness fell upon the girl's emotion. It came over her with a greater force that Mrs. Penniman had enjoyed a whole year of her lover's society, and it was not a pleasure to her to hear her aunt explain and interpret the young man, speaking of him as if her own knowledge of him were supreme. It was not that Catherine was jealous; but her sense of Mrs. Penniman's innocent falsity, which had lain dormant, began to haunt her again, and she was glad that she was safely at home. With this, however, it was a blessing to be able to talk of Morris, to sound his name, to be with a person who was not unjust to him.

"You have been very kind to him," said Catherine. "He has written me that, often. I shall never forget that, Aunt Lavinia."

"I have done what I could; it has been very little. To let him come and talk to me, and give him his cup of tea—that was all. Your Aunt Almond thought it was too much, and used to scold me terribly; but she promised me, at least, not to betray me."

"To betray you?"

"Not to tell your father. He used to sit in your father's study!" said Mrs. Penniman, with a little laugh.

Catherine was silent a moment. This idea was disagreeable to her, and she was reminded again, with pain, of her aunt's secretive habits. Morris, the reader may be informed, had had the tact not to tell her that he sat in her father's study. He had known her but for a few months, and her aunt had known her for fifteen years; and yet he would not have made the mistake of thinking that Catherine would see the joke of the thing. "I am sorry you made him go into father's room," she said, after a while.

"I didn't make him go; he went himself. He liked to look at the books, and all those things in the glass cases. He knows all about them; he knows all about everything."

Catherine was silent again; then, "I wish he had found some employment," she said.

"He has found some employment! It's beautiful news, and he told me to tell you as soon as you arrived. He has gone into partnership with a commission merchant. It was all settled, quite suddenly, a week ago."

This seemed to Catherine indeed beautiful news; it had a fine prosperous air. "Oh, I'm so glad!" she said; and now, for a moment, she was disposed to throw herself on Aunt Lavinia's neck.

"It's much better than being under some one; and he has never been used to that," Mrs. Penniman went on. "He is just as good as his partner— they are perfectly equal! You see how right he was to wait. I should like to know what your father can say now! They have got an office in Duane Street, and little printed cards; he brought me one to show me. I have got it in my room, and you shall see it to-morrow. That's what he said to me the last time he was here—'You see how right I was to wait!' He has got other people under him, instead of being a subordinate. He could never be a subordinate; I have often told him I could never think of him in that way."

Catherine assented to this proposition, and was very happy to know that Morris was his own master; but she was deprived of the satisfaction of thinking that she might communicate this news in triumph to her father. Her father would care equally little whether Morris were established in business or transported for life. Her trunks had been brought into her room, and further reference to her lover was for a short time suspended, while she opened them and displayed to her aunt some of the spoils of foreign travel. These were rich and abundant; and Catherine had brought home a present to every one— to every one save Morris, to whom she had brought simply her undiverted heart. To Mrs. Penniman she had been lavishly generous, and Aunt Lavinia spent half an hour in unfolding and folding again, with little ejaculations of gratitude and taste. She marched about for some time in a splendid cashmere shawl, which Catherine had begged her to accept, settling it on her shoulders, and twisting down her head to see how low the point descended behind.

"I shall regard it only as a loan," she said. "I will leave it to you again when I die; or rather," she added, kissing her niece again, "I will leave it to your first-born little girl!" And draped in her shawl, she stood there smiling.

"You had better wait till she comes," said Catherine.

"I don't like the way you say that," Mrs. Penniman rejoined, in a moment. "Catherine, are you changed?"

"No; I am the same."

"You have not swerved a line?"

"I am exactly the same," Catherine repeated, wishing her aunt were a little less sympathetic.

"Well, I am glad!" and Mrs. Penniman surveyed her cashmere in the glass. Then, "How is your father?" she asked in a moment, with her eyes on her niece. "Your letters were so meagre—I could never tell!"

"Father is very well."

"Ah, you know what I mean," said Mrs. Penniman, with a dignity to which the cashmere gave a richer effect. "Is he still implacable!"

"Oh yes!"

"Quite unchanged?"

"He is, if possible, more firm."

Mrs. Penniman took off her great shawl, and slowly folded it up. "That is very bad. You had no success with your little project?"

"What little project?"

"Morris told me all about it. The idea of turning the tables on him, in Europe; of watching him, when he was agreeably impressed by some celebrated sight—he pretends to be so artistic, you know—and then just pleading with him and bringing him round."

"I never tried it. It was Morris's idea; but if he had been with us, in Europe, he would have seen that father was never impressed in that way. He *is* artistic—tremendously artistic; but the more celebrated places we visited, and the more he admired them, the less use it would have been to plead with him. They seemed only to make him more determined—more terrible," said poor Catherine. "I shall never bring him round, and I expect nothing now."

"Well, I must say," Mrs. Penniman answered, "I never supposed you were going to give it up."

"I have given it up. I don't care now."

"You have grown very brave," said Mrs. Penniman, with a short laugh. "I didn't advise you to sacrifice your property."

"Yes, I am braver than I was. You asked me if I had changed; I have changed in that way. Oh," the girl went on, "I have changed very much. And it isn't my property. If *he* doesn't care for it, why should I?"

Mrs. Penniman hesitated. "Perhaps he does care for it."

"He cares for it for my sake, because he doesn't want to injure me. But he will know—he knows already—how little he need be afraid about that. Besides," said Catherine, "I have got plenty of money of my own. We shall be very well off; and now hasn't he got his business? I am delighted about that business." She went on talking, showing a good deal of excitement as she proceeded. Her aunt had never seen her with just this manner, and Mrs. Penniman, observing her, set it down to foreign travel, which had made her more positive, more mature. She thought also that Catherine had improved in appearance; she looked rather handsome. Mrs. Penniman wondered whether Morris Townsend would be struck with that. While she was engaged in this speculation, Catherine broke out, with a certain sharpness, "Why are you so contradictory, Aunt Penniman? You seem to think one thing at one time, and another at another. A year ago, before I went away, you wished me not to mind about displeasing father; and now you seem to recommend me to take another line. You change about so."

This attack was unexpected, for Mrs. Penniman was not used, in any discussion, to seeing the war carried into her own country—possibly because the enemy generally had doubts of finding subsistence there. To her own consciousness, the flowery fields of her reason had rarely been ravaged by a hostile force. It was perhaps on this account that in defending them she was majestic rather than agile.

"I don't know what you accuse me of, save of being too deeply interested in your happiness. It is the first time I have been told I am capricious. That fault is not what I am usually reproached with."

"You were angry last year that I wouldn't marry immediately, and now you talk about my winning my father over. You told me it would serve him right if he should take me to Europe for nothing. Well, he has taken me for nothing, and you ought to be satisfied. Nothing is changed—nothing but my feeling about father. I don't mind nearly so much now. I have been as good as I could, but he doesn't care. Now I don't care either. I don't know whether I have grown bad; perhaps I have. But I don't care for that. I have come home to be married—that's all I know. That ought to please you, unless you have taken up some new idea; you are so strange. You may do as you please; but you must never speak to me again about pleading with father. I shall never plead with him for anything; that is all over. He has put me off. I am come home to be married."

This was a more authoritative speech than she had ever heard on her niece's lips, and Mrs. Penniman was proportionately startled. She was indeed a little awestruck, and the force of the girl's emotion and resolution left her nothing to reply. She was easily frightened, and she always carried off her discomfiture by a concession; a concession which was often accompanied, as in the present case, by a little nervous laugh.

XXVI

IF she had disturbed her niece's temper—she began from this moment forward to talk a good deal about Catherine's temper, an article which up to that time had never been mentioned in connexion with our heroine—Catherine had opportunity, on the morrow, to recover her serenity. Mrs. Penniman had given her a message from Morris Townsend, to the effect that he would come and welcome her home on the day after her arrival. He came in the afternoon; but, as may be imagined, he was not on this occasion made free of Dr. Sloper's study. He had been coming and going, for the past year, so comfortably and irresponsibly, that he had a certain sense of being wronged by finding himself reminded that he must now limit his horizon to the front parlour, which was Catherine's particular province.

"I am very glad you have come back," he said; "it makes me very happy to see you again." And he looked at her, smiling, from head to foot; though it did not appear, afterwards, that he agreed with Mrs. Penniman (who, womanlike, went more into details) in thinking her embellished.

To Catherine he appeared resplendent; it was some time before she could believe again that this beautiful young man was her own exclusive property. They had a great deal of characteristic lovers' talk—a soft exchange of inquiries and assurances. In these matters Morris had an excellent grace, which flung a picturesque interest even over the account of his début in the commission business—a subject as to which his companion earnestly questioned him. From time to time he got up from the sofa where they sat together, and walked about the room; after which he came back, smiling and passing his hand through his hair. He was unquiet, as was natural in a young man who has just been reunited to a long-absent mistress, and Catherine made the reflexion that she had never seen him so excited. It gave her pleasure, somehow, to note this fact. He asked her questions about her travels, to some of which she was unable to reply, for she had forgotten the names of places, and the order of her father's journey. But for the moment she was so happy, so lifted up by the belief that her troubles at last were over, that she forgot to be ashamed of her meagre answers. It seemed to her now that she could marry him without the remnant of a scruple or a single tremor save those that belonged to joy. Without waiting for him to ask, she told him that her father had come back in exactly the same state of mind—that he had not yielded an inch.

"We must not expect it now," she said, "and we must do without it."

Morris sat looking and smiling. "My poor dear girl!" he exclaimed.

"You mustn't pity me," said Catherine; "I don't mind it now—I am used to it."

Morris continued to smile, and then he got up and walked about again. "You had better let me try him!"

"Try to bring him over? You would only make him worse," Catherine answered resolutely.

"You say that because I managed it so badly before. But I should manage it differently now. I am much wiser; I have had a year to think of it. I have more tact."

"Is that what you have been thinking of for a year?"

"Much of the time. You see, the idea sticks in my crop. I don't like to be beaten."

"How are you beaten if we marry?"

"Of course, I am not beaten on the main issue; but I am, don't you see, on all the rest of it—on the question of my reputation, of my relations with your father, of my relations with my own children, if we should have any."

"We shall have enough for our children—we shall have enough for everything. Don't you expect to succeed in business?"

"Brilliantly, and we shall certainly be very comfortable. But it isn't of the mere material comfort I speak; it is of the moral comfort," said Morris— "of the intellectual satisfaction!"

"I have great moral comfort now," Catherine declared, very simply.

"Of course you have. But with me it is different. I have staked my pride on proving to your father that he is wrong; and now that I am at the head of a flourishing business, I can deal with him as an equal. I have a capital plan—do let me go at him!"

He stood before her with his bright face, his jaunty air, his hands in his pockets; and she got up, with her eyes resting on his own. "Please don't, Morris; please don't," she said; and there was a certain mild, sad firmness in her tone which he heard for the first time. "We must ask no favours of him— we must ask nothing more. He won't relent, and nothing good will come of it. I know it now—I have a very good reason."

"And pray; what is your reason?"

She hesitated to bring it out, but at last it came. "He is not very fond of me!"

"Oh, bother!" cried Morris angrily.

"I wouldn't say such a thing without being sure. I saw it, I felt it, in England, just before he came away. He talked to me one night—the last night; and then it came over me. You can tell when a person feels that way. I wouldn't accuse him if he hadn't made me feel that way. I don't accuse him; I just tell you that that's how it is. He can't help it; we can't govern our affections. Do I govern mine? mightn't he say that to me? It's because he is so fond of my mother, whom we lost so long ago. She was beautiful, and very, very brilliant; he is always thinking of her. I am not at all like her; Aunt Penniman has told me that. Of course, it isn't my fault; but neither is it his fault. All I mean is, it's true; and it's a stronger reason for his never being reconciled than simply his dislike for you."

"'Simply?'" cried Morris, with a laugh, "I am much obliged for that!"

"I don't mind about his disliking you now; I mind everything less. I feel differently; I feel separated from my father."

"Upon my word," said Morris, "you are a queer family!"

"Don't say that—don't say anything unkind," the girl entreated. "You must be very kind to me now, because, Morris—because," and she hesitated a moment—"because I have done a great deal for you."

"Oh, I know that, my dear!"

She had spoken up to this moment without vehemence or outward sign of emotion, gently, reasoningly, only trying to explain. But her emotion had been ineffectually smothered, and it betrayed itself at last in the trembling of her voice. "It is a great thing to be separated like that from your father, when you have worshipped him before. It has made me very unhappy; or it would have made me so if I didn't love you. You can tell when a person speaks to you as if—as if—"

"As if what?"

"As if they despised you!" said Catherine passionately. "He spoke that way the night before we sailed. It wasn't much, but it was enough, and I thought of it on the voyage, all the time. Then I made up my mind. I will never ask him for anything again, or expect anything from him. It would not be natural now. We must be very happy together, and we must not seem to depend upon his forgiveness. And Morris, Morris, you must never despise me!"

This was an easy promise to make, and Morris made it with fine effect. But for the moment he undertook nothing more onerous.

XXVII

THE Doctor, of course, on his return, had a good deal of talk with his sisters. He was at no great pains to narrate his travels or to communicate his impressions of distant lands to Mrs. Penniman, upon whom he contented himself with bestowing a memento of his enviable experience, in the shape of a velvet gown. But he conversed with her at some length about matters nearer home, and lost no time in assuring her that he was still an inflexible father.

"I have no doubt you have seen a great deal of Mr. Townsend, and done your best to console him for Catherine's absence," he said. "I don't ask you, and you needn't deny it. I wouldn't put the question to you for the world, and expose you to the inconvenience of having to—a—excogitate an answer. No one has betrayed you, and there has been no spy upon your proceedings. Elizabeth has told no tales, and has never mentioned you except to praise your good looks and good spirits. The thing is simply an inference of my own—an induction, as the philosophers say. It seems to me likely that you would have offered an asylum to an interesting sufferer. Mr. Townsend has been a good deal in the house; there is something in the house that tells me so. We doctors, you know, end by acquiring fine perceptions, and it is impressed upon my sensorium that he has sat in these chairs, in a very easy attitude, and warmed himself at that fire. I don't grudge him the comfort of it; it is the only one he will ever enjoy at my expense. It seems likely, indeed, that I shall be able to economise at his own. I don't know what you may have said to him, or what you may say hereafter; but I should like you to know that if you have encouraged him to believe that he will gain anything by hanging on, or that I have budged a hair's-breadth from the position I took up a year ago, you have played him a trick for which he may exact reparation. I'm not sure that he may not bring a suit against you. Of course you have done it conscientiously; you have made yourself believe that I can be tired out. This is the most baseless hallucination that ever visited the brain of a genial optimist. I am not in the least tired; I am as fresh as when I started; I am good for fifty years yet. Catherine appears not to have budged an inch either; she is equally fresh; so we are about where we were before. This, however, you know as well as I. What I wish is simply to give you notice of my own state of mind! Take it to heart, dear Lavinia. Beware of the just resentment of a deluded fortune-hunter!"

"I can't say I expected it," said Mrs. Penniman. "And I had a sort of foolish hope that you would come home without that odious ironical tone with which you treat the most sacred subjects."

"Don't undervalue irony, it is often of great use. It is not, however, always necessary, and I will show you how gracefully I can lay it aside. I should like to know whether you think Morris Townsend will hang on."

"I will answer you with your own weapons," said Mrs. Penniman. "You had better wait and see!"

"Do you call such a speech as that one of my own weapons? I never said anything so rough."

"He will hang on long enough to make you very uncomfortable, then."

"My dear Lavinia," exclaimed the Doctor, "do you call that irony? I call it pugilism."

Mrs. Penniman, however, in spite of her pugilism, was a good deal frightened, and she took counsel of her fears. Her brother meanwhile took counsel, with many reservations, of Mrs. Almond, to whom he was no less generous than to Lavinia, and a good deal more communicative.

"I suppose she has had him there all the while," he said. "I must look into the state of my wine! You needn't mind telling me now; I have already said all I mean to say to her on the subject."

"I believe he was in the house a good deal," Mrs. Almond answered. "But you must admit that your leaving Lavinia quite alone was a great change for her, and that it was natural she should want some society."

"I do admit that, and that is why I shall make no row about the wine; I shall set it down as compensation to Lavinia. She is capable of telling me that she drank it all herself. Think of the inconceivable bad taste, in the circumstances, of that fellow making free with the house—or coming there at all! If that doesn't describe him, he is indescribable."

"His plan is to get what he can. Lavinia will have supported him for a year," said Mrs. Almond. "It's so much gained."

"She will have to support him for the rest of his life, then!" cried the Doctor. "But without wine, as they say at the *tables d'hôte*."

"Catherine tells me he has set up a business, and is making a great deal of money."

The Doctor stared. "She has not told me that—and Lavinia didn't deign. Ah!" he cried, "Catherine has given me up. Not that it matters, for all that the business amounts to."

"She has not given up Mr. Townsend," said Mrs. Almond. "I saw that in the first half minute. She has come home exactly the same."

"Exactly the same; not a grain more intelligent. She didn't notice a stick or a stone all the while we were away—not a picture nor a view, not a statue nor a cathedral."

"How could she notice? She had other things to think of; they are never for an instant out of her mind. She touches me very much."

"She would touch me if she didn't irritate me. That's the effect she has upon me now. I have tried everything upon her; I really have been quite merciless. But it is of no use whatever; she is absolutely *glued*. I have passed, in consequence, into the exasperated stage. At first I had a good deal of a certain genial curiosity about it; I wanted to see if she really would stick. But, good Lord, one's curiosity is satisfied! I see she is capable of it, and now she can let go."

"She will never let go," said Mrs. Almond.

"Take care, or you will exasperate me too. If she doesn't let go, she will be shaken off—sent tumbling into the dust! That's a nice position for my daughter. She can't see that if you are going to be pushed you had better jump. And then she will complain of her bruises."

"She will never complain," said Mrs. Almond.

"That I shall object to even more. But the deuce will be that I can't prevent anything."

"If she is to have a fall," said Mrs. Almond, with a gentle laugh, "we must spread as many carpets as we can." And she carried out this idea by showing a great deal of motherly kindness to the girl.

Mrs. Penniman immediately wrote to Morris Townsend. The intimacy between these two was by this time consummate, but I must content myself with noting but a few of its features. Mrs. Penniman's own share in it was a singular sentiment, which might have been misinterpreted, but which in itself was not discreditable to the poor lady. It was a romantic interest in this attractive and unfortunate young man, and yet it was not such an interest as Catherine might have been jealous of. Mrs. Penniman had not a particle of jealousy of her niece. For herself, she felt as if she were Morris's mother or sister—a mother or sister of an emotional temperament—and she had an absorbing desire to make him comfortable and happy. She had striven to do so during the year that her brother left her an open field, and her efforts had been attended with the success that has been pointed out. She had never had a child of her own, and Catherine, whom she had done her best to invest with the importance that would naturally belong to a youthful Penniman, had only partly rewarded her zeal. Catherine, as an object of affection and solicitude, had never had that picturesque charm which (as it seemed to her) would have been a natural attribute of her own progeny. Even the maternal passion in Mrs. Penniman would have been romantic and factitious, and Catherine was not constituted to inspire a romantic passion. Mrs. Penniman was as fond of her as ever, but she had grown to feel that with Catherine she lacked opportunity. Sentimentally speaking, therefore, she had (though she had not disinherited her niece) adopted Morris Townsend, who gave her opportunity in abundance. She would have been very happy to have a handsome and tyrannical son, and would have taken an extreme interest in his love affairs. This was the light in which she had come to regard Morris, who had conciliated her at first, and made his impression by his delicate and calculated deference—a sort of exhibition to which Mrs. Penniman was particularly sensitive. He had largely abated his deference afterwards, for he economised his resources, but the impression was made, and the young man's very brutality came to have a sort of filial value. If Mrs. Penniman had had a son, she would probably have been afraid of him, and at this stage of our narrative she was certainly afraid of Morris Townsend. This was one of the results of his domestication in Washington Square. He took his ease with her—as, for that matter, he would certainly have done with his own mother.

XXVIII

THE letter was a word of warning; it informed him that the Doctor had come home more impracticable than ever. She might have reflected that Catherine would supply him with all the information he needed on this point; but we know that Mrs. Penniman's reflexions were rarely just; and, moreover, she felt that it was not for her to depend on what Catherine might do. She was to do her duty, quite irrespective of Catherine. I have said that her young friend took his ease with her, and it is an illustration of the fact that he made no answer to her letter. He took note of it, amply; but he lighted his cigar with it, and he waited, in tranquil confidence that he should receive another. "His state of mind really freezes my blood," Mrs. Penniman had written, alluding to her brother; and it would have seemed that upon this statement she could hardly improve. Nevertheless, she wrote again, expressing herself with the aid of a different figure. "His hatred of you burns with a lurid flame—the flame that never dies," she wrote. "But it doesn't light up the darkness of your future. If my affection could do so, all the years of your life would be an eternal sunshine. I can extract nothing from C.; she is so terribly secretive, like her father. She seems to expect to be married very soon, and has evidently made preparations in Europe—quantities of clothing, ten pairs of shoes, etc. My dear friend, you cannot set up in married life simply with a few pairs of shoes, can you? Tell me what you think of this. I am intensely anxious to see you; I have so much to say. I miss you dreadfully; the house seems so empty without you. What is the news down town? Is the business extending? That dear little business—I think it's so brave of you! Couldn't I come to your office?—just for three minutes? I might pass for a customer—is that what you call them? I might come in to buy something—some shares or some railroad things. *Tell me what you think of this plan.* I would carry a little reticule, like a woman of the people."

In spite of the suggestion about the reticule, Morris appeared to think poorly of the plan, for he gave Mrs. Penniman no encouragement whatever to visit his office, which he had already represented to her as a place peculiarly and unnaturally difficult to find. But as she persisted in desiring an interview—up to the last, after months of intimate colloquy, she called these meetings "interviews"—he agreed that they should take a walk together, and was even kind enough to leave his office for this purpose, during the hours at which business might have been supposed to be liveliest. It was no surprise to him, when they met at a street corner, in a region of empty lots and undeveloped pavements (Mrs. Penniman being attired as much as possible like a "woman of the people"), to find that, in spite of her urgency, what she chiefly had to convey to him was the assurance of her sympathy. Of such assurances, however, he had already a voluminous collection, and it would not have been worth his while to forsake a fruitful avocation merely to hear Mrs. Penniman say, for the thousandth time, that she had made his cause her own. Morris had something of his own to say. It was not an easy thing to bring out, and while he turned it over the difficulty made him acrimonious.

"Oh yes, I know perfectly that he combines the properties of a lump of ice and a red-hot coal," he observed. "Catherine has made it thoroughly clear, and you have told me so till I am sick of it. You needn't tell me again; I am perfectly satisfied. He will never give us a penny; I regard that as mathematically proved."

Mrs. Penniman at this point had an inspiration.

"Couldn't you bring a lawsuit against him?" She wondered that this simple expedient had never occurred to her before.

"I will bring a lawsuit against *you*," said Morris, "if you ask me any more such aggravating questions. A man should know when he is beaten," he added, in a moment. "I must give her up!"

Mrs. Penniman received this declaration in silence, though it made her heart beat a little. It found her by no means unprepared, for she had accustomed herself to the thought that, if Morris should decidedly not be able to get her brother's money, it would not do for him to marry Catherine without it. "It would not do" was a vague way of putting the thing; but Mrs. Penniman's natural affection completed the idea, which, though it had not as yet been so crudely expressed between them as in the form that Morris had just given it, had nevertheless been implied so often, in certain easy intervals of talk, as he sat stretching his legs in the Doctor's well-stuffed armchairs, that she had grown first to regard it with an emotion which she flattered herself was philosophic, and then to have a secret tenderness for it. The fact that she kept her tenderness secret proves, of course, that she was ashamed of it; but she managed to blink her shame by reminding herself that she was, after all, the official protector of her niece's marriage. Her logic would scarcely have passed muster with the Doctor. In the first place, Morris *must* get the money, and she would help him to it. In the second, it was plain it would never come to him, and it would be a grievous pity he should marry without it—a young man who might so easily find something better. After her brother had delivered himself, on his return from Europe, of that incisive little address that has been quoted, Morris's cause seemed so hopeless that Mrs. Penniman fixed her attention exclusively upon the latter branch of her argument. If Morris had been her son, she would certainly have sacrificed Catherine to a superior conception of his future; and to be ready to do so as the case stood was therefore even a finer degree of devotion. Nevertheless, it checked her breath a little to have the sacrificial knife, as it were, suddenly thrust into her hand.

Morris walked along a moment, and then he repeated harshly: "I must give her up!"

"I think I understand you," said Mrs. Penniman gently.

"I certainly say it distinctly enough—brutally and vulgarly enough."

He was ashamed of himself, and his shame was uncomfortable; and as he was extremely intolerant of discomfort, he felt vicious and cruel. He wanted to abuse somebody, and he began, cautiously—for he was always cautious—with himself.

"Couldn't you take her down a little?" he asked.

"Take her down?"

"Prepare her—try and ease me off."

Mrs. Penniman stopped, looking at him very solemnly.

"My poor Morris, do you know how much she loves you?"

"No, I don't. I don't want to know. I have always tried to keep from knowing. It would be too painful."

"She will suffer much," said Mrs. Penniman.

"You must console her. If you are as good a friend to me as you pretend to be, you will manage it."

Mrs. Penniman shook her head sadly.

"You talk of my 'pretending' to like you; but I can't pretend to hate you. I can only tell her I think very highly of you; and how will that console her for losing you?"

"The Doctor will help you. He will be delighted at the thing being broken off, and, as he is a knowing fellow, he will invent something to comfort her."

"He will invent a new torture!" cried Mrs. Penniman. "Heaven deliver her from her father's comfort. It will consist of his crowing over her and saying, 'I always told you so!'"

Morris coloured a most uncomfortable red.

"If you don't console her any better than you console me, you certainly won't be of much use! It's a damned disagreeable necessity; I feel it extremely, and you ought to make it easy for me."

"I will be your friend for life!" Mrs. Penniman declared.

"Be my friend *now*!" And Morris walked on.

She went with him; she was almost trembling.

"Should you like me to tell her?" she asked. "You mustn't tell her, but you can—you can—" And he hesitated, trying to think what Mrs. Penniman could do. "You can explain to her why it is. It's because I can't bring myself to step in between her and her father—to give him the pretext he grasps at—so eagerly (it's a hideous sight) for depriving her of her rights."

Mrs. Penniman felt with remarkable promptitude the charm of this formula.

"That's so like you," she said; "it's so finely felt."

Morris gave his stick an angry swing.

"Oh, botheration!" he exclaimed perversely.

Mrs. Penniman, however, was not discouraged.

"It may turn out better than you think. Catherine is, after all, so very peculiar." And she thought she might take it upon herself to assure him that, whatever happened, the girl would be very quiet—she wouldn't make a noise. They extended their walk, and, while they proceeded, Mrs. Penniman took upon herself other things besides, and ended by having assumed a considerable burden; Morris being ready enough, as may be imagined, to put everything off upon her. But he was not for a single instant the dupe of her blundering alacrity; he knew that of what she promised she was competent to perform but an insignificant fraction, and the more she professed her willingness to serve him, the greater fool he thought her.

"What will you do if you don't marry her?" she ventured to inquire in the course of this conversation.

"Something brilliant," said Morris. "Shouldn't you like me to do something brilliant?"

The idea gave Mrs. Penniman exceeding pleasure.

"I shall feel sadly taken in if you don't."

"I shall have to, to make up for this. This isn't at all brilliant, you know."

Mrs. Penniman mused a little, as if there might be some way of making out that it was; but she had to give up the attempt, and, to carry off the awkwardness of failure, she risked a new inquiry.

"Do you mean—do you mean another marriage?"

Morris greeted this question with a reflexion which was hardly the less impudent from being inaudible. "Surely, women are more crude than men!" And then he answered audibly:

"Never in the world!"

Mrs. Penniman felt disappointed and snubbed, and she relieved herself in a little vaguely-sarcastic cry. He was certainly perverse.

"I give her up, not for another woman, but for a wider career!" Morris announced.

This was very grand; but still Mrs. Penniman, who felt that she had exposed herself, was faintly rancorous.

"Do you mean never to come to see her again?" she asked, with some sharpness.

"Oh no, I shall come again; but what is the use of dragging it out? I have been four times since she came back, and it's terribly awkward work. I can't keep it up indefinitely; she oughtn't to expect that, you know. A woman should never keep a man dangling!" he added finely.

"Ah, but you must have your last parting!" urged his companion, in whose imagination the idea of last partings occupied a place inferior in dignity only to that of first meetings.

XXIX

HE came again, without managing the last parting; and again and again, without finding that Mrs. Penniman had as yet done much to pave the path of retreat with flowers. It was devilish awkward, as he said, and he felt a lively animosity for Catherine's aunt, who, as he had now quite formed the habit of saying to himself, had dragged him into the mess and was bound in common charity to get him out of it. Mrs. Penniman, to tell the truth, had, in the seclusion of her own apartment—and, I may add, amid the suggestiveness of Catherine's, which wore in those days the appearance of that of a young lady laying out her *trousseau*—Mrs. Penniman had measured her responsibilities, and taken fright at their magnitude. The task of preparing Catherine and easing off Morris presented difficulties which increased in the execution, and even led the impulsive Lavinia to ask herself whether the modification of the young man's original project had been conceived in a happy spirit. A brilliant future, a wider career, a conscience exempt from the reproach of interference between a young lady and her natural rights—these excellent things might be too troublesomely purchased. From Catherine herself Mrs. Penniman received no assistance whatever; the poor girl was apparently without suspicion of her danger. She looked at her lover with eyes of undiminished trust, and though she had less confidence in her aunt than in a young man with whom she had exchanged so many tender vows, she gave her no handle for explaining or confessing. Mrs. Penniman, faltering and wavering, declared Catherine was very stupid, put off the great scene, as she would have called it, from day to day, and wandered about very uncomfortably, primed, to repletion, with her apology, but unable to bring it to the light. Morris's own scenes were very small ones just now; but even these were beyond his strength. He made his visits as brief as possible, and while he sat with his mistress, found terribly little to talk about. She was waiting for him, in vulgar parlance, to name the day; and so long as he was unprepared to be explicit on this point it seemed a mockery to pretend to talk about matters more abstract. She had no airs and no arts; she never attempted to disguise her expectancy. She was waiting on his good pleasure, and would wait modestly and patiently; his hanging back at this supreme time might appear strange, but of course he must have a good reason for it. Catherine would have made a wife of the gentle old-fashioned pattern—regarding reasons as favours and windfalls, but no more expecting one every day than she would have expected a bouquet of camellias. During the period of her engagement, however, a young lady even of the most slender pretensions counts upon more bouquets than at other times; and there was a want of perfume in the air at this moment which at last excited the girl's alarm.

"Are you sick?" she asked of Morris. "You seem so restless, and you look pale."

"I am not at all well," said Morris; and it occurred to him that, if he could only make her pity him enough, he might get off.

"I am afraid you are overworked; you oughtn't to work so much."

"I must do that." And then he added, with a sort of calculated brutality, "I don't want to owe you everything!"

"Ah, how can you say that?"

"I am too proud," said Morris.

"Yes—you are too proud!"

"Well, you must take me as I am," he went on, "you can never change me."

"I don't want to change you," she said gently. "I will take you as you are!" And she stood looking at him.

"You know people talk tremendously about a man's marrying a rich girl," Morris remarked. "It's excessively disagreeable."

"But I am not rich?" said Catherine.

"You are rich enough to make me talked about!"

"Of course you are talked about. It's an honour!"

"It's an honour I could easily dispense with."

She was on the point of asking him whether it were not a compensation for this annoyance that the poor girl who had the misfortune to bring it upon him, loved him so dearly and believed in him so truly; but she hesitated, thinking that this would perhaps seem an exacting speech, and while she hesitated, he suddenly left her.

The next time he came, however, she brought it out, and she told him again that he was too proud. He repeated that he couldn't change, and this time she felt the impulse to say that with a little effort he might change.

Sometimes he thought that if he could only make a quarrel with her it might help him; but the question was how to quarrel with a young woman who had such treasures of concession. "I suppose you think the effort is all on your side!" he was reduced to exclaiming. "Don't you believe that I have my own effort to make?"

"It's all yours now," she said. "My effort is finished and done with!"

"Well, mine is not."

"We must bear things together," said Catherine. "That's what we ought to do."

Morris attempted a natural smile. "There are some things which we can't very well bear together—for instance, separation."

"Why do you speak of separation?"

"Ah! you don't like it; I knew you wouldn't!"

"Where are you going, Morris?" she suddenly asked.

He fixed his eye on her for a moment, and for a part of that moment she was afraid of it. "Will you promise not to make a scene?"

"A scene!—do I make scenes?"

"All women do!" said Morris, with the tone of large experience.

"I don't. Where are you going?"

"If I should say I was going away on business, should you think it very strange?"

She wondered a moment, gazing at him. "Yes—no. Not if you will take me with you."

"Take you with me—on business?"

"What is your business? Your business is to be with me."

"I don't earn my living with you," said Morris. "Or rather," he cried with a sudden inspiration, "that's just what I do—or what the world says I do!"

This ought perhaps to have been a great stroke, but it miscarried. "Where are you going?" Catherine simply repeated.

"To New Orleans. About buying some cotton."

"I am perfectly willing to go to New Orleans," Catherine said.

"Do you suppose I would take you to a nest of yellow fever?" cried Morris. "Do you suppose I would expose you at such a time as this?"

"If there is yellow fever, why should you go? Morris, you must not go!"

"It is to make six thousand dollars," said Morris. "Do you grudge me that satisfaction?"

"We have no need of six thousand dollars. You think too much about money!"

"You can afford to say that? This is a great chance; we heard of it last night." And he explained to her in what the chance consisted; and told her a long story, going over more than once several of the details, about the remarkable stroke of business which he and his partner had planned between them.

But Catherine's imagination, for reasons best known to herself, absolutely refused to be fired. "If you can go to New Orleans, I can go," she said. "Why shouldn't you catch yellow fever quite as easily as I? I am every bit as strong as you, and not in the least afraid of any fever. When we were in Europe, we were in very unhealthy places; my father used to make me take some pills. I never caught anything, and I never was nervous. What will be the use of six thousand dollars if you die of a fever? When persons are going to be married they oughtn't to think so much about business. You shouldn't think about cotton, you should think about me. You can go to New Orleans some other time—there will always be plenty of cotton. It isn't the moment to choose—we have waited too long already." She spoke more forcibly and volubly than he had ever heard her, and she held his arm in her two hands.

"You said you wouldn't make a scene!" cried Morris. "I call this a scene."

"It's you that are making it! I have never asked you anything before. We have waited too long already." And it was a comfort to her to think that she had hitherto asked so little; it seemed to make her right to insist the greater now.

Morris bethought himself a little. "Very well, then; we won't talk about it any more. I will transact my business by letter." And he began to smooth his hat, as if to take leave.

"You won't go?" And she stood looking up at him.

He could not give up his idea of provoking a quarrel; it was so much the simplest way! He bent his eyes on her upturned face, with the darkest frown he could achieve. "You are not discreet. You mustn't bully me!"

But, as usual, she conceded everything. "No, I am not discreet; I know I am too pressing. But isn't it natural? It is only for a moment."

"In a moment you may do a great deal of harm. Try and be calmer the next time I come."

"When will you come?"

"Do you want to make conditions?" Morris asked. "I will come next Saturday."

"Come to-morrow," Catherine begged; "I want you to come to-morrow. I will be very quiet," she added; and her agitation had by this time become so great that the assurance was not becoming. A sudden fear had come over her; it was like the solid conjunction of a dozen disembodied doubts, and her imagination, at a single bound, had traversed an enormous distance. All her being, for the moment, centred in the wish to keep him in the room.

Morris bent his head and kissed her forehead. "When you are quiet, you are perfection," he said; "but when you are violent, you are not in character."

It was Catherine's wish that there should be no violence about her save the beating of her heart, which she could not help; and she went on, as gently as possible, "Will you promise to come to-morrow?"

"I said Saturday!" Morris answered, smiling. He tried a frown at one moment, a smile at another; he was at his wit's end.

"Yes, Saturday too," she answered, trying to smile. "But to-morrow first." He was going to the door, and she went with him quickly. She leaned her shoulder against it; it seemed to her that she would do anything to keep him.

"If I am prevented from coming to-morrow, you will say I have deceived you!" he said.

"How can you be prevented? You can come if you will."

"I am a busy man—I am not a dangler!" cried Morris sternly.

His voice was so hard and unnatural that, with a helpless look at him, she turned away; and then he quickly laid his hand on the door-knob. He felt as if he were absolutely running away from her. But in an instant she was close to him again, and murmuring in a tone none the less penetrating for being low, "Morris, you are going to leave me."

"Yes, for a little while."

"For how long?"

"Till you are reasonable again."

"I shall never be reasonable in that way!" And she tried to keep him longer; it was almost a struggle. "Think of what I have done!" she broke out. "Morris, I have given up everything!"

"You shall have everything back!"

"You wouldn't say that if you didn't mean something. What is it?— what has happened?—what have I done?—what has changed you?"

"I will write to you—that is better," Morris stammered.

"Ah, you won't come back!" she cried, bursting into tears.

"Dear Catherine," he said, "don't believe that I promise you that you shall see me again!" And he managed to get away and to close the door behind him.

XXX

It was almost her last outbreak of passive grief; at least, she never indulged in another that the world knew anything about. But this one was long and terrible; she flung herself on the sofa and gave herself up to her misery. She hardly knew what had happened; ostensibly she had only had a difference with her lover, as other girls had had before, and the thing was not only not a rupture, but she was under no obligation to regard it even as a menace. Nevertheless, she felt a wound, even if he had not dealt it; it seemed to her that a mask had suddenly fallen from his face. He had wished to get away from her; he had been angry and cruel, and said strange things, with strange looks. She was smothered and stunned; she buried her head in the cushions, sobbing and talking to herself. But at last she raised herself, with the fear that either her father or Mrs. Penniman would come in; and then she sat there, staring before her, while the room grew darker. She said to herself that perhaps he would come back to tell her he had not meant what he said; and she listened for his ring at the door, trying to believe that this was probable. A long time passed, but Morris remained absent; the shadows gathered; the evening settled down on the meagre elegance of the light, clear-coloured room; the fire went out. When it had grown dark, Catherine went to the window and looked out; she stood there for half an hour, on the mere chance that he would come up the steps. At last she turned away, for she saw her father come in. He had seen her at the window looking out, and he stopped a moment at the bottom of the white steps, and gravely, with an air of exaggerated courtesy, lifted his hat to her. The gesture was so incongruous to the condition she was in, this stately tribute of respect to a poor girl despised and forsaken was so out of place, that the thing gave her a kind of horror, and she hurried away to her room. It seemed to her that she had given Morris up.

She had to show herself half an hour later, and she was sustained at table by the immensity of her desire that her father should not perceive that anything had happened. This was a great help to her afterwards, and it served her (though never as much as she supposed) from the first. On this occasion Dr. Sloper was rather talkative. He told a great many stories about a wonderful poodle that he had seen at the house of an old lady whom he visited professionally. Catherine not only tried to appear to listen to the anecdotes of the poodle, but she endeavoured to interest herself in them, so as not to think of her scene with Morris. That perhaps was an hallucination; he was mistaken, she was jealous; people didn't change like that from one day to another. Then she knew that she had had doubts before—strange suspicions, that were at once vague and acute—and that he had been different ever since her return from Europe: whereupon she tried again to listen to her father, who told a story so remarkably well. Afterwards she went straight to her own room; it was beyond her strength to undertake to spend the evening with her aunt. All the evening, alone, she questioned herself. Her trouble was terrible; but was it a thing of her imagination, engendered by an extravagant sensibility, or did it represent a clear-cut reality, and had the worst that was possible actually come to pass? Mrs. Penniman, with a degree of tact that was as unusual as it was commendable, took the line of leaving her alone. The truth is, that her suspicions having been aroused, she indulged a desire, natural to a timid person, that the explosion should be localised. So long as the air still vibrated she kept out of the way.

She passed and repassed Catherine's door several times in the course of the evening, as if she expected to hear a plaintive moan behind it. But the room remained perfectly still; and accordingly, the last thing before retiring to her own couch, she applied for admittance. Catherine was sitting up, and had a book that she pretended to be reading. She had no wish to go to bed, for she had no expectation of sleeping. After Mrs. Penniman had left her she sat up half the night, and she offered her visitor no inducement to remain. Her aunt came stealing in very gently, and approached her with great solemnity.

"I am afraid you are in trouble, my dear. Can I do anything to help you?"

"I am not in any trouble whatever, and do not need any help," said Catherine, fibbing roundly, and proving thereby that not only our faults, but our most involuntary misfortunes, tend to corrupt our morals.

"Has nothing happened to you?"

"Nothing whatever."

"Are you very sure, dear?"

"Perfectly sure."

"And can I really do nothing for you?"

"Nothing, aunt, but kindly leave me alone," said Catherine.

Mrs. Penniman, though she had been afraid of too warm a welcome before, was now disappointed at so cold a one; and in relating afterwards, as she did to many persons, and with considerable variations of detail, the history of the termination of her niece's engagement, she was usually careful to mention that the young lady, on a certain occasion, had "hustled" her out of the room. It was characteristic of Mrs. Penniman that she related this fact, not in the least out of malignity to Catherine, whom she very sufficiently pitied, but simply from a natural disposition to embellish any subject that she touched.

Catherine, as I have said, sat up half the night, as if she still expected to hear Morris Townsend ring at the door. On the morrow this expectation was less unreasonable; but it was not gratified by the reappearance of the young man. Neither had he written; there was not a word of explanation or reassurance. Fortunately for Catherine she could take refuge from her excitement, which had now become intense, in her determination that her father should see nothing of it. How well she deceived her father we shall have occasion to learn; but her innocent arts were of little avail before a person of the rare perspicacity of Mrs. Penniman. This lady easily saw that she was agitated, and if there was any agitation going forward, Mrs. Penniman was not a person to forfeit her natural share in it. She returned to the charge the next evening, and requested her niece to lean upon her—to unburden her heart. Perhaps she should be able to explain certain things that now seemed dark, and that she knew more about than Catherine supposed. If Catherine had been frigid the night before, to-day she was haughty.

"You are completely mistaken, and I have not the least idea what you mean. I don't know what you are trying to fasten on me, and I have never had less need of any one's explanations in my life."

In this way the girl delivered herself, and from hour to hour kept her aunt at bay. From hour to hour Mrs. Penniman's curiosity grew. She would have given her little finger to know what Morris had said and done, what tone he had taken, what pretext he had found. She wrote to him, naturally, to request an interview; but she received, as naturally, no answer to her petition. Morris was not in a writing mood; for Catherine had addressed him two short notes which met with no acknowledgment. These notes were so brief that I may give them entire. "Won't you give me some sign that you didn't mean to be so cruel as you seemed on Tuesday?"—that was the first; the other was a little longer. "If I was unreasonable or suspicious on Tuesday—if I annoyed you or troubled you in any way—I beg your forgiveness, and I promise never again to be so foolish. I am punished enough, and I don't understand. Dear Morris, you are killing me!" These notes were despatched on the Friday and Saturday; but Saturday and Sunday passed without bringing the poor girl the satisfaction she desired. Her punishment accumulated; she continued to bear it, however, with a good deal of superficial fortitude. On Saturday morning the Doctor, who had been watching in silence, spoke to his sister Lavinia.

"The thing has happened—the scoundrel has backed out!"

"Never!" cried Mrs. Penniman, who had bethought herself what she should say to Catherine, but was not provided with a line of defence against her brother, so that indignant negation was the only weapon in her hands.

"He has begged for a reprieve, then, if you like that better!"

"It seems to make you very happy that your daughter's affections have been trifled with."

"It does," said the Doctor; "for I had foretold it! It's a great pleasure to be in the right."

"Your pleasures make one shudder!" his sister exclaimed.

Catherine went rigidly through her usual occupations; that is, up to the point of going with her aunt to church on Sunday morning. She generally went to afternoon service as well; but on this occasion her courage faltered, and she begged of Mrs. Penniman to go without her.

"I am sure you have a secret," said Mrs. Penniman, with great significance, looking at her rather grimly.

"If I have, I shall keep it!" Catherine answered, turning away.

Mrs. Penniman started for church; but before she had arrived, she stopped and turned back, and before twenty minutes had elapsed she re-entered the house, looked into the empty parlours, and then went upstairs and knocked at Catherine's door. She got no answer; Catherine was not in her room, and Mrs. Penniman presently ascertained that she was not in the house. "She has gone to him, she has fled!" Lavinia cried, clasping her hands with admiration and envy. But she soon perceived that Catherine had taken nothing with her—all her personal property in her room was intact—and then she jumped at the hypothesis that the girl had gone forth, not in tenderness, but in resentment. "She has followed him to his own door—she has burst upon him in his own apartment!" It was in these terms that Mrs. Penniman depicted to herself her niece's errand, which, viewed in this light, gratified her sense of the picturesque only a shade less strongly than the idea of a clandestine marriage. To visit one's lover, with tears and reproaches, at his own residence, was an image so agreeable to Mrs. Penniman's mind that she felt a sort of æsthetic disappointment at its lacking, in this case, the harmonious accompaniments of darkness and storm. A quiet Sunday afternoon appeared an inadequate setting for it; and, indeed, Mrs. Penniman was quite out of humour with the conditions of the time, which passed very slowly as she sat in the front parlour in her bonnet and her cashmere shawl, awaiting Catherine's return.

This event at last took place. She saw her—at the window—mount the steps, and she went to await her in the hall, where she pounced upon her as soon as she had entered the house, and drew her into the parlour, closing the door with solemnity. Catherine was flushed, and her eye was bright. Mrs. Penniman hardly knew what to think.

"May I venture to ask where you have been?" she demanded.

"I have been to take a walk," said Catherine. "I thought you had gone to church."

"I did go to church; but the service was shorter than usual. And pray, where did you walk?"

"I don't know!" said Catherine.

"Your ignorance is most extraordinary! Dear Catherine, you can trust me."

"What am I to trust you with?"

"With your secret—your sorrow."

"I have no sorrow!" said Catherine fiercely.

"My poor child," Mrs. Penniman insisted, "you can't deceive me. I know everything. I have been requested to—a—to converse with you."

"I don't want to converse!"

"It will relieve you. Don't you know Shakespeare's lines?—'the grief that does not speak!' My dear girl, it is better as it is."

"What is better?" Catherine asked.

She was really too perverse. A certain amount of perversity was to be allowed for in a young lady whose lover had thrown her over; but not such an amount as would prove inconvenient to his apologists. "That you should be reasonable," said Mrs. Penniman, with some sternness. "That you should take counsel of worldly prudence, and submit to practical considerations. That you should agree to—a—separate."

Catherine had been ice up to this moment, but at this word she flamed up. "Separate? What do you know about our separating?"

Mrs. Penniman shook her head with a sadness in which there was almost a sense of injury. "Your pride is my pride, and your susceptibilities are mine. I see your side perfectly, but I also"—and she smiled with melancholy suggestiveness—"I also see the situation as a whole!"

This suggestiveness was lost upon Catherine, who repeated her violent inquiry. "Why do you talk about separation; what do you know about it?"

"We must study resignation," said Mrs. Penniman, hesitating, but sententious at a venture.

"Resignation to what?"

"To a change of—of our plans."

"My plans have not changed!" said Catherine, with a little laugh.

"Ah, but Mr. Townsend's have," her aunt answered very gently.

"What do you mean?"

There was an imperious brevity in the tone of this inquiry, against which Mrs. Penniman felt bound to protest; the information with which she had undertaken to supply her niece was, after all, a favour. She had tried sharpness, and she had tried sternness: but neither would do; she was shocked at the girl's obstinacy. "Ah, well," she said, "if he hasn't told you! . . . " and she turned away.

Catherine watched her a moment in silence; then she hurried after her, stopping her before she reached the door. "Told me what? What do you mean? What are you hinting at and threatening me with?"

"Isn't it broken off?" asked Mrs. Penniman.

"My engagement? Not in the least!"

"I beg your pardon in that case. I have spoken too soon!"

"Too soon! Soon or late," Catherine broke out, "you speak foolishly and cruelly!"

"What has happened between you, then?" asked her aunt, struck by the sincerity of this cry. "For something certainly has happened."

"Nothing has happened but that I love him more and more!"

Mrs. Penniman was silent an instant. "I suppose that's the reason you went to see him this afternoon."

Catherine flushed as if she had been struck. "Yes, I did go to see him! But that's my own business."

"Very well, then; we won't talk about it." And Mrs. Penniman moved towards the door again. But she was stopped by a sudden imploring cry from the girl.

"Aunt Lavinia, *where* has he gone?"

"Ah, you admit, then, that he has gone away? Didn't they know at his house?"

"They said he had left town. I asked no more questions; I was ashamed," said Catherine, simply enough.

"You needn't have taken so compromising a step if you had had a little more confidence in me," Mrs. Penniman observed, with a good deal of grandeur.

"Is it to New Orleans?" Catherine went on irrelevantly.

It was the first time Mrs. Penniman had heard of New Orleans in this connexion; but she was averse to letting Catherine know that she was in the dark. She attempted to strike an illumination from the instructions she had received from Morris. "My dear Catherine," she said, "when a separation has been agreed upon, the farther he goes away the better."

"Agreed upon? Has he agreed upon it with you?" A consummate sense of her aunt's meddlesome folly had come over her during the last five minutes, and she was sickened at the thought that Mrs. Penniman had been let loose, as it were, upon her happiness.

"He certainly has sometimes advised with me," said Mrs. Penniman.

"Is it you, then, that have changed him and made him so unnatural?" Catherine cried. "Is it you that have worked on him and taken him from me? He doesn't belong to you, and I don't see how you have anything to do with what is between us! Is it you that have made this plot and told him to leave me? How could you be so wicked, so cruel? What have I ever done to you; why can't you leave me alone? I was afraid you would spoil everything; for you *do* spoil everything you touch; I was afraid of you all the time we were abroad; I had no rest when I thought that you were always talking to him." Catherine went on with growing vehemence, pouring out in her bitterness and in the clairvoyance of her passion (which suddenly, jumping all processes, made her judge her aunt finally and without appeal) the uneasiness which had lain for so many months upon her heart.

Mrs. Penniman was scared and bewildered; she saw no prospect of introducing her little account of the purity of Morris's motives. "You are a most ungrateful girl!" she cried. "Do you scold me for talking with him? I am sure we never talked of anything but you!"

"Yes; and that was the way you worried him; you made him tired of my very name! I wish you had never spoken of me to him; I never asked your help!"

"I am sure if it hadn't been for me he would never have come to the house, and you would never have known what he thought of you," Mrs. Penniman rejoined, with a good deal of justice.

"I wish he never had come to the house, and that I never had known it! That's better than this," said poor Catherine.

"You are a very ungrateful girl," Aunt Lavinia repeated.

Catherine's outbreak of anger and the sense of wrong gave her, while they lasted, the satisfaction that comes from all assertion of force; they hurried her along, and there is always a sort of pleasure in cleaving the air. But at the bottom she hated to be violent, and she was conscious of no aptitude for organised resentment. She calmed herself with a great effort, but with great rapidity, and walked about the room a few moments, trying to say to herself that her aunt had meant everything for the best. She did not succeed in saying it with much conviction, but after a little she was able to speak quietly enough.

"I am not ungrateful, but I am very unhappy. It's hard to be grateful for that," she said. "Will you please tell me where he is?"

"I haven't the least idea; I am not in secret correspondence with him!" And Mrs. Penniman wished indeed that she were, so that she might let him know how Catherine abused her, after all she had done.

"Was it a plan of his, then, to break off—?" By this time Catherine had become completely quiet.

Mrs. Penniman began again to have a glimpse of her chance for explaining. "He shrank—he shrank," she said. "He lacked courage, but it was the courage to injure you! He couldn't bear to bring down on you your father's curse."

Catherine listened to this with her eyes fixed upon her aunt, and continued to gaze at her for some time afterwards. "Did he tell you to say that?"

"He told me to say many things—all so delicate, so discriminating. And he told me to tell you he hoped you wouldn't despise him."

"I don't," said Catherine. And then she added: "And will he stay away for ever?"

"Oh, for ever is a long time. Your father, perhaps, won't live for ever."

"Perhaps not."

"I am sure you appreciate—you understand—even though your heart bleeds," said Mrs. Penniman. "You doubtless think him too scrupulous. So do I, but I respect his scruples. What he asks of you is that you should do the same."

Catherine was still gazing at her aunt, but she spoke at last, as if she had not heard or not understood her. "It has been a regular plan, then. He has broken it off deliberately; he has given me up."

"For the present, dear Catherine. He has put it off only."

"He has left me alone," Catherine went on.

"Haven't you *me?*" asked Mrs. Penniman, with much expression.

Catherine shook her head slowly. "I don't believe it!" and she left the room.

XXXI

Though she had forced herself to be calm, she preferred practising this virtue in private, and she forbore to show herself at tea—a repast which, on Sundays, at six o'clock, took the place of dinner. Dr. Sloper and his sister sat face to face, but Mrs. Penniman never met her brother's eye. Late in the evening she went with him, but without Catherine, to their sister Almond's, where, between the two ladies, Catherine's unhappy situation was discussed with a frankness that was conditioned by a good deal of mysterious reticence on Mrs. Penniman's part.

"I am delighted he is not to marry her," said Mrs. Almond, "but he ought to be horsewhipped all the same."

Mrs. Penniman, who was shocked at her sister's coarseness, replied that he had been actuated by the noblest of motives—the desire not to impoverish Catherine.

"I am very happy that Catherine is not to be impoverished—but I hope he may never have a penny too much! And what does the poor girl say to *you*?" Mrs. Almond asked.

"She says I have a genius for consolation," said Mrs. Penniman.

This was the account of the matter that she gave to her sister, and it was perhaps with the consciousness of genius that, on her return that evening to Washington Square, she again presented herself for admittance at Catherine's door. Catherine came and opened it; she was apparently very quiet.

"I only want to give you a little word of advice," she said. "If your father asks you, say that everything is going on."

Catherine stood there, with her hand on the knob looking at her aunt, but not asking her to come in. "Do you think he will ask me?"

"I am sure he will. He asked me just now, on our way home from your Aunt Elizabeth's. I explained the whole thing to your Aunt Elizabeth. I said to your father I know nothing about it."

"Do you think he will ask me when he sees—when he sees—?" But here Catherine stopped.

"The more he sees the more disagreeable he will be," said her aunt.

"He shall see as little as possible!" Catherine declared.

"Tell him you are to be married."

"So I am," said Catherine softly; and she closed the door upon her aunt.

She could not have said this two days later—for instance, on Tuesday, when she at last received a letter from Morris Townsend. It was an epistle of considerable length, measuring five large square pages, and written at Philadelphia. It was an explanatory document, and it explained a great many things, chief among which were the considerations that had led the writer to take advantage of an urgent "professional" absence to try and banish from his mind the image of one whose path he had crossed only to scatter it with ruins. He ventured to expect but partial success in this attempt, but he could promise her that, whatever his failure, he would never again interpose between her generous heart and her brilliant prospects and filial duties. He closed with an intimation that his professional pursuits might compel him to travel for some months, and with the hope that when they should each have accommodated themselves to what was sternly involved in their respective positions—even should this result not be reached for years—they should meet as friends, as fellow-sufferers, as innocent but philosophic victims of a great social law. That her life should be peaceful and happy was the dearest wish of him who ventured still to subscribe himself her most obedient servant. The letter was beautifully written, and Catherine, who kept it for many years after this, was able, when her sense of the bitterness of its meaning and the hollowness of its tone had grown less acute, to admire its grace of expression. At present, for a long time after she received it, all she had to help her was the determination, daily more rigid, to make no appeal to the compassion of her father.

He suffered a week to elapse, and then one day, in the morning, at an hour at which she rarely saw him, he strolled into the back parlour. He had watched his time, and he found her alone. She was sitting with some work, and he came and stood in front of her. He was going out, he had on his hat and was drawing on his gloves.

"It doesn't seem to me that you are treating me just now with all the consideration I deserve," he said in a moment.

"I don't know what I have done," Catherine answered, with her eyes on her work.

"You have apparently quite banished from your mind the request I made you at Liverp

ool, before we sailed; the request that you would notify me in advance before leaving my house."

"I have not left your house!" said Catherine.

"But you intend to leave it, and by what you gave me to understand, your departure must be impending. In fact, though you are still here in body, you are already absent in spirit. Your mind has taken up its residence with your prospective husband, and you might quite as well be lodged under the conjugal roof, for all the benefit we get from your society."

"I will try and be more cheerful!" said Catherine.

"You certainly ought to be cheerful, you ask a great deal if you are not. To the pleasure of marrying a brilliant young man, you add that of having your own way; you strike me as a very lucky young lady!"

Catherine got up; she was suffocating. But she folded her work, deliberately and correctly, bending her burning face upon it. Her father stood where he had planted himself; she hoped he would go, but he smoothed and buttoned his gloves, and then he rested his hands upon his hips.

"It would be a convenience to me to know when I may expect to have an empty house," he went on. "When you go, your aunt marches."

She looked at him at last, with a long silent gaze, which, in spite of her pride and her resolution, uttered part of the appeal she had tried not to make. Her father's cold grey eye sounded her own, and he insisted on his point.

"Is it to-morrow? Is it next week, or the week after?"

"I shall not go away!" said Catherine.

The Doctor raised his eyebrows. "Has he backed out?"

"I have broken off my engagement."

"Broken it off?"

"I have asked him to leave New York, and he has gone away for a long time."

The Doctor was both puzzled and disappointed, but he solved his perplexity by saying to himself that his daughter simply misrepresented—justifiably, if one would? but nevertheless misrepresented—the facts; and he eased off his disappointment, which was that of a man losing a chance for a little triumph that he had rather counted on, by a few words that he uttered aloud.

"How does he take his dismissal?"

"I don't know!" said Catherine, less ingeniously than she had hitherto spoken.

"You mean you don't care? You are rather cruel, after encouraging him and playing with him for so long!"

The Doctor had his revenge, after all.

XXXII

OUR story has hitherto moved with very short steps, but as it approaches its termination it must take a long stride. As time went on, it might have appeared to the Doctor that his daughter's account of her rupture with Morris Townsend, mere bravado as he had deemed it, was in some degree justified by the sequel. Morris remained as rigidly and unremittingly absent as if he had died of a broken heart, and Catherine had apparently buried the memory of this fruitless episode as deep as if it had terminated by her own choice. We know that she had been deeply and incurably wounded, but the Doctor had no means of knowing it. He was certainly curious about it, and would have given a good deal to discover the exact truth; but it was his punishment that he never knew—his punishment, I mean, for the abuse of sarcasm in his relations with his daughter. There was a good deal of effective sarcasm in her keeping him in the dark, and the rest of the world conspired with her, in this sense, to be sarcastic. Mrs. Penniman told him nothing, partly because he never questioned her—he made too light of Mrs. Penniman for that—and partly because she flattered herself that a tormenting reserve, and a serene profession of ignorance, would avenge her for his theory that she had meddled in the matter. He went two or three times to see Mrs. Montgomery, but Mrs. Montgomery had nothing to impart. She simply knew that her brother's engagement was broken off, and now that Miss Sloper was out of danger she preferred not to bear witness in any way against Morris. She had done so before—however unwillingly—because she was sorry for Miss Sloper; but she was not sorry for Miss Sloper now—not at all sorry. Morris had told her nothing about his relations with Miss Sloper at the time, and he had told her nothing since. He was always away, and he very seldom wrote to her; she believed he had gone to California. Mrs. Almond had, in her sister's phrase, "taken up" Catherine violently since the recent catastrophe; but though the girl was very grateful to her for her kindness, she revealed no secrets, and the good lady could give the Doctor no satisfaction. Even, however, had she been able to narrate to him the private history of his daughter's unhappy love affair, it would have given her a certain comfort to leave him in ignorance; for Mrs. Almond was at this time not altogether in sympathy with her brother. She had guessed for herself that Catherine had been cruelly jilted—she knew nothing from Mrs. Penniman, for Mrs. Penniman had not ventured to lay the famous explanation of Morris's motives before Mrs. Almond, though she had thought it good enough for Catherine—and she pronounced her brother too consistently indifferent to what the poor creature must have suffered and must still be suffering. Dr. Sloper had his theory, and he rarely altered his theories. The marriage would have been an abominable one, and the girl had had a blessed escape. She was not to be pitied for that, and to pretend to condole with her would have been to make concessions to the idea that she had ever had a right to think of Morris.

"I put my foot on this idea from the first, and I keep it there now," said the Doctor. "I don't see anything cruel in that; one can't keep it there too long." To this Mrs. Almond more than once replied that if Catherine had got rid of her incongruous lover, she deserved the credit of it, and that to bring herself to her father's enlightened view of the matter must have cost her an effort that he was bound to appreciate.

"I am by no means sure she has got rid of him," the Doctor said. "There is not the smallest probability that, after having been as obstinate as a mule for two years, she suddenly became amenable to reason. It is infinitely more probable that he got rid of her."

"All the more reason you should be gentle with her."

"I *am* gentle with her. But I can't do the pathetic; I can't pump up tears, to look graceful, over the most fortunate thing that ever happened to her."

"You have no sympathy," said Mrs. Almond; "that was never your strong point. You have only to look at her to see that, right or wrong, and whether the rupture came from herself or from him, her poor little heart is grievously bruised."

"Handling bruises—and even dropping tears on them—doesn't make them any better! My business is to see she gets no more knocks, and that

I shall carefully attend to. But I don't at all recognise your description of Catherine. She doesn't strike me in the least as a young woman going about in search of a moral poultice. In fact, she seems to me much better than while the fellow was hanging about. She is perfectly comfortable and blooming; she eats and sleeps, takes her usual exercise, and overloads herself, as usual, with finery. She is always knitting some purse or embroidering some handkerchief, and it seems to me she turns these articles out about as fast as ever. She hasn't much to say; but when had she anything to say? She had her little dance, and now she is sitting down to rest. I suspect that, on the whole, she enjoys it."

"She enjoys it as people enjoy getting rid of a leg that has been crushed. The state of mind after amputation is doubtless one of comparative repose."

"If your leg is a metaphor for young Townsend, I can assure you he has never been crushed. Crushed? Not he! He is alive and perfectly intact, and that's why I am not satisfied."

"Should you have liked to kill him?" asked Mrs. Almond.

"Yes, very much. I think it is quite possible that it is all a blind."

"A blind?"

"An arrangement between them. *Il fait le mort*, as they say in France; but he is looking out of the corner of his eye. You can depend upon it he has not burned his ships; he has kept one to come back in. When I am dead, he will set sail again, and then she will marry him."

"It is interesting to know that you accuse your only daughter of being the vilest of hypocrites," said Mrs. Almond.

"I don't see what difference her being my only daughter makes. It is better to accuse one than a dozen. But I don't accuse any one. There is not the smallest hypocrisy about Catherine, and I deny that she even pretends to be miserable."

The Doctor's idea that the thing was a "blind" had its intermissions and revivals; but it may be said on the whole to have increased as he grew older; together with his impression of Catherine's blooming and comfortable condition. Naturally, if he had not found grounds for viewing her as a lovelorn maiden during the year or two that followed her great trouble, he found none at a time when she had completely recovered her self-possession. He was obliged to recognise the fact that if the two young people were waiting for him to get out of the way, they were at least waiting very patiently. He had heard from time to time that Morris was in New York; but he never remained there long, and, to the best of the Doctor's belief, had no communication with Catherine. He was sure they never met, and he had reason to suspect that Morris never wrote to her. After the letter that has been mentioned, she heard from him twice again, at considerable intervals; but on none of these occasions did she write herself. On the other hand, as the Doctor observed, she averted herself rigidly from the idea of marrying other people. Her opportunities for doing so were not numerous, but they occurred often enough to test her disposition. She refused a widower, a man with a genial temperament, a handsome fortune, and three little girls (he had heard that she was very fond of children, and he pointed to his own with some confidence); and she turned a deaf ear to the solicitations of a clever young lawyer, who, with the prospect of a great practice, and the reputation of a most agreeable man, had had the shrewdness, when he came to look about him for a wife, to believe that she would suit him better than several younger and prettier girls. Mr. Macalister, the widower, had desired to make a marriage of reason, and had chosen Catherine for what he supposed to be her latent matronly qualities; but John Ludlow, who was a year the girl's junior, and spoken of always as a young man who might have his "pick," was seriously in love with her. Catherine, however, would never look at him; she made it plain to him that she thought he came to see her too often. He afterwards consoled himself, and married a very different person, little Miss Sturtevant, whose attractions were obvious to the dullest comprehension. Catherine, at the time of these events, had left her thirtieth year well behind her, and had quite taken her place as an old maid. Her father would have preferred she should marry, and he once told her that he hoped she would not be too fastidious. "I should like to see you an honest man's wife before I die," he said. This was after John Ludlow had been compelled to give it up, though the Doctor had advised him to persevere. The Doctor exercised no further pressure, and had the credit of not "worrying" at all over his daughter's singleness. In fact he worried rather more than appeared, and there were considerable periods during which he felt sure that Morris Townsend was hidden behind some door. "If he is not, why doesn't she marry?" he asked himself. "Limited as her intelligence may be, she must understand perfectly well that she is made to do the usual thing." Catherine, however, became an admirable old maid. She formed habits, regulated her days upon a system of her own, interested herself in charitable institutions, asylums, hospitals, and aid societies; and went generally, with an even and noiseless step, about the rigid business of her life. This life had, however, a secret history as well as a public one—if I may talk of the public history of a mature and diffident spinster for whom publicity had always a combination of terrors. From her own point of view the great facts of her career were that Morris Townsend had trifled with her affection, and that her father had broken its spring. Nothing could ever alter these facts; they were always there, like her name, her age, her plain face. Nothing could ever undo the wrong or cure the pain that Morris had inflicted on her, and nothing could ever make her feel towards her father as she felt in her younger years. There was something dead in her life, and her duty was to try and fill the void. Catherine recognised this duty to the utmost; she had a great disapproval of brooding and moping. She had, of course, no faculty for quenching memory in dissipation; but she mingled freely in the usual gaieties of the town, and she became at last an inevitable figure at all respectable entertainments. She was greatly liked, and as time went on she grew to be a sort of kindly maiden aunt to the younger portion of society. Young girls were apt to confide to her their love affairs (which they never did to Mrs. Penniman), and young men to be fond of her without knowing why. She developed a few harmless eccentricities; her habits, once formed, were rather stiffly maintained; her opinions, on all moral and social matters, were extremely conservative; and before she was forty she was regarded as an old-fashioned person, and an authority on customs that had passed away. Mrs. Penniman, in comparison, was quite a girlish figure; she grew younger as she advanced in life. She lost none of her relish for beauty and mystery, but she had little opportunity to exercise it. With Catherine's later wooers she failed to establish relations as intimate as those which had given her so many interesting hours in the society of Morris Townsend. These gentlemen had an indefinable mistrust of her good offices, and they never talked to her about Catherine's charms. Her ringlets, her buckles and bangles, glistened more brightly with each succeeding year, and she remained quite the same officious and imaginative Mrs. Penniman, and the odd mixture of impetuosity and circumspection, that we have hitherto known. As regards one point, however, her circumspection prevailed, and she must be given due credit for it. For upwards of seventeen years she never mentioned Morris Townsend's name to her niece. Catherine was grateful to her, but this consistent silence, so little in accord with her aunt's character, gave her a certain alarm, and she could never wholly rid herself of a suspicion that Mrs. Penniman sometimes had news of him.

XXXIII

LITTLE by little Dr. Sloper had retired from his profession; he visited only those patients in whose symptoms he recognised a certain originality. He went again to Europe, and remained two years; Catherine went with him, and on this occasion Mrs. Penniman was of the party. Europe apparently had few surprises for Mrs. Penniman, who frequently remarked, in the most romantic sites—"You know I am very familiar with all this." It should be added that such remarks were usually not addressed to her brother, or yet to her niece, but to fellow-tourists who happened to be at hand, or even to the cicerone or the goat-herd in the foreground.

One day, after his return from Europe, the Doctor said something to his daughter that made her start—it seemed to come from so far out of the past.

"I should like you to promise me something before I die."

"Why do you talk about your dying?" she asked.

"Because I am sixty-eight years old."

"I hope you will live a long time," said Catherine.

"I hope I shall! But some day I shall take a bad cold, and then it will not matter much what any one hopes. That will be the manner of my exit, and when it takes place, remember I told you so. Promise me not to marry Morris Townsend after I am gone."

This was what made Catherine start, as I have said; but her start was a silent one, and for some moments she said nothing. "Why do you speak of him?" she asked at last.

"You challenge everything I say. I speak of him because he's a topic, like any other. He's to be seen, like any one else, and he is still looking for a wife—having had one and got rid of her, I don't know by what means. He has lately been in New York, and at your cousin Marian's house; your Aunt Elizabeth saw him there."

"They neither of them told me," said Catherine.

"That's their merit; it's not yours. He has grown fat and bald, and he has not made his fortune. But I can't trust those facts alone to steel your heart against him, and that's why I ask you to promise."

"Fat and bald": these words presented a strange image to Catherine's mind, out of which the memory of the most beautiful young man in the world had never faded. "I don't think you understand," she said. "I very seldom think of Mr. Townsend."

"It will be very easy for you to go on, then. Promise me, after my death, to do the same."

Again, for some moments, Catherine was silent; her father's request deeply amazed her; it opened an old wound and made it ache afresh. "I don't think I can promise that," she answered.

"It would be a great satisfaction," said her father.

"You don't understand. I can't promise that."

The Doctor was silent a minute. "I ask you for a particular reason. I am altering my will."

This reason failed to strike Catherine; and indeed she scarcely understood it. All her feelings were merged in the sense that he was trying to treat her as he had treated her years before. She had suffered from it then; and now all her experience, all her acquired tranquillity and rigidity, protested. She had been so humble in her youth that she could now afford to have a little pride, and there was something in this request, and in her father's thinking himself so free to make it, that seemed an injury to her dignity. Poor Catherine's dignity was not aggressive; it never sat in state; but if you pushed far enough you could find it. Her father had pushed very far.

"I can't promise," she simply repeated.

"You are very obstinate," said the Doctor.

"I don't think you understand."

"Please explain, then."

"I can't explain," said Catherine. "And I can't promise."

"Upon my word," her father explained, "I had no idea how obstinate you are!"

She knew herself that she was obstinate, and it gave her a certain joy. She was now a middle-aged woman.

About a year after this, the accident that the Doctor had spoken of occurred; he took a violent cold. Driving out to Bloomingdale one April day to see a patient of unsound mind, who was confined in a private asylum for the insane, and whose family greatly desired a medical opinion from an eminent source, he was caught in a spring shower, and being in a buggy, without a hood, he found himself soaked to the skin. He came home with an ominous chill, and on the morrow he was seriously ill. "It is congestion of the lungs," he said to Catherine; "I shall need very good nursing. It will make no difference, for I shall not recover; but I wish everything to be done, to the smallest detail, as if I should. I hate an ill-conducted sick-room; and you will be so good as to nurse me on the hypothesis that I shall get well." He told her which of his fellow-physicians to send for, and gave her a multitude of minute directions; it was quite on the optimistic hypothesis that she nursed him. But he had never been wrong in his life, and he was not wrong now. He was touching his seventieth year, and though he had a very well-tempered constitution, his hold upon life had lost its firmness. He died after three weeks' illness, during which Mrs. Penniman, as well as his daughter, had been assiduous at his bedside.

On his will being opened after a decent interval, it was found to consist of two portions. The first of these dated from ten years back, and consisted of a series of dispositions by which he left the great mass of property to his daughter, with becoming legacies to his two sisters. The second was a codicil, of recent origin, maintaining the annuities to Mrs. Penniman and Mrs. Almond, but reducing Catherine's share to a fifth of what he had first bequeathed her. "She is amply provided for from her mother's side," the document ran, "never having spent more than a fraction of her income from this source; so that her fortune is already more than sufficient to attract those unscrupulous adventurers whom she has given me reason to believe that she persists in regarding as an interesting class." The large remainder of his property, therefore, Dr. Sloper had divided into seven unequal parts, which he left, as endowments, to as many different hospitals and schools of medicine, in various cities of the Union.

To Mrs. Penniman it seemed monstrous that a man should play such tricks with other people's money; for after his death, of course, as she said, it was other people's. "Of course, you will dispute the will," she remarked, fatuously, to Catherine.

"Oh no," Catherine answered, "I like it very much. Only I wish it had been expressed a little differently!"

XXXIV

It was her habit to remain in town very late in the summer; she preferred the house in Washington Square to any other habitation whatever, and it was under protest that she used to go to the seaside for the month of August. At the sea she spent her month at an hotel. The year that her father died she intermitted this custom altogether, not thinking it consistent with deep mourning; and the year after that she put off her departure till so late that the middle of August found her still in the heated solitude of Washington Square. Mrs. Penniman, who was fond of a change, was usually eager for a visit to the country; but this year she appeared quite content with such rural impressions as she could gather, at the parlour window, from the ailantus-trees behind the wooden paling. The peculiar fragrance of this vegetation used to diffuse itself in the evening air, and Mrs. Penniman, on the warm nights of July, often sat at the open window and inhaled it. This was a happy moment for Mrs. Penniman; after the death of her brother she felt more free to obey her impulses. A vague oppression had disappeared from her life, and she enjoyed a sense of freedom of which she had not been conscious since the memorable time, so long ago, when the Doctor went abroad with Catherine and left her at home to entertain Morris Townsend. The year that had elapsed since her brother's death reminded her—of that happy time, because, although Catherine, in growing older, had become a person to be reckoned with, yet her society was a very different thing, as Mrs. Penniman said, from that of a tank of cold water. The elder lady hardly knew what use to make of this larger margin of her life; she sat and looked at it very much as she had often sat, with her poised needle in her hand, before her tapestry frame. She had a confident hope, however, that her rich impulses, her talent for embroidery, would still find their application, and this confidence was justified before many months had elapsed.

Catherine continued to live in her father's house in spite of its being represented to her that a maiden lady of quiet habits might find a more convenient abode in one of the smaller dwellings, with brown stone fronts, which had at this time begun to adorn the transverse thoroughfares in the upper part of the town. She liked the earlier structure—it had begun by this time to be called an "old" house—and proposed to herself to end her days in it. If it was too large for a pair of unpretending gentlewomen, this was better than the opposite fault; for Catherine had no desire to find herself in closer quarters with her aunt. She expected to spend the rest of her life in Washington Square, and to enjoy Mrs. Penniman's society for the whole of this period; as she had a conviction that, long as she might live, her aunt would live at least as long, and always retain her brilliancy and activity. Mrs. Penniman suggested to her the idea of a rich vitality.

On one of those warm evenings in July of which mention has been made, the two ladies sat together at an open window, looking out on the quiet Square. It was too hot for lighted lamps, for reading, or for work; it might have appeared too hot even for conversation, Mrs. Penniman having long been speechless. She sat forward in the window, half on the balcony, humming a little song. Catherine was within the room, in a low rocking-chair, dressed in white, and slowly using a large palmetto fan. It was in this way, at this season, that the aunt and niece, after they had had tea, habitually spent their evenings.

"Catherine," said Mrs. Penniman at last, "I am going to say something that will surprise you."

"Pray do," Catherine answered; "I like surprises. And it is so quiet now."

"Well, then, I have seen Morris Townsend."

If Catherine was surprised, she checked the expression of it; she gave neither a start nor an exclamation. She remained, indeed, for some moments intensely still, and this may very well have been a symptom of emotion. "I hope he was well," she said at last.

"I don't know; he is a great deal changed. He would like very much to see you."

"I would rather not see him," said Catherine quickly.

"I was afraid you would say that. But you don't seem surprised!"

"I am—very much."

"I met him at Marian's," said Mrs. Penniman. "He goes to Marian's, and they are so afraid you will meet him there. It's my belief that that's why he goes. He wants so much to see you." Catherine made no response to this, and Mrs. Penniman went on. "I didn't know him at first; he is so remarkably changed. But he knew me in a minute. He says I am not in the least changed. You know how polite he always was. He was coming away when I came, and we walked a little distance together. He is still very handsome, only, of course, he looks older, and he is not so—so animated as he used to be. There was a touch of sadness about him; but there was a touch of sadness about him before—especially when he went away. I am afraid he has not been very successful—that he has never got thoroughly established. I don't suppose he is sufficiently plodding, and that, after all, is what succeeds in this world." Mrs. Penniman had not mentioned Morris Townsend's name to her niece for upwards of the fifth of a century; but now that she had broken the spell, she seemed to wish to make up for lost time, as if there had been a sort of exhilaration in hearing herself talk of him. She proceeded, however, with considerable caution, pausing occasionally to let Catherine give some sign. Catherine gave no other sign than to stop the rocking of her chair and the swaying of her fan; she sat motionless and silent. "It was on Tuesday last," said Mrs. Penniman, "and I have been hesitating ever since about telling you. I didn't know how you might like it. At last I thought that it was so long ago that you would probably not have any particular feeling. I saw him again, after meeting him at Marian's. I met him in the street, and he went a few steps with me. The first thing he said was about you; he asked ever so many questions. Marian didn't want me to speak to you; she didn't want you to know that they receive him. I told him I was sure that after all these years you couldn't have any feeling about that; you couldn't grudge him the hospitality of his own cousin's house. I said you would be bitter indeed if you did that. Marian has the most extraordinary ideas about what happened between you; she seems to think he behaved in some very unusual manner. I took the liberty of reminding her of the real facts, and placing the story in its true light. *He* has no bitterness, Catherine, I can assure you; and he might be excused for it, for things have not gone well with him. He has been all over the world, and tried to establish himself everywhere; but his evil star was against him. It is most interesting to hear him talk of his evil star. Everything failed; everything but his—you know, you remember—his proud, high spirit. I believe he married some lady somewhere in Europe. You know they marry in such a peculiar matter-of-course way in Europe; a marriage of reason they call it. She died soon afterwards; as he said to me, she only flitted across his life. He has not been in New York for ten years; he came back a few days ago. The first thing he did was to ask me about you. He had heard you had never married; he seemed very much interested about that. He said you had been the real romance of his life."

Catherine had suffered her companion to proceed from point to point, and pause to pause, without interrupting her; she fixed her eyes on the ground and listened. But the last phrase I have quoted was followed by a pause of peculiar significance, and then, at last, Catherine spoke. It will be observed that before doing so she had received a good deal of information about Morris Townsend. "Please say no more; please don't follow up that subject."

"Doesn't it interest you?" asked Mrs. Penniman, with a certain timorous archness.

"It pains me," said Catherine.

"I was afraid you would say that. But don't you think you could get used to it? He wants so much to see you."

"Please don't, Aunt Lavinia," said Catherine, getting up from her seat. She moved quickly away, and went to the other window, which stood open to the balcony; and here, in the embrasure, concealed from her aunt by the white curtains, she remained a long time, looking out into the warm darkness. She had had a great shock; it was as if the gulf of the past had suddenly opened, and a spectral figure had risen out of it. There were some things she believed she had got over, some feelings that she had thought of as dead; but apparently there was a certain vitality in them still. Mrs. Penniman had made them stir themselves. It was but a momentary agitation, Catherine said to herself; it would presently pass away. She was trembling, and her heart was beating so that she could feel it; but this also would subside. Then, suddenly, while she waited for a return of her calmness, she burst into tears. But her tears flowed very silently, so that Mrs. Penniman had no observation of them. It was perhaps, however, because Mrs. Penniman suspected them that she said no more that evening about Morris Townsend.

XXXV

HER refreshed attention to this gentleman had not those limits of which Catherine desired, for herself, to be conscious; it lasted long enough to enable her to wait another week before speaking of him again. It was under the same circumstances that she once more attacked the subject. She had been sitting with her niece in the evening; only on this occasion, as the night was not so warm, the lamp had been lighted, and Catherine had placed herself near it with a morsel of fancy-work. Mrs. Penniman went and sat alone for half an hour on the balcony; then she came in, moving vaguely about the room. At last she sank into a seat near Catherine, with clasped hands, and a little look of excitement.

"Shall you be angry if I speak to you again about *him*?" she asked.

Catherine looked up at her quietly. "Who is *he*?"

"He whom you once loved."

"I shall not be angry, but I shall not like it."

"He sent you a message," said Mrs. Penniman. "I promised him to deliver it, and I must keep my promise."

In all these years Catherine had had time to forget how little she had to thank her aunt for in the season of her misery; she had long ago forgiven Mrs. Penniman for taking too much upon herself. But for a moment this attitude of interposition and disinterestedness, this carrying of messages and redeeming of promises, brought back the sense that her companion was a dangerous woman. She had said she would not be angry; but for an instant she felt sore. "I don't care what you do with your promise!" she answered.

Mrs. Penniman, however, with her high conception of the sanctity of pledges, carried her point. "I have gone too far to retreat," she said, though precisely what this meant she was not at pains to explain. "Mr. Townsend wishes most particularly to see you, Catherine; he believes that if you knew how much, and why, he wishes it, you would consent to do so."

"There can be no reason," said Catherine; "no good reason."

"His happiness depends upon it. Is not that a good reason?" asked Mrs. Penniman impressively.

"Not for me. My happiness does not."

"I think you will be happier after you have seen him. He is going away again—going to resume his wanderings. It is a very lonely, restless, joyless life. Before he goes he wishes to speak to you; it is a fixed idea with him—he is always thinking of it. He has something very important to say to you. He believes that you never understood him—that you never judged him rightly, and the belief has always weighed upon him terribly. He wishes to justify himself; he believes that in a very few words he could do so. He wishes to meet you as a friend."

Catherine listened to this wonderful speech without pausing in her work; she had now had several days to accustom herself to think of Morris Townsend again as an actuality. When it was over she said simply, "Please say to Mr. Townsend that I wish he would leave me alone."

She had hardly spoken when a sharp, firm ring at the door vibrated through the summer night. Catherine looked up at the clock; it marked a quarter-past nine—a very late hour for visitors, especially in the empty condition of the town. Mrs. Penniman at the same moment gave a little start, and then Catherine's eyes turned quickly to her aunt. They met Mrs. Penniman's and sounded them for a moment, sharply. Mrs. Penniman was blushing; her look was a conscious one; it seemed to confess something. Catherine guessed its meaning, and rose quickly from her chair.

"Aunt Penniman," she said, in a tone that scared her companion, "have you taken the *liberty* . . . ?"

"My dearest Catherine," stammered Mrs. Penniman, "just wait till you see him!"

Catherine had frightened her aunt, but she was also frightened herself; she was on the point of rushing to give orders to the servant, who was passing to the door, to admit no one; but the fear of meeting her visitor checked her.

"Mr. Morris Townsend."

This was what she heard, vaguely but recognisably articulated by the domestic, while she hesitated. She had her back turned to the door of the parlour, and for some moments she kept it turned, feeling that he had come in. He had not spoken, however, and at last she faced about. Then she saw a gentleman standing in the middle of the room, from which her aunt had discreetly retired.

She would never have known him. He was forty-five years old, and his figure was not that of the straight, slim young man she remembered. But it was a very fine person, and a fair and lustrous beard, spreading itself upon a well-presented chest, contributed to its effect. After a moment Catherine recognised the upper half of the face, which, though her visitor's clustering locks had grown thin, was still remarkably handsome. He stood in a deeply deferential attitude, with his eyes on her face. "I have ventured—I have ventured," he said; and then he paused, looking about him, as if he expected her to ask him to sit down. It was the old voice, but it had not the old charm. Catherine, for a minute, was conscious of a distinct determination not to invite him to take a seat. Why had he come? It was wrong for him to come. Morris was embarrassed, but Catherine gave him no help. It was not that she was glad of his embarrassment; on the contrary, it excited all her own liabilities of this kind, and gave her great pain. But how could she welcome him when she felt so vividly that he ought not to have come? "I wanted so much—I was determined," Morris went on. But he stopped again; it was not easy. Catherine still said nothing, and he may well have recalled with apprehension her ancient faculty of silence. She continued to look at him, however, and as she did so she made the strangest observation. It seemed to be he, and yet not he; it was the man who had been everything, and yet this person was nothing. How long ago it was—how old she had grown—how much she had lived! She had lived on something that was connected with *him*, and she had consumed it in doing so. This person did not look unhappy. He was fair and well-preserved, perfectly dressed, mature and complete. As Catherine looked at him, the story of his life defined itself in his eyes; he had made himself comfortable, and he had never been caught. But even while her perception opened itself to this, she had no desire to catch him; his presence was painful to her, and she only wished he would go.

"Will you not sit down?" he asked.

"I think we had better not," said Catherine.

"I offend you by coming?" He was very grave; he spoke in a tone of the richest respect.

"I don't think you ought to have come."

"Did not Mrs. Penniman tell you—did she not give you my message?"

"She told me something, but I did not understand."

"I wish you would let *me* tell you—let me speak for myself."

"I don't think it is necessary," said Catherine.

"Not for you, perhaps, but for me. It would be a great satisfaction—and I have not many." He seemed to be coming nearer; Catherine turned away. "Can we not be friends again?" he said.

"We are not enemies," said Catherine. "I have none but friendly feelings to you."

"Ah, I wonder whether you know the happiness it gives me to hear you say that!" Catherine uttered no intimation that she measured the influence of her words; and he presently went on, "You have not changed—the years have passed happily for you."

"They have passed very quietly," said Catherine.

"They have left no marks; you are admirably young." This time he succeeded in coming nearer—he was close to her; she saw his glossy perfumed beard, and his eyes above it looking strange and hard. It was very different from his old—from his young—face. If she had first seen him this way she would not have liked him. It seemed to her that he was smiling, or trying to smile. "Catherine," he said, lowering his voice, "I have never ceased to think of you."

"Please don't say those things," she answered.

"Do you hate me?"

"Oh no," said Catherine.

Something in her tone discouraged him, but in a moment he recovered himself. "Have you still some kindness for me, then?"

"I don't know why you have come here to ask me such things!" Catherine exclaimed.

"Because for many years it has been the desire of my life that we should be friends again."

"That is impossible."

"Why so? Not if you will allow it."

"I will not allow it!" said Catherine.

He looked at her again in silence. "I see; my presence troubles you and pains you. I will go away; but you must give me leave to come again."

"Please don't come again," she said.

"Never?—never?"

She made a great effort; she wished to say something that would make it impossible he should ever again cross her threshold. "It is wrong of you. There is no propriety in it—no reason for it."

"Ah, dearest lady, you do me injustice!" cried Morris Townsend. "We have only waited, and now we are free."

"You treated me badly," said Catherine.

"Not if you think of it rightly. You had your quiet life with your father—which was just what I could not make up my mind to rob you of."

"Yes; I had that."

Morris felt it to be a considerable damage to his cause that he could not add that she had had something more besides; for it is needless to say that he had learnt the contents of Dr. Sloper's will. He was nevertheless not at a loss. "There are worse fates than that!" he exclaimed, with expression; and he might have been supposed to refer to his own unprotected situation. Then he added, with a deeper tenderness, "Catherine, have you never forgiven me?"

"I forgave you years ago, but it is useless for us to attempt to be friends."

"Not if we forget the past. We have still a future, thank God!"

"I can't forget—I don't forget," said Catherine. "You treated me too badly. I felt it very much; I felt it for years." And then she went on, with her wish to show him that he must not come to her this way, "I can't begin again—I can't take it up. Everything is dead and buried. It was too serious; it made a great change in my life. I never expected to see you here."

"Ah, you are angry!" cried Morris, who wished immensely that he could extort some flash of passion from her mildness. In that case he might hope.

"No, I am not angry. Anger does not last, that way, for years. But there are other things. Impressions last, when they have been strong. But I can't talk."

Morris stood stroking his beard, with a clouded eye. "Why have you never married?" he asked abruptly. "You have had opportunities."

"I didn't wish to marry."

"Yes, you are rich, you are free; you had nothing to gain."

"I had nothing to gain," said Catherine.

Morris looked vaguely round him, and gave a deep sigh. "Well, I was in hopes that we might still have been friends."

"I meant to tell you, by my aunt, in answer to your message—if you had waited for an answer—that it was unnecessary for you to come in that hope."

"Good-bye, then," said Morris. "Excuse my indiscretion."

He bowed, and she turned away—standing there, averted, with her eyes on the ground, for some moments after she had heard him close the door of the room.

In the hall he found Mrs. Penniman, fluttered and eager; she appeared to have been hovering there under the irreconcilable promptings of her curiosity and her dignity.

"That was a precious plan of yours!" said Morris, clapping on his hat.

"Is she so hard?" asked Mrs. Penniman.

"She doesn't care a button for me—with her confounded little dry manner."

"Was it very dry?" pursued Mrs. Penniman, with solicitude.

Morris took no notice of her question; he stood musing an instant, with his hat on. "But why the deuce, then, would she never marry?"

"Yes—why indeed?" sighed Mrs. Penniman. And then, as if from a sense of the inadequacy of this explanation, "But you will not despair—you will come back?"

"Come back? Damnation!" And Morris Townsend strode out of the house, leaving Mrs. Penniman staring.

Catherine, meanwhile, in the parlour, picking up her morsel of fancy work, had seated herself with it again—for life, as it were.

About Author

Henry James OM (15 April 1843 – 28 February 1916) was an American-British author regarded as a key transitional figure between literary realism and literary modernism, and is considered by many to be among the greatest novelists in the English language. He was the son of Henry James Sr. and the brother of renowned philosopher and psychologist William James and diarist Alice James.

He is best known for a number of novels dealing with the social and marital interplay between émigré Americans, English people, and continental Europeans. Examples of such novels include The Portrait of a Lady, The Ambassadors, and The Wings of the Dove. His later works were increasingly experimental. In describing the internal states of mind and social dynamics of his characters, James often made use of a style in which ambiguous or contradictory motives and impressions were overlaid or juxtaposed in the discussion of a character's psyche. For their unique ambiguity, as well as for other aspects of their composition, his late works have been compared to impressionist painting.

His novella The Turn of the Screw has garnered a reputation as the most analysed and ambiguous ghost story in the English language and remains his most widely adapted work in other media. He also wrote a number of other highly regarded ghost stories and is considered one of the greatest masters of the field.

James published articles and books of criticism, travel, biography, autobiography, and plays. Born in the United States, James largely relocated to Europe as a young man and eventually settled in England, becoming a British subject in 1915, one year before his death. James was nominated for the Nobel Prize in Literature in 1911, 1912 and 1916.

Life

Early years, 1843–1883

James was born at 2 Washington Place in New York City on 15 April 1843. His parents were Mary Walsh and Henry James Sr. His father was intelligent and steadfastly congenial. He was a lecturer and philosopher who had inherited independent means from his father, an Albany banker and investor. Mary came from a wealthy family long settled in New York City. Her sister Katherine lived with her adult family for an extended period of time. Henry Jr. had three brothers, William, who was one year his senior, and younger brothers Wilkinson (Wilkie) and Robertson. His younger sister was Alice. Both of his parents were of Irish and Scottish descent.

The family first lived in Albany, at 70 N. Pearl St., and then moved to Fourteenth Street in New York City when James was still a young boy. His education was calculated by his father to expose him to many influences, primarily scientific and philosophical; it was described by Percy Lubbock, the editor of his selected letters, as "extraordinarily haphazard and promiscuous." James did not share the usual education in Latin and Greek classics. Between 1855 and 1860, the James' household traveled to London, Paris, Geneva, Boulogne-sur-Mer and Newport, Rhode Island, according to the father's current interests and publishing ventures, retreating to the United States when funds were low. Henry studied primarily with tutors and briefly attended schools while the family traveled in Europe. Their longest stays were in France, where Henry began to feel at home and became fluent in French. He was afflicted with a stutter, which seems to have manifested itself only when he spoke English; in French, he did not stutter.

In 1860 the family returned to Newport. There Henry became a friend of the painter John La Farge, who introduced him to French literature, and in particular, to Balzac. James later called Balzac his "greatest master," and said that he had learned more about the craft of fiction from him than from anyone else.

In the autumn of 1861 Henry received an injury, probably to his back, while fighting a fire. This injury, which resurfaced at times throughout his life, made him unfit for military service in the American Civil War.

In 1864 the James family moved to Boston, Massachusetts to be near William, who had enrolled first in the Lawrence Scientific School at Harvard and then in the medical school. In 1862 Henry attended Harvard Law School, but realised that he was not interested in studying law. He pursued his interest in literature and associated with authors and critics William Dean Howells and Charles Eliot Norton in Boston and Cambridge, formed lifelong friendships with Oliver Wendell Holmes Jr., the future Supreme Court Justice, and with James and Annie Fields, his first professional mentors.

His first published work was a review of a stage performance, "Miss Maggie Mitchell in Fanchon the Cricket," published in 1863. About a year later, A Tragedy of Error, his first short story, was published anonymously. James's first payment was for an appreciation of Sir Walter Scott's novels, written for the North American Review. He wrote fiction and non-fiction pieces for The Nation and Atlantic Monthly, where Fields was editor. In 1871 he published his first novel, Watch and Ward, in serial form in the Atlantic Monthly. The novel was later published in book form in 1878.

During a 14-month trip through Europe in 1869–70 he met Ruskin, Dickens, Matthew Arnold, William Morris, and George Eliot. Rome impressed him profoundly. "Here I am then in the Eternal City," he wrote to his brother William. "At last—for the first time—I live!" He attempted to support himself as a freelance writer in Rome, then secured a position as Paris correspondent for the New York Tribune, through the influence of its editor John Hay. When these efforts failed he returned to New York City. During 1874 and 1875 he published Transatlantic Sketches, A Passionate Pilgrim, and Roderick Hudson. During this early period in his career he was influenced by Nathaniel Hawthorne.

In 1869 he settled in London. There he established relationships with Macmillan and other publishers, who paid for serial installments that they would later publish in book form. The audience for these serialized novels was largely made up of middle-class women, and James struggled to fashion serious literary work within the strictures imposed by editors' and publishers' notions of what was suitable for young women to read. He lived in rented rooms but was able to join gentlemen's clubs that had libraries and where he could entertain male friends. He was introduced to English society by Henry Adams and Charles Milnes Gaskell, the latter introducing him to the Travellers' and the Reform Clubs.

In the fall of 1875 he moved to the Latin Quarter of Paris. Aside from two trips to America, he spent the next three decades—the rest of his life—in Europe. In Paris he met Zola, Alphonse Daudet, Maupassant, Turgenev, and others. He stayed in Paris only a year before moving to London.

In England he met the leading figures of politics and culture. He continued to be a prolific writer, producing The American (1877), The Europeans (1878), a revision of Watch and Ward (1878), French Poets and Novelists (1878), Hawthorne (1879), and several shorter works of fiction. In 1878 Daisy Miller established his fame on both sides of the Atlantic. It drew notice perhaps mostly because it depicted a woman whose behavior is outside the social norms of Europe. He also began his first masterpiece, The Portrait of a Lady, which would appear in 1881.

In 1877 he first visited Wenlock Abbey in Shropshire, home of his friend Charles Milnes Gaskell whom he had met through Henry Adams. He was much inspired by the darkly romantic Abbey and the surrounding countryside, which features in his essay Abbeys and Castles. In particular the gloomy monastic fishponds behind the Abbey are said to have inspired the lake in The Turn of the Screw.

While living in London, James continued to follow the careers of the "French realists", Émile Zola in particular. Their stylistic methods influenced his own work in the years to come. Hawthorne's influence on him faded during this period, replaced by George Eliot and Ivan Turgenev. 1879–1882 saw the publication of The Europeans, Washington Square, Confidence, and The Portrait of a Lady. He visited America in 1882–1883, then returned to London.

The period from 1881 to 1883 was marked by several losses. His mother died in 1881, followed by his father a few months later, and then by his brother Wilkie. Emerson, an old family friend, died in 1882. His friend Turgenev died in 1883.

Middle years, 1884–1897

In 1884 James made another visit to Paris. There he met again with Zola, Daudet, and Goncourt. He had been following the careers of the French "realist" or "naturalist" writers, and was increasingly influenced by them. In 1886, he published The Bostonians and The Princess Casamassima, both influenced by the French writers he'd studied assiduously. Critical reaction and sales were poor. He wrote to Howells that the books had hurt his career rather than helped because they had "reduced the desire, and demand, for my productions to zero". During this time he became friends with Robert Louis Stevenson, John Singer Sargent, Edmund Gosse, George du Maurier, Paul Bourget, and Constance Fenimore Woolson. His third novel from the 1880s was The Tragic Muse. Although he was following the precepts of Zola in his novels of the '80s, their tone and attitude are closer to the fiction of Alphonse Daudet. The lack of critical and financial success for his novels during this period led him to try writing for the theatre. (His dramatic works and his experiences with theatre are discussed below.)

In the last quarter of 1889, he started translating "for pure and copious lucre" Port Tarascon, the third volume of Alphonse Daudet adventures of Tartarin de Tarascon. Serialized in Harper's Monthly Magazine from June 1890, this translation praised as "clever" by The Spectator was published in January 1891 by Sampson Low, Marston, Searle & Rivington.

After the stage failure of Guy Domville in 1895, James was near despair and thoughts of death plagued him. The years spent on dramatic works were not entirely a loss. As he moved into the last phase of his career he found ways to adapt dramatic techniques into the novel form.

In the late 1880s and throughout the 1890s James made several trips through Europe. He spent a long stay in Italy in 1887. In that year the short novel The Aspern Papers and The Reverberator were published.

Late years, 1898–1916

In 1897–1898 he moved to Rye, Sussex, and wrote The Turn of the Screw. 1899–1900 saw the publication of The Awkward Age and The Sacred

Fount. During 1902–1904 he wrote The Ambassadors, The Wings of the Dove, and The Golden Bowl.

In 1904 he revisited America and lectured on Balzac. In 1906–1910 he published The American Scene and edited the "New York Edition", a 24-volume collection of his works. In 1910 his brother William died; Henry had just joined William from an unsuccessful search for relief in Europe on what then turned out to be his (Henry's) last visit to the United States (from summer 1910 to July 1911), and was near him, according to a letter he wrote, when he died.

In 1913 he wrote his autobiographies, A Small Boy and Others, and Notes of a Son and Brother. After the outbreak of the First World War in 1914 he did war work. In 1915 he became a British subject and was awarded the Order of Merit the following year. He died on 28 February 1916, in Chelsea, London. As he requested, his ashes were buried in Cambridge Cemetery in Massachusetts.

Biographers

James regularly rejected suggestions that he should marry, and after settling in London proclaimed himself "a bachelor". F. W. Dupee, in several volumes on the James family, originated the theory that he had been in love with his cousin Mary ("Minnie") Temple, but that a neurotic fear of sex kept him from admitting such affections: "James's invalidism ... was itself the symptom of some fear of or scruple against sexual love on his part." Dupee used an episode from James's memoir A Small Boy and Others, recounting a dream of a Napoleonic image in the Louvre, to exemplify James's romanticism about Europe, a Napoleonic fantasy into which he fled.

Dupee had not had access to the James family papers and worked principally from James's published memoir of his older brother, William, and the limited collection of letters edited by Percy Lubbock, heavily weighted toward James's last years. His account therefore moved directly from James's childhood, when he trailed after his older brother, to elderly invalidism. As more material became available to scholars, including the diaries of contemporaries and hundreds of affectionate and sometimes erotic letters written by James to younger men, the picture of neurotic celibacy gave way to a portrait of a closeted homosexual.

Between 1953 and 1972, Leon Edel authored a major five-volume biography of James, which accessed unpublished letters and documents after Edel gained the permission of James's family. Edel's portrayal of James included the suggestion he was celibate. It was a view first propounded by critic Saul Rosenzweig in 1943. In 1996 Sheldon M. Novick published Henry James: The Young Master, followed by Henry James: The Mature Master (2007). The first book "caused something of an uproar in Jamesian circles" as it challenged the previous received notion of celibacy, a once-familiar paradigm in biographies of homosexuals when direct evidence was non-existent. Novick also criticised Edel for following the discounted Freudian interpretation of homosexuality "as a kind of failure." The difference of opinion erupted in a series of exchanges between Edel and Novick which were published by the online magazine Slate, with the latter arguing that even the suggestion of celibacy went against James's own injunction "live!"—not "fantasize!"

A letter James wrote in old age to Hugh Walpole has been cited as an explicit statement of this. Walpole confessed to him of indulging in "high jinks", and James wrote a reply endorsing it: "We must know, as much as possible, in our beautiful art, yours & mine, what we are talking about — & the only way to know it is to have lived & loved & cursed & floundered & enjoyed & suffered — I don't think I regret a single 'excess' of my responsive youth".

The interpretation of James as living a less austere emotional life has been subsequently explored by other scholars. The often intense politics of Jamesian scholarship has also been the subject of studies. Author Colm Tóibín has said that Eve Kosofsky Sedgwick's Epistemology of the Closet made a landmark difference to Jamesian scholarship by arguing that he be read as a homosexual writer whose desire to keep his sexuality a secret shaped his layered style and dramatic artistry. According to Tóibín such a reading "removed James from the realm of dead white males who wrote about posh people. He became our contemporary."

James's letters to expatriate American sculptor Hendrik Christian Andersen have attracted particular attention. James met the 27-year-old Andersen in Rome in 1899, when James was 56, and wrote letters to Andersen that are intensely emotional: "I hold you, dearest boy, in my innermost love, & count on your feeling me—in every throb of your soul". In a letter of 6 May 1904, to his brother William, James referred to himself as "always your hopelessly celibate even though sexagenarian Henry". How accurate that description might have been is the subject of contention among James's biographers, but the letters to Andersen were occasionally quasi-erotic: "I put, my dear boy, my arm around you, & feel the pulsation, thereby, as it were, of our excellent future & your admirable endowment." To his homosexual friend Howard Sturgis, James could write: "I repeat, almost to indiscretion, that I could live with you. Meanwhile I can only try to live without you."

His numerous letters to the many young gay men among his close male friends are more forthcoming. In a letter to Howard Sturgis, following a long visit, James refers jocularly to their "happy little congress of two" and in letters to Hugh Walpole he pursues convoluted jokes and puns about their relationship, referring to himself as an elephant who "paws you oh so benevolently" and winds about Walpole his "well meaning old trunk". His letters to Walter Berry printed by the Black Sun Press have long been celebrated for their lightly veiled eroticism.

He corresponded in almost equally extravagant language with his many female friends, writing, for example, to fellow novelist Lucy Clifford: "Dearest Lucy! What shall I say? when I love you so very, very much, and see you nine times for once that I see Others! Therefore I think that—if you want it made clear to the meanest intelligence—I love you more than I love Others." To his New York friend Mary Cadwalader Jones: "Dearest Mary Cadwalader. I yearn over you, but I yearn in vain; & your long silence really breaks my heart, mystifies, depresses, almost alarms me, to the point even of making me wonder if poor unconscious & doting old Célimare [Jones's pet name for James] has 'done' anything, in some dark somnambulism of the spirit, which has ... given you a bad moment, or a wrong impression, or a 'colourable pretext' ... However these things may be, he loves you as tenderly as ever;

nothing, to the end of time, will ever detach him from you, & he remembers those Eleventh St. matutinal intimes hours, those telephonic matinées, as the most romantic of his life ..." His long friendship with American novelist Constance Fenimore Woolson, in whose house he lived for a number of weeks in Italy in 1887, and his shock and grief over her suicide in 1894, are discussed in detail in Edel's biography and play a central role in a study by Lyndall Gordon. (Edel conjectured that Woolson was in love with James and killed herself in part because of his coldness, but Woolson's biographers have objected to Edel's account.)

Works

Style and themes

James is one of the major figures of trans-Atlantic literature. His works frequently juxtapose characters from the Old World (Europe), embodying a feudal civilisation that is beautiful, often corrupt, and alluring, and from the New World (United States), where people are often brash, open, and assertive and embody the virtues—freedom and a more highly evolved moral character—of the new American society. James explores this clash of personalities and cultures, in stories of personal relationships in which power is exercised well or badly. His protagonists were often young American women facing oppression or abuse, and as his secretary Theodora Bosanquet remarked in her monograph Henry James at Work:

> When he walked out of the refuge of his study and into the world and looked around him, he saw a place of torment, where creatures of prey perpetually thrust their claws into the quivering flesh of doomed, defenseless children of light ... His novels are a repeated exposure of this wickedness, a reiterated and passionate plea for the fullest freedom of development, unimperiled by reckless and barbarous stupidity.

Critics have jokingly described three phases in the development of James's prose: "James I, James II, and The Old Pretender." He wrote short stories and plays. Finally, in his third and last period he returned to the long, serialised novel. Beginning in the second period, but most noticeably in the third, he increasingly abandoned direct statement in favour of frequent double negatives, and complex descriptive imagery. Single paragraphs began to run for page after page, in which an initial noun would be succeeded by pronouns surrounded by clouds of adjectives and prepositional clauses, far from their original referents, and verbs would be deferred and then preceded by a series of adverbs. The overall effect could be a vivid evocation of a scene as perceived by a sensitive observer. It has been debated whether this change of style was engendered by James's shifting from writing to dictating to a typist, a change made during the composition of What Maisie Knew.

In its intense focus on the consciousness of his major characters, James's later work foreshadows extensive developments in 20th century fiction. Indeed, he might have influenced stream-of-consciousness writers such as Virginia Woolf, who not only read some of his novels but also wrote essays about them. Both contemporary and modern readers have found the late style difficult and unnecessary; his friend Edith Wharton, who admired him greatly, said that there were passages in his work that were all but incomprehensible. James was harshly portrayed by H. G. Wells as a hippopotamus laboriously attempting to pick up a pea that had got into a corner of its cage. The "late James" style was ably parodied by Max Beerbohm in "The Mote in the Middle Distance".

More important for his work overall may have been his position as an expatriate, and in other ways an outsider, living in Europe. While he came from middle-class and provincial beginnings (seen from the perspective of European polite society) he worked very hard to gain access to all levels of society, and the settings of his fiction range from working class to aristocratic, and often describe the efforts of middle-class Americans to make their way in European capitals. He confessed he got some of his best story ideas from gossip at the dinner table or at country house weekends. He worked for a living, however, and lacked the experiences of select schools, university, and army service, the common bonds of masculine society. He was furthermore a man whose tastes and interests were, according to the prevailing standards of Victorian era Anglo-American culture, rather feminine, and who was shadowed by the cloud of prejudice that then and later accompanied suspicions of his homosexuality. Edmund Wilson famously compared James's objectivity to Shakespeare's:

One would be in a position to appreciate James better if one compared him with the dramatists of the seventeenth century—Racine and Molière, whom he resembles in form as well as in point of view, and even Shakespeare, when allowances are made for the most extreme differences in subject and form. These poets are not, like Dickens and Hardy, writers of melodrama—either humorous or pessimistic, nor secretaries of society like Balzac, nor prophets like Tolstoy: they are occupied simply with the presentation of conflicts of moral character, which they do not concern themselves about softening or averting. They do not indict society for these situations: they regard them as universal and inevitable. They do not even blame God for allowing them: they accept them as the conditions of life.

It is also possible to see many of James's stories as psychological thought-experiments. In his preface to the New York edition of The American he describes the development of the story in his mind as exactly such: the "situation" of an American, "some robust but insidiously beguiled and betrayed, some cruelly wronged, compatriot..." with the focus of the story being on the response of this wronged man. The Portrait of a Lady may be an experiment to see what happens when an idealistic young woman suddenly becomes very rich. In many of his tales, characters seem to exemplify alternative futures and possibilities, as most markedly in "The Jolly Corner", in which the protagonist and a ghost-doppelganger live alternative American and European lives; and in others, like The Ambassadors, an older James seems fondly to regard his own younger self facing a crucial moment.

Major novels

The first period of James's fiction, usually considered to have culminated in The Portrait of a Lady, concentrated on the contrast between Europe and America. The style of these novels is generally straightforward and, though personally characteristic, well within the norms of 19th-century fiction. Roderick Hudson (1875) is a Künstlerroman that traces the development of the title character, an extremely talented sculptor. Although the book shows some signs of immaturity—this was James's first serious attempt at a full-length novel—it has attracted favourable comment due to the vivid realisation of the three major characters: Roderick Hudson, superbly gifted but unstable and unreliable; Rowland Mallet, Roderick's limited but much more mature friend and patron; and Christina Light, one of James's most enchanting and maddening femmes fatales. The pair of Hudson and Mallet has been seen as representing the two sides of James's own nature: the wildly imaginative artist and the brooding conscientious mentor.

In The Portrait of a Lady (1881) James concluded the first phase of his career with a novel that remains his most popular piece of long fiction. The story is of a spirited young American woman, Isabel Archer, who "affronts her destiny" and finds it overwhelming. She inherits a large amount of money and subsequently becomes the victim of Machiavellian scheming by two American expatriates. The narrative is set mainly in Europe, especially in England and Italy. Generally regarded as the masterpiece of his early phase, The Portrait of a Lady is described as a psychological novel, exploring the minds of his characters, and almost a work of social science, exploring the differences between Europeans and Americans, the old and the new worlds.

The second period of James's career, which extends from the publication of The Portrait of a Lady through the end of the nineteenth century, features less popular novels including The Princess Casamassima, published serially in The Atlantic Monthly in 1885–1886, and The Bostonians, published serially in The Century Magazine during the same period. This period also featured James's celebrated Gothic novella, The Turn of the Screw.

The third period of James's career reached its most significant achievement in three novels published just around the start of the 20th century: The Wings of the Dove (1902), The Ambassadors (1903), and The Golden Bowl (1904). Critic F. O. Matthiessen called this "trilogy" James's major phase, and these novels have certainly received intense critical study. It was the second-written of the books, The Wings of the Dove (1902) that was the first published because it attracted no serialization. This novel tells the story of Milly Theale, an American heiress stricken with a serious disease, and her impact on the people around her. Some of these people befriend Milly with honourable motives, while others are more self-interested. James stated in his autobiographical books that Milly was based on Minny Temple, his beloved cousin who died at an early age of tuberculosis. He said that he attempted in the novel to wrap her memory in the "beauty and dignity of art".

Shorter narratives

James was particularly interested in what he called the "beautiful and blest nouvelle", or the longer form of short narrative. Still, he produced a number of very short stories in which he achieved notable compression of sometimes complex subjects. The following narratives are representative of James's achievement in the shorter forms of fiction.

- "A Tragedy of Error" (1864), short story
- "The Story of a Year" (1865), short story
- A Passionate Pilgrim (1871), novella
- Madame de Mauves (1874), novella
- Daisy Miller (1878), novella
- The Aspern Papers (1888), novella
- The Lesson of the Master (1888), novella
- The Pupil (1891), short story
- "The Figure in the Carpet" (1896), short story
- The Beast in the Jungle (1903), novella
- An International Episode (1878)
- Picture and Text
- Four Meetings (1885)
- A London Life, and Other Tales (1889)
- The Spoils of Poynton (1896)

- Embarrassments (1896)

- The Two Magics: The Turn of the Screw, Covering End (1898)

- A Little Tour of France (1900)

- The Sacred Fount (1901)

- Views and Reviews (1908)

- The Wings of the Dove, Volume I (1902)

- The Wings of the Dove, Volume II (1909)

- The Finer Grain (1910)

- The Outcry (1911)

- Lady Barbarina: The Siege of London, An International Episode and Other Tales (1922)

- The Birthplace (1922)

Plays

At several points in his career James wrote plays, beginning with one-act plays written for periodicals in 1869 and 1871 and a dramatisation of his popular novella Daisy Miller in 1882. From 1890 to 1892, having received a bequest that freed him from magazine publication, he made a strenuous effort to succeed on the London stage, writing a half-dozen plays of which only one, a dramatisation of his novel The American, was produced. This play was performed for several years by a touring repertory company and had a respectable run in London, but did not earn very much money for James. His other plays written at this time were not produced.

In 1893, however, he responded to a request from actor-manager George Alexander for a serious play for the opening of his renovated St. James's Theatre, and wrote a long drama, Guy Domville, which Alexander produced. There was a noisy uproar on the opening night, 5 January 1895, with hissing from the gallery when James took his bow after the final curtain, and the author was upset. The play received moderately good reviews and had a modest run of four weeks before being taken off to make way for Oscar Wilde's The Importance of Being Earnest, which Alexander thought would have better prospects for the coming season.

After the stresses and disappointment of these efforts James insisted that he would write no more for the theatre, but within weeks had agreed to write a curtain-raiser for Ellen Terry. This became the one-act "Summersoft", which he later rewrote into a short story, "Covering End", and then expanded into a full-length play, The High Bid, which had a brief run in London in 1907, when James made another concerted effort to write for the stage. He wrote three new plays, two of which were in production when the death of Edward VII on 6 May 1910 plunged London into mourning and theatres closed. Discouraged by failing health and the stresses of theatrical work, James did not renew his efforts in the theatre, but recycled his plays as successful novels. The Outcry was a best-seller in the United States when it was published in 1911. During the years 1890–1893 when he was most engaged with the theatre, James wrote a good deal of theatrical criticism and assisted Elizabeth Robins and others in translating and producing Henrik Ibsen for the first time in London.

Leon Edel argued in his psychoanalytic biography that James was traumatised by the opening night uproar that greeted Guy Domville, and that it plunged him into a prolonged depression. The successful later novels, in Edel's view, were the result of a kind of self-analysis, expressed in fiction, which partly freed him from his fears. Other biographers and scholars have not accepted this account, however; the more common view being that of F.O. Matthiessen, who wrote: "Instead of being crushed by the collapse of his hopes [for the theatre]... he felt a resurgence of new energy."

Non-fiction

Beyond his fiction, James was one of the more important literary critics in the history of the novel. In his classic essay The Art of Fiction (1884), he argued against rigid prescriptions on the novelist's choice of subject and method of treatment. He maintained that the widest possible freedom in content and approach would help ensure narrative fiction's continued vitality.

James wrote many valuable critical articles on other novelists; typical is his book-length study of Nathaniel Hawthorne, which has been the subject of critical debate. Richard Brodhead has suggested that the study was emblematic of James's struggle with Hawthorne's influence, and constituted an effort to place the elder writer "at a disadvantage." Gordon Fraser, meanwhile, has suggested that the study was part of a more commercial effort by James to introduce himself to British readers as Hawthorne's natural successor.

When James assembled the New York Edition of his fiction in his final years, he wrote a series of prefaces that subjected his own work to searching, occasionally harsh criticism.

At 22 James wrote The Noble School of Fiction for The Nation's first issue in 1865. He would write, in all, over 200 essays and book, art, and theatre reviews for the magazine.

For most of his life James harboured ambitions for success as a playwright. He converted his novel The American into a play that enjoyed modest returns in the early 1890s. In all he wrote about a dozen plays, most of which went unproduced. His costume drama Guy Domville failed disastrously on its opening night in 1895. James then largely abandoned his efforts to conquer the stage and returned to his fiction. In his Notebooks he maintained that his theatrical experiment benefited his novels and tales by helping him dramatise his characters' thoughts and emotions. James produced a small but valuable amount of theatrical criticism, including perceptive appreciations of Henrik Ibsen.

With his wide-ranging artistic interests, James occasionally wrote on the visual arts. Perhaps his most valuable contribution was his favourable assessment of fellow expatriate John Singer Sargent, a painter whose critical status has improved markedly in recent decades. James also wrote sometimes charming, sometimes brooding articles about various places he visited and lived in. His most famous books of travel writing include Italian Hours (an example of the charming approach) and The American Scene (most definitely on the brooding side).

James was one of the great letter-writers of any era. More than ten thousand of his personal letters are extant, and over three thousand have been published in a large number of collections. A complete edition of James's letters began publication in 2006, edited by Pierre Walker and Greg Zacharias. As of 2014, eight volumes have been published, covering the period from 1855 to 1880. James's correspondents included celebrated contemporaries like Robert Louis Stevenson, Edith Wharton and Joseph Conrad, along with many others in his wide circle of friends and acquaintances. The letters range from the "mere twaddle of graciousness" to serious discussions of artistic, social and personal issues.

Very late in life James began a series of autobiographical works: A Small Boy and Others, Notes of a Son and Brother, and the unfinished The Middle Years. These books portray the development of a classic observer who was passionately interested in artistic creation but was somewhat reticent about participating fully in the life around him.

Reception

Criticism, biographies and fictional treatments

James's work has remained steadily popular with the limited audience of educated readers to whom he spoke during his lifetime, and has remained firmly in the canon, but, after his death, some American critics, such as Van Wyck Brooks, expressed hostility towards James for his long expatriation and eventual naturalisation as a British subject. Other critics such as E. M. Forster complained about what they saw as James's squeamishness in the treatment of sex and other possibly controversial material, or dismissed his late style as difficult and obscure, relying heavily on extremely long sentences and excessively latinate language. Similarly Oscar Wilde criticised him for writing "fiction as if it were a painful duty". Vernon Parrington, composing a canon of American literature, condemned James for having cut himself off from America. Jorge Luis Borges wrote about him, "Despite the scruples and delicate complexities of James, his work suffers from a major defect: the absence of life." And Virginia Woolf, writing to Lytton Strachey, asked, "Please tell me what you find in Henry James. ... we have his works here, and

I read, and I can't find anything but faintly tinged rose water, urbane and sleek, but vulgar and pale as Walter Lamb. Is there really any sense in it?" The novelist W. Somerset Maugham wrote, "He did not know the English as an Englishman instinctively knows them and so his English characters never to my mind quite ring true," and argued "The great novelists, even in seclusion, have lived life passionately. Henry James was content to observe it from a window." Maugham nevertheless wrote, "The fact remains that those last novels of his, notwithstanding their unreality, make all other novels, except the very best, unreadable." Colm Tóibín observed that James "never really wrote about the English very well. His English characters don't work for me."

Despite these criticisms, James is now valued for his psychological and moral realism, his masterful creation of character, his low-key but playful humour, and his assured command of the language. In his 1983 book, The Novels of Henry James, Edward Wagenknecht offers an assessment that echoes Theodora Bosanquet's:

> "To be completely great," Henry James wrote in an early review, "a work of art must lift up the heart," and his own novels do this to an outstanding degree ... More than sixty years after his death, the great novelist who sometimes professed to have no opinions stands foursquare in the great Christian humanistic and democratic tradition. The men and women who, at the height of World War II, raided the secondhand shops for his out-of-print books knew what they were about. For no writer ever raised a braver banner to which all who love freedom might adhere.

William Dean Howells saw James as a representative of a new realist school of literary art which broke with the English romantic tradition epitomised by the works of Charles Dickens and William Makepeace Thackeray. Howells wrote that realism found "its chief exemplar in Mr. James... A novelist he is not, after the old fashion, or after any fashion but his own." F.R. Leavis championed Henry James as a novelist of "established pre-eminence" in The Great Tradition (1948), asserting that The Portrait of a Lady and The Bostonians were "the two most brilliant novels in the language." James is now prized as a master of point of view who moved literary fiction forward by insisting in showing, not telling, his stories to the reader. (Source: Wikipedia)

NOTABLE WORKS

NOVELS

Watch and Ward (1871)

Roderick Hudson (1875)

The American (1877)

The Europeans (1878)

Confidence (1879)

Washington Square (1880)

The Portrait of a Lady (1881)

The Bostonians (1886)

The Princess Casamassima (1886)

The Reverberator (1888)

The Tragic Muse (1890)

The Other House (1896)

The Spoils of Poynton (1897)

What Maisie Knew (1897)

The Awkward Age (1899)

The Sacred Fount (1901)

The Wings of the Dove (1902)

The Ambassadors (1903)

The Golden Bowl (1904)

The Whole Family (collaborative novel with eleven other authors, 1908)

The Outcry (1911)

The Ivory Tower (unfinished, published posthumously 1917)

The Sense of the Past (unfinished, published posthumously 1917)

SHORT STORIES AND NOVELLAS

A Tragedy of Error (1864)

The Story of a Year (1865)

A Landscape Painter (1866)

A Day of Days (1866)

My Friend Bingham (1867)

Poor Richard (1867)

The Story of a Masterpiece (1868)

A Most Extraordinary Case (1868)

A Problem (1868)

De Grey: A Romance (1868)

Osborne's Revenge (1868)

The Romance of Certain Old Clothes (1868)

A Light Man (1869)

Gabrielle de Bergerac (1869)

Travelling Companions (1870)

A Passionate Pilgrim (1871)

At Isella (1871)

Master Eustace (1871)

Guest's Confession (1872)

The Madonna of the Future (1873)

The Sweetheart of M. Briseux (1873)

The Last of the Valerii (1874)

Madame de Mauves (1874)

Adina (1874)

Professor Fargo (1874)

Eugene Pickering (1874)

Benvolio (1875)

Crawford's Consistency (1876)

The Ghostly Rental (1876)

Four Meetings (1877)

Rose-Agathe (1878, as Théodolinde)

Daisy Miller (1878)

Longstaff's Marriage (1878)

An International Episode (1878)

The Pension Beaurepas (1879)

A Diary of a Man of Fifty (1879)

A Bundle of Letters (1879)

The Point of View (1882)

The Siege of London (1883)

Impressions of a Cousin (1883)

Lady Barberina (1884)

Pandora (1884)

The Author of Beltraffio (1884)

Georgina's Reasons (1884)

A New England Winter (1884)

The Path of Duty (1884)

Mrs. Temperly (1887)

Louisa Pallant (1888)

The Aspern Papers (1888)

The Liar (1888)

The Modern Warning (1888, originally published as The Two Countries)

A London Life (1888)

The Patagonia (1888)

The Lesson of the Master (1888)

The Solution (1888)

The Pupil (1891)

Brooksmith (1891)

The Marriages (1891)

The Chaperon (1891)

Sir Edmund Orme (1891)

Nona Vincent (1892)

The Real Thing (1892)

The Private Life (1892)

Lord Beaupré (1892)

The Visits (1892)

Sir Dominick Ferrand (1892)

Greville Fane (1892)

Collaboration (1892)

Owen Wingrave (1892)

The Wheel of Time (1892)

The Middle Years (1893)

The Death of the Lion (1894)

The Coxon Fund (1894)

The Next Time (1895)

Glasses (1896)

The Altar of the Dead (1895)

The Figure in the Carpet (1896)

The Way It Came (1896, also published as The Friends of the Friends)

The Turn of the Screw (1898)

Covering End (1898)

In the Cage (1898)

John Delavoy (1898)

The Given Case (1898)

Europe (1899)

The Great Condition (1899)

The Real Right Thing (1899)

Paste (1899)

The Great Good Place (1900)

Maud-Evelyn (1900)

Miss Gunton of Poughkeepsie (1900)

The Tree of Knowledge (1900)

The Abasement of the Northmores (1900)

The Third Person (1900)

The Special Type (1900)

The Tone of Time (1900)

Broken Wings (1900)

The Two Faces (1900)

Mrs. Medwin (1901)

The Beldonald Holbein (1901)

The Story in It (1902)

Flickerbridge (1902)

The Birthplace (1903)

The Beast in the Jungle (1903)

The Papers (1903)

Fordham Castle (1904)

Julia Bride (1908)

The Jolly Corner (1908)

The Velvet Glove (1909)

Mora Montravers (1909)

Crapy Cornelia (1909)

The Bench of Desolation (1909)

A Round of Visits (1910)

OTHER

Transatlantic Sketches (1875)

French Poets and Novelists (1878)

Hawthorne (1879)

Portraits of Places (1883)

A Little Tour in France (1884)

Partial Portraits (1888)

Essays in London and Elsewhere (1893)

Picture and Text (1893)

Terminations (1893)

Theatricals (1894)

Theatricals: Second Series (1895)

Guy Domville (1895)

The Soft Side (1900)

William Wetmore Story and His Friends (1903)

The Better Sort (1903)

English Hours (1905)

The Question of our Speech; The Lesson of Balzac. Two Lectures (1905)

The American Scene (1907)

Views and Reviews (1908)

Italian Hours (1909)

A Small Boy and Others (1913)

Notes on Novelists (1914)

Notes of a Son and Brother (1914)

Within the Rim (1918)

Travelling Companions (1919)

Notebooks (various, published posthumously)

The Middle Years (unfinished, published posthumously 1917)

A Most Unholy Trade (1925, published posthumously)

The Art of the Novel : Critical Prefaces (1934)

CPSIA information can be obtained
at www.ICGtesting.com
Printed in the USA
LVHW091945261020
669863LV00002B/50